I0055217

Introduction to the Boost C++ Libraries

Volume I – Foundations

Robert Demming
Daniel J. Duffy

Datasim Education BV

Published by Datasim Education BV, 't Veer 1, 1832 AK Koedijk The Netherlands

Email for orders and customer service enquiries: info@datasim.nl
Phone +31 (0)72 2204802

You can also visit our home pages **www.datasimfinancial.com** or
www.datasim-press.com

All rights reserved. No part of this publication may be reproduced, stored in a retrieval system or transmitted in any form or by any means, electronic, mechanical, photocopying, recording, scanning or otherwise without permission in writing of the publisher.

Request to the publisher should be addressed to:
Datasim Education BV
't Veer 1
1832 AK Koedijk
The Netherlands

Copyright 2010 Datasim Education BV

Dutch library

A copy of this book is available from the Koninklijke Bibliotheek
ISBN/EAN 978-94-91028-01-4

History:
November 2010: First printing
April 2011:   Second printing with corrections

Table of Contents

Preface

C++ Boost Libraries

Boost is a collection of C++ libraries, each one focusing on a particular issue of concern to software developers. There are approximately one hundred libraries that can be classified into one or more categories. The functionality corresponds to text and string processing, input/output, multi-threading and higher-order functions, to name a few. Most of the libraries are licensed under the Boost Software License and this allows Boost code to be used with both free and proprietary software projects. The libraries can be used by C++ developers and in many kinds of application domains. Furthermore, several Boost libraries have been incorporated into the new C++ standard. Boost makes extensive use of templates in order to ensure efficiency and flexibility.

The approach in this book is based on the assumption that readers wish to use the Boost libraries as soon as possible in their applications. In particular, we adopt the following strategies; first, we give examples that contain code to help you become acquainted with a given library. Second, we discuss more advanced features of the Boost libraries and we create code to show how to apply these features. Finally, we show how to use the Boost libraries as building blocks in applications that use design patterns. In fact, a number of these libraries are implementations of some well-known patterns. However, you can skip the discussion of design patterns in Boost without loss of continuity.

We feel that it is important to actually use, modify and run the code examples that accompany the book if you wish to get a good understanding of how to use the libraries, in particular the mundane but time-consuming issues such as resolving compiler errors and getting used to the syntax of each library. Furthermore, the code should help those developers who wish to improve their knowledge of C++ templates and generic programming.

The Boost site is **www.boost.org** where the reader can find all relevant information, including software downloads, installation guidelines, Boost mailing-lists, documentation and other technical information.

Goals of this Book

This book describes approximately thirty C++ libraries in Boost. We focus mainly on categories for higher-order functions, data types and data structures, text and string processing and a number of libraries for smart pointers, serialisation, multi-threading, flyweight objects and random number generation. We have deliberately included these libraries (and excluded others) because we wish to appeal to a wide range of C++ developers and we hope that the 18 chapters in this book will be useful to them in their daily work.

The main goals of this book are: first, to describe the Boost libraries in such a way that readers can understand and learn how to use them. In each chapter we introduce essential syntax in combination with simple examples and we then progress to more extended examples. The second goal is to introduce a number of software techniques and methods that can be directly implemented in Boost, for example reference-counted memory pointers, multi-threading concepts and their implementation, multi-dimensional array structures and regular expressions. Finally, we discuss how several popular design patterns are directly supported in Boost.

Structure of the book
There are 18 chapters in the book that we group into several major categories:
- Higher-order functions.
- Data types and data structures.
- Text and string processing.
- System libraries (for example smart pointers).
- Miscellaneous libraries.

Since there are many libraries in Boost we have made an attempt to discuss the libraries that we think will be of benefit to developers most of the time. It is for this reason that we decided not to include the more mathematically-oriented libraries and libraries for meta-programming in this volume. On the other hand, we include a chapter on multi-threading because of the increasing interest in parallel programming models for multi-core and multi-processor CPUs.

In order to retain the relationship with software design and application development we have included a chapter and three appendices on migrating legacy code to code that uses Boost libraries for serialisation and for smart pointers in combination with object-oriented and generic design patterns.

For whom is this book?
This book is for C++ developers and programmers who have several years experience with small, medium and large applications. We assume that the reader knows how the object-oriented model is supported in C++ (encapsulation, inheritance, polymorphic functions) and knows STL containers, algorithms and iterators. Working experience with these techniques is assumed. Advanced generics – such as traits and policy based design – will be reviewed in appendices A and B for those readers for whom these topics are new. Appendix C contains exercises and projects to test your knowledge of the Boost libraries.

In our experience an incremental approach to learning the libraries is best. In particular, concentrating on the most important functionality in each library in the short term is an approach that we recommend. When you have succeeded in compiling and running the code you can then concentrate on optimising it in addition to resolving exceptional and pathological use cases. It is also useful to take examples that relate to your own application area or area of interest.

Using the Boost Libraries
How can we use these libraries? In general, it is better to use them rather than implementing the same functionality yourself in our opinion. For example, instead of writing code to do string manipulation we prefer to use the String Algo library. Likewise, we use Boost.MultiArray instead of creating our own n-dimensional data structures. Furthermore, the Pareto rule will probably be applicable; a number of libraries will be important in a given software project and for each of these libraries you will see that some classes are more often used than other ones. Finally, we can use the Boost libraries directly in new projects. A second scenario is to replace code by similar Boost code in legacy applications.

The chapters in this book should hopefully appeal to a wide audience. We have resisted discussing more advanced and domain-specific libraries, for example networking, graph and mathematical libraries as well as libraries for advanced data structures, interoperability and advanced parsers. We discuss these libraries in Volume II and their applications to engineering, optimisation, mixed language development (C#, C++/CLI), computer graphics and computational finance.

You can study the chapters in this book in any order because there are few dependencies between them. In order to learn a library we suggest one possible approach. First, you can read the Introduction and Summary sections to get an overview of what a given library has to offer, then you can compile and run the 'Hello World/101' examples to make sure that compiler settings are correct and then you can read the sections in the book that discuss advanced functionality in the library. Having done that, doing the exercises in Appendix C is a good way to test what you have learned.

Practical Hints and Guidelines
In order to help the reader become acquainted with Boost as quickly as possible we recommend that you download the Boost libraries for Windows/Visual Studio distribution. We also recommend using Microsoft's Visual Studio. Of course, other compilers and development environments can be used but we emphasise that our code was written and tested using Visual Studio 2008 and Visual Studio 2010. Finally, reading Appendices A and B before commencing with chapter 1 will provide you with relevant background knowledge of C++ templates and generic programming concepts.

The full source code becomes available to the owner of this book by completing the (original) Book Registration Form and sending it to Datasim Education. We shall then send you the code. The code is runnable and we have provided Visual Studio projects.

We wish to thank Ilona Hooft Graafland of Datasim Education who produced this book and made it production-ready.

www.datasimfinancial.com

Robert Demming
Daniel J. Duffy

1 Modelling Functions

1.1 Goals and Objectives

The first four chapters of this book are devoted to the topic of how to define and use functions. In particular, we introduce the Boost.Function library that allows us to create function types as objects. Having introduced Boost.Function we then show how to bind function input arguments to specific values using the Boost.Bind library. This is an improvement on the STL Bind in terms of ease of use and extendibility. For completeness, we also give an account of STL Bind.

Boost.Function and Boost.Bind libraries provide the basis for applications and specialised libraries. In particular, we discuss how to define callback functions that we apply in notification and event-handling applications. To this end, the Boost.Signals library provides mechanisms that support the *Observer* pattern (see GOF 1995). Furthermore, the Signals library resolves some of the limitations of the GOF version of *Observer* because it is based on generic interface design principles rather than the object-oriented approach that employs class hierarchies and dynamic polymorphism.

We include a chapter on the Boost.Phoenix library.

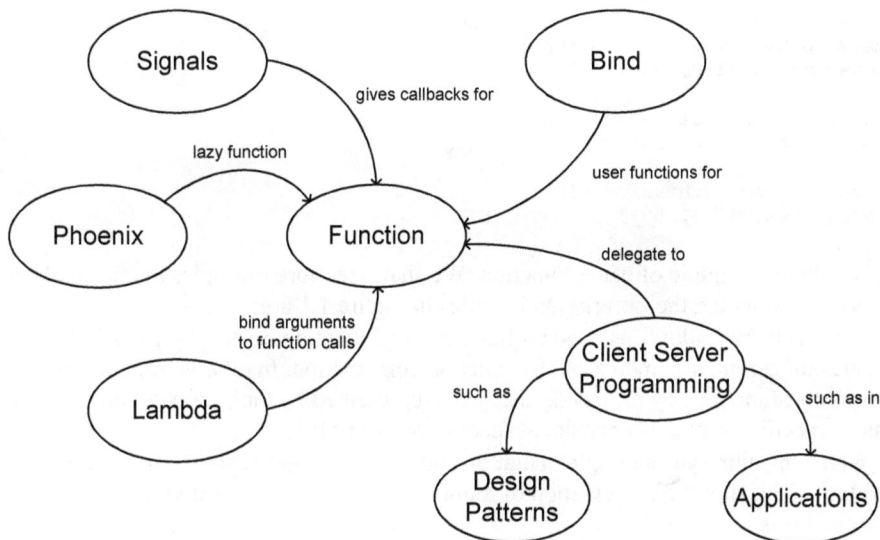

Figure 1.1 Categories of higher order functions

We have drawn a concept map in Figure 1.1 showing the main libraries as concepts and the semantic relationships between them as links. This is a high-level preview of what we discuss in the next four chapters.

We take an initial example:

```cpp
// Include Function header file
#include <boost/function.hpp>

// Define prototype object
boost::function<void (double, long)> metaFunction;
```

This is an abstract function specification in the sense that is has no body and it cannot be called. It describes functions whose return type is `void` and that have input arguments of type `double` and `long`. We can assign this object to specific functions and we then call these functions with given values of the arguments. To this end, we define three global functions that print their input arguments in some way:

```
void firstFunction(double d, long lp)
{
    cout << "print numbers: " << d << ", " << lp << endl;
}

void secondFunction(double d, long lp)
{
    cout << "product: " << d * double(lp) << endl;
}

void thirdFunction(double d, long lp)
{
    cout << "sum: " << d + double(lp) << endl;
}
```

We can now assign the function object to each of these functions by providing specific input arguments:

```
// Assign specific functions to the prototype; call them
metaFunction = firstFunction;
metaFunction(2.0, 55);

metaFunction = secondFunction;
metaFunction(2.0, 55);

metaFunction = thirdFunction;
metaFunction(2.0, 55);
```

This is a simple example of using Function. We shall see more examples in this and later chapters. In particular, the libraries and entities in Figure 1.1 are:
- *Bind*: this library allows us to adapt functions and function objects by choosing specific values for certain arguments and by function composition. In other words, we can customise functions by projecting the space represented by their input arguments into more specific or lower-dimensional spaces, for example.
- *Signals*: this library is an implementation and generalisation of the *Observer* design pattern and it supports the creation of multicast callbacks and event notification mechanisms.
- *Phoenix*: this library is closely related to Bind and Function and it allows clients to create unnamed functions. Phoenix subsumes the Lambda library. It supports the functional programming model.
- *Client-server programming*: objects call member functions in other objects.

1.2   What is a Function and why do we need Functions?

In general, a function is an algorithm that produces output data from input data. It describes the series of steps that transform the input to output. In C++ we have two main function classes:
- *Free (global) functions*: these are the modular functions in languages such as C. All input is via data in the function argument list but these functions can also access global data. We can model free functions using function pointers, in which case all input takes

place via the argument list, or by using function objects that overload the 'function call operator' (), in which case the input is a combination of function arguments and object state.

- *Member functions*: input is a combination of function arguments and object state. The return type of a member function may be `void`, in which case the member function (usually) modifies object state.

We prefer to create functions whose input data is not modified in the body of the functions, although in special cases we may loosen this restriction. To this end, atomic type arguments are called by value and user-defined arguments are `const` reference in general. Furthermore, both input and output data types can be generic. The flexibility of code is determined in no small part by the ability to model a range of algorithms and data types; ideally, all data and function bodies should be customisable. We draw up a list of areas where the libraries in this book can be used to promote the flexibility and extendibility of applications:

- Avoiding hard-coded algorithms in classes: we externalise hard-coded algorithms in classes by using design patterns such as *Strategy* and *Template Method* patterns (GOF 1995, Josuttis 2003), template member functions and template template parameters.
- Inter-object communication: an application is a network of inter-connected objects. An object can call a member function of another object that it 'knows'. Furthermore, an object can be registered with another object so that an update takes place when some event occurs.
- The object-oriented paradigm can lead to tightly-coupled and inflexible object networks and we use the libraries in this book to model interface and plug-and-socket architectures, thus promoting flexibility of code and applications (Leavens 2000).

We now discuss these issues in the context of the Function library. As motivation, we show how to define and use functions in C and having done that we shall see that the transition to understanding the syntax in Function is one of generalisation.

1.3 Function Pointers in C

We give an introduction to function pointers. In order to motivate the use of function pointers in applications, let us consider the model problem of solving an algebraic equation in one variable:

$$A(x)u = F(x)$$

where $A()$ and $F()$ are scalar functions. The solution of this algebraic equation is given by $u = F(x)/A(x)$ for a given value of x. We model this problem as a class containing two function pointers:

```
class AlgebraicEquation
{ // Scalar zero-order problem. Mainly for test cases and illustration

private:
    double (*rhs)(double t);    // Forcing term f(t)
    double (*a)(double t);      // Coefficient of zero order term

    AlgebraicEquation(const AlgebraicEquation& source) {}
    AlgebraicEquation& operator = (const AlgebraicEquation& source) {}

public:
    AlgebraicEquation() { rhs = a = 0; }
```

```
        virtual ~AlgebraicEquation() {}

        // Choosing functions in equation
        void Rhs(double (*fp)(double x))
        { // Choose the function f(t)

            rhs = fp;
        }

        void Coeff(double (*fp)(double x))
        { // Choose the function a(t)

            a = fp;
        }

        // Selector functions
        double value(double x) const
        { // The solution at a certain point

            // Exception 1: pointers must be initialized
            if (rhs == 0 || a == 0)
            {
                throw string("Function pointers not initialised");
            }

            // Exception 2: Cannot divide by zero
            if (a(x) == 0.0)
            {
                throw string("Cannot solve equation");
            }

            return rhs(x)/a(x);
        }
};
```

This class has a default constructor and modifier functions to set the functions $A()$ and $F()$. Furthermore, we compute the solution of the algebraic equation for a given value x by calling the member function `value(double x)`. In order to use the class we define two functions and we then assign the function pointers:

```
double F(double x)
{ // Right-hand side

    return x;
}

double A(double x)
{ // Coefficient of the unknown function

    return x*x;
}
```

The following code shows how to use the class and functions:

```
int main()
{
    AlgebraicEquation myEquation;
    myEquation.Rhs(&F);
    myEquation.Coeff(&A);

    try
    {
        cout << "Value: " << myEquation.value(2.0)<<endl;
```

```
    }
    catch(string& exception)
    {
        cout << exception << endl;
    }
    return 0;
}
```

This concludes our discussion of function pointers. We note some disadvantages:
- Function pointers can be slower than function objects.
- They have no state (if we exclude static variables from this discussion); all data input must take place using input arguments.
- They can be difficult to integrate in object-oriented frameworks and applications.

In the following section we discuss how to support function pointers, function objects and pointers to member functions in Function. We shall then create the code for a class that models algebraic expressions in section 1.5.

1.4 Function Essentials

Creating a Boost function is similar to defining a function pointer; in this case we define an object by instantiating a template. Here is an example of a function that has one input argument of type double and a double return type:

```
#include <boost/function.hpp>

// Declare 'empty' functions
boost::function<double (double x)> f;
```

At this stage, this object has not been assigned to specific functions and a placeholder for any function that has double as input and double as output. You can check if it has been assigned to a specific function by calling the empty() member function:

```
// Do functions contain a function object?
cout << f.empty() << endl;
```

The function f will return true if it has not been assigned. We can assign f to any one of the following:
- Global (free) functions.
- Function objects.
- Member functions of classes.

We now give examples of the first two function types and to this end let us consider a global function and a function object:

```
double myFunc(double x)
{
    return x*x;
}

struct FO
{ // Function object

    double operator () (double x)
    {
        return 23.0 * x;
    }
```

```
double doit(double x)
{
    return exp(x);
}

double doSomethingElse(double x)
{
    return log(x);
}
};
```

We can now assign the object f to these functions (note the two forms of assignment):

```
// Assign to a global function
f = &myFunc;    // Address of function syntax
f = myFunc;     // Also possible
cout << "First function: " << f(2.0) << endl;

// Assignment to a stateful function object
FO fo;
f = fo;
cout << "function object assignment: " << f(2.0) << endl;
```

We can remove the dependencies of f on specific functions by calling the clear() member function:

```
// Remove embedded function object, now a 'null' function
f.clear();
```

If we now call f we will get a run-time error and we need to catch this error, as the following code shows:

```
// Execute the 'emptied' function, need exception handling
try
{
    cout << f(2.0) << endl;
}
catch(boost::bad_function_call& error)
{
    cout << error.what() << endl; // Call to empty boost::function
}
```

We now discuss the assignment of functions to member functions. First, we define the syntax:

```
boost::function<double (FO*, double)> fMember;
```

What does this syntax mean? In this case we define a member function pointer to the struct FO which returns a double and has an input argument of type double. Thus, the instance fMember can call any member function of FO as long as the latter's member function conforms to the above signature. For example, the following code shows how to choose between two member functions at run-time:

```
// Assignment to a stateful object
FO fo;

// Assign to a member function
boost::function<double (FO*, double)> fMember;
cout << "Choose 1) exponential, 2) logarithmic: ";
int choice; cin >> choice;
fMember = &FO::doit;
```

```
if (choice != 1)
fMember = &FO::doSomethingElse;

cout << fMember(&fo, 2.0) << endl;
```

We conclude this section by giving an example of a function with three input arguments and `bool` as return type:

```
boost::function<bool (int, string, double)> F;     // Preferred form
```

We define a specific function:

```
// Function with three input parameters
bool funcA(int a, string s, double d)
{
    return false;
}
```

We can now assign `F` to this specific function:

```
// Assign the function
F = &funcA;

try
{
    cout << F(1, string("F"), 2.0) << endl;
}
catch(boost::bad_function_call& error)
{
    cout << error.what() << endl;
}
```

This completes the initial discussion of the syntax in Function. We see that it is possible to define functions and assign them to global functions, pointers to member functions and to function objects.

1.5 Modelling Algebraic Expressions using Function

We revisit the example from section 1.3 and we redesign it using Function. We have a number of new requirements relating to the functions in the algebraic equation $A(x)u = F(x)$, for example:

- S1: The function $A()$ can have a removable singularity at some point x.
- S2: The input variable x to $A()$ needs to be perturbed by a given amount when `value()` is called.

Modelling these requirements is not possible when using function pointers unless we allow extra parameters as input arguments, a decision which destroys the reusability of the design. Instead, we employ a class that contains the data relating to scenarios S1 and S2 and that implements $A()$ and $F()$ as functions. The new class structure is:

```
class AlgebraicEquation
{ // Scalar zero order problem. Boost implementation

private:

    // New data
    double tol;            // Some tolerance factor
    double X, Y;           // Removable singularity and its value
```

```
      // Functions with double as output and input
      boost::function<double (double)> rhs;  // Forcing term f(t)
      boost::function<double (double)> a;     // Zero order term

      AlgebraicEquation(const AlgebraicEquation& source) {}
      AlgebraicEquation& operator = (const AlgebraicEquation& source) {}
public:
      AlgebraicEquation() { rhs = a = 0; tol = X = Y = 0.0; }
      AlgebraicEquation(double tolerance, double SingularX, double SingularY)
      { rhs = a = 0; tol = tolerance; X = SingularX; Y = SingularY; }
      virtual ~AlgebraicEquation() {}

      // Choosing objects from Function in equation
      void Rhs(const boost::function<double (double)>& fp)
      { // Choose the function f(t)

          rhs = fp;
      }

      void Coeff(const boost::function<double (double)>& fp)
      {
          // Choose the function a(t)
          a = fp;
      }

      // Selector functions
      double value(double x) const
      { // The solution at a certain point

          // Exception 1: function objects defined
          if (rhs.empty() == true || a.empty() == true)
          {
              throw string("Function pointers not initialised");
          }

          // Check at singularity point
          if (a(x) == X)
          { // At the singularity?

              return Y;
          }

          return rhs(x+tol)/a(x+tol);
      }
};
```

We see that this solution is more flexible than the solution in section 1.3 because we can use both global functions and function objects to create the algebraic expression. An example of use is:

```
int main()
{
    // Boost version of algebraic equation
    AlgebraicEquation myEquation;

    myEquation.Rhs(&F);
    myEquation.Coeff(&A);

    try
    {
        cout << "Value using C function for A coefficient : "
             << myEquation.value(2.0) << endl;
```

```
        }
    catch(string& exception)
    {
        cout << exception << endl;
    }

    // Now use function object to define A
    double tol = 0.001; double X = 0.0; double Y = 1.0;
    AStructure myA(0.01);
    myEquation.Coeff(myA);

    cout << "Give x value: "; double val; cin >> val;

    try
    {
        cout << "Value using Boost Function: " << myEquation.value(val);
    }
    catch(string& exception)
    {
        cout << exception << endl;
    }
    return 0;
}
```

In this example we have used the following function object:

```
class AStructure
{   // In this we add a tolerance to test perturbation effects
    // In general this could have even more hidden details.

private:
    double tol;

public:
    AStructure(double tolerance) { tol = tolerance;}
    double operator () (double x) { return (x-tol)*(x+tol); }
};
```

Finally, we remark that the example in this section is a model for more complex cases, such as the solution of linear and nonlinear systems of equations.

1.6   Generic Functions and Functions as Data Members

The examples in the previous section used specific data types – such as double, string and int – as input parameters. We can define functions that use generic data types and it is possible to create classes that contain generic functions as data members. To this end, we consider the *model problem*:

```
template <typename T>
struct GenericClass
{ // Class with a generic boost function

    boost::function<T (T)> func;

    GenericClass(const boost::function<T (T)>& function)
    {
        func = function;
    }

    void function(const boost::function<T (T)>& newFunction)
    {
        func = newFunction;
```

```
    }

    // Member function using Function
    double calculate(const boost::function<T (T)>& algorithm, const T& t)
    {
        return func(t) * algorithm(t);
    }

    void print(const T& t)
    {
        cout << "Calculate boost: " << func(t) << endl;
    }
};
```

This class uses Function in different ways. It is composed of a function that is initialised in the constructor. This means that each instance of GenericClass can have its own internal algorithm. For example, we take the cases of algorithms for squaring a number and taking the square root of a number:

```
double Square(double x)
{
    return x*x;
}

double SquareRoot(double x)
{
    return sqrt(x);
}
```

We now create an instance of GenericClass as follows:

```
// Using classes that have generic functions in state
GenericClass<double> myGen(Square);
myGen.print(2.0);

// Choose another algorithm (global function)
myGen.function(SquareRoot);
myGen.print(2.0);
```

We can also modify an internal algorithm in a class by assigning it to a function object, for example using the function object FO from section 1.4:

```
// Choose another algorithm (function object)
FO myFO;
myGen.function(myFO);
myGen.print(2.0);
```

The second way is to define a member function with a Function instance as an input argument:

```
// Member function using Function
double calculate(const boost::function<T (T)>& algorithm, const T& t)
{
    return func(t) * algorithm(t);
}
```

An example of use is:

```
// Calling an algorithm
GenericClass<double> myGen2(SquareRoot);
cout << myGen2.calculate(Square, 2.0) << endl;
```

We summarise the advantages of using Function:

- *Functionality*: clients wishing to use `GenericClass` only need to define function objects that have the same signature as expected by that class. In an object-oriented approach, `GenericClass` would typically have a pointer to some base class B and clients need to define derived classes of B that implement one or more pure `virtual` functions. This approach leads to inflexible software because of the potential profusion of class hierarchies.
- *Reliability*: in contrast to function pointers, it is not possible to have a null function object; clients must create the function objects and then deliver them as function arguments.
- *Portability*: function objects can be assigned to free functions, to STL function objects and to member functions. This makes them usable in a variety of software environments.

Some of the generalisations are:

- Using function objects to implement part or all of the body of member functions is a form of *policy-based design*; clients can customise a class by providing it with their own algorithms.
- The approach in this section allows us to generalise and improve object-oriented behavioural design patterns. We are no longer forced to use pointers to base classes in combination with dynamic polymorphism but now we can use function objects to promote loose coupling. In this sense the technique is similar to the *Delegates* mechanism in C#.
- Many applications use classes that are aggregates of functions and we can model these as function objects. For example, we model a partial differential equation (PDE) as a collection of functions for the diffusion and convection terms as well as the related boundary and initial conditions. In particular, in many kinds of applications we wish to model certain mathematical entities such as arrays and matrices of functions and we may wish to project these entities into lower-dimensional spaces (Duffy 2004).

1.7   Callback Functions and Notification Patterns

A typical C++ application implements an object dependency graph. This implies that events that take place in certain objects can lead to notifications in other (dependent) objects. We can model these notification patterns using *callback functions*. In this case we define two roles; first, the *subject* or *observable* that contains changeable state and that emits events to registered *observers* (also known as *subscribers*). In general, the multiplicity relationship between subject and observer is many-to-many but we restrict the scope by assuming that the multiplicity is one-to-many.

As a first example, consider the model problem in which a class calls a number of functions when its member data is changed. In this case, we print the new data value, compute its square root and save the value to a database (in that order).

The three functions that will be called when change in state occurs are:

```
void Print(double x)
{
    cout << "I am a printer " << x << endl;
}

void MathsWhiz(double x)
{
    cout << "I am a whiz sqrt,answer: " << sqrt(x) << endl;
}
```

```
void Database(double x)
{
    cout << "In due time, I save " << x << " to a database " << endl;
}
```

We now discuss the class that contains changeable data; it contains a list of registered observables (functions in this case) and it has a member function `ChangeEvent()` that implements the change propagation mechanism:

```
class Subject
{ // The notifier (Observable) class in Publisher-Subscriber pattern

private:
    // Assume functions of a certain signature
    typedef void (*FunctionType) (double);
    list<FunctionType> attentionList;

public:
    Subject() { attentionList = list<FunctionType>(); }

    // Register a functiopn for future possible updating
    void AddObserver(const FunctionType& ft)
    {
        attentionList.push_back(ft);
    }

    void ChangeEvent(double x)
    { // Change propagation mechanism

        list<FunctionType>::const_iterator it;
        for (it=attentionList.begin();it!=attentionList.end(); ++it)
        {
            (*it)(x);
        }
    }
};
```

Finally, the following code shows how to use these callback functions:

```
int main()
{
    // Create the notifier
    Subject mySubject;

    // Create the attention list
    mySubject.AddObserver(&Print);
    mySubject.AddObserver(&MathsWhiz);
    mySubject.AddObserver(&Database);

    // Trigger the event
    cout << "Give the value: "; double val; cin >> val;
    mySubject.ChangeEvent(val);
    return 0;
}
```

1.8   Class-based Callback Functions

We generalise the discussion in section 1.7 by allowing the observers to be function objects in addition to global functions. This implies that we can still use the same function signature as before while allowing the function objects to have state. For example, we create one global function and three function objects:

```cpp
void CPrint(double x)
{
   cout << "C function: " << x << endl;
}

struct Print
{
   void operator () (double x)
   {
      cout << "I am a printer " << x << endl;
   }
};

struct MathsWhiz
{
   double fac;

   MathsWhiz(double factor) { fac = factor; }

   void operator () (double x)
   {
      cout << "I am a whiz sqrt: " << fac * sqrt(x) << endl;
   }

   void print(double x)
   {
      cout << "I am a whiz sqrt, option II: " << fac * sqrt(x) << endl;
   }
};

struct Database
{
   void operator () (double x)
   {
      cout << "In due time, I save " << x << " to a database " << endl;
   }
};
```

For readability reasons, we include the code for the class that implements the Subject again:

```cpp
class Subject
{ // The notifier (Observable) class in Publisher-Subscriber pattern

private:
   // Using boost Function library
   typedef boost::function<void (double)> FunctionType;
   list<FunctionType> attentionList;

public:
   Subject() { attentionList = list<FunctionType>(); }

   void AddObserver(const FunctionType& ft)
   {
      attentionList.push_back(ft);
   }

   void ChangeEvent(double x)
   {
      list<FunctionType>::const_iterator it;
      for (it = attentionList.begin(); it != attentionList.end(); ++it)
      {
         (*it)(x);
      }
   }
};
```

Finally, we give an example of use:

```
int main()
{
    // Create the notifier
    Subject mySubject;

    // Create the attention list
    Print myPrint;
    MathsWhiz myMaths(10.0);
    Database myDatabase;

    mySubject.AddObserver(myPrint);
    mySubject.AddObserver(myMaths);
    mySubject.AddObserver(myDatabase);
    mySubject.AddObserver(&CPrint);

    // Trigger the event
    cout << "Give the value: "; double val; cin >> val;
    mySubject.ChangeEvent(val);
    return 0;
}
```

Running the code is probably the best way to see what is happening as it helps in our understanding of the source code.

1.9   Scalar, Vector and Vector-valued Functions

The Function library can be used and extended to model functions for a wide range of applications. In particular, a function's input arguments and return type can be specialised and adapted to model well-known data structures. In this section we discuss a category of functions that are used in mathematics:

- *Scalar-valued functions*: these are functions having an array input argument and a single return type. Both types are generic.
- *Vector functions*: these functions map a single argument into an array type.
- *Real-valued functions*: these functions map arrays into a single variable of real type.
- *Vector-valued functions*: these functions map arrays of size n into arrays of size m, where n and m are positive integers.

Before we describe how we have implemented these functions in C++ we need to have template classes that model one-dimensional arrays. We can use the STL `vector` class or the authors' class `Vector<V, I>` (see Duffy 2004, Duffy 2009). We decided to use `boost::array<T,N>` because it models vectors of fixed-size. The class has two template parameters namely, one for the underlying data type and one for the size of the array. It is easy to use as the following examples show in which we construct an array and access its elements (note that indexing starts at index 0). (We discuss `boost::array<T,N>` in chapter 14):

```
boost::array<long, 4> myArr = {1, 2, 3, 4};

// Using iterators
boost::array<long, 4>::const_iterator it;

for (it = myArr.begin(); it != myArr.end(); ++it)
{
    cout << *it << endl;
}
```

```
// Indexing operator
for (long i = 0; i < myArr.size(); ++i)
{
    cout << myArr[i] << endl;
}

boost::array<Point, 4> myPointArr;
myPointArr[0] = Point();
myPointArr[1] = Point();
myPointArr[2] = Point();
myPointArr[3] = Point();

// Testing function objects and boost compile-time arrays
boost::array<double, 4> myArr2 = {1.0, 2.0, 3.0, 4.0};
```

We now discuss the C++ hierarchy that models the function types that we introduced at the beginning of this section. At the highest level we see that a function is a mapping from the elements in one set (called the *domain* D) to the elements in another set (called the *range* R). The base class that represents these mappings is a function object:

```
// Mathematical function
template <typename R, typename D>   // D == Domain, R == Range
class GenericFunction
{
private:
    // OLD R (*f) (const D& d);
    boost::function<R (D)> f;

protected:
    GenericFunction();

public:
    GenericFunction(const boost::function<R (D)>& myFunction);

    R evaluate(const D& value) const;

    // Using STL function object; competitor of evaluate()
    R operator () (const D& value) const;
};
```

We now specialise the sets D and R. First, scalar-valued functions are defined as:

```
// Mapping from Array to Scalar
template <typename R, typename D, int n>
class ScalarValuedFunction: public GenericFunction<R, boost::array<D, n> >
{
public:
    ScalarValuedFunction(
        const boost::function<R (const boost::array<D, n>)>& myF);
};
```

In other words, these functions map an array of domain types to a scalar type.

Vector functions are defined by:

```
// Mapping from Scalar to Array
template <typename R, int n, typename D>
class VectorFunction: public GenericFunction<boost::array<R, n>, D>
{
public:
    VectorFunction(
        const boost::function<boost::array<R, n> (D)>& myFunction);
};
```

Finally, vector-valued functions are defined by:

```
// Mapping from Array to Array
template <typename R, int m, typename D, int n>
class VectorValuedFunction:
    public GenericFunction<boost::array<R, m>, boost::array<D, n> >
{
public:
    VectorValuedFunction(const boost::function<boost::array<R, m>
        (boost::array<D, n>)>& myFunction);
};
```

Having described the interfaces for these classes we now give examples on how to use them. In general, the steps are:
a) Define the specific function that you wish to use.
b) Create an instance of the function class.
c) Use the instance in some way, for example computing the value of the function with a given input argument.

We define two constants:

```
const int TWO = 2;
const int THREE = 3;
```

1.9.1   Scalar-valued Function

This function type is used when we compute a single value from an algorithm that uses an array of homogeneous data as input argument. As an example, we examine a generic function to calculate the *Euclidean norm* of an array. The input is a Boost `array` and the output is a scalar value:

```
// Scalar-valued function
template <typename Numeric, std::size_t N>
Numeric Norm(const boost::array<Numeric, N>& vec)
{
    Numeric result = vec[0] * vec[0];
    for (std::size_t i = 1; i < vec.size(); ++i)
    {
        result += fabs(vec[i] * vec[i]);
    }

    return sqrt(result);
}
```

We create an instance of `boost::array`:

```
// Get the norm of an array
const int N = 4;
boost::array<double, N> vec = {1.0, 2.0, 2.0, -1.0};
```

We now create a scalar-valued function and we compute its norm by invoking the function call operator (notice that it is a function object):

```
ScalarValuedFunction<double, double, N> myScalarValFunc(Norm<double, N>);
cout << "Norm: " << myScalarValFunc(vec) << endl;
```

1.9.2   Vector Function

In this case we define functions that accept a single parameter as input and produce an n-dimensional array as output. These functions arise when modelling curves in differential geometry, for example. We take an example of a curve that is defined by a scalar parameter t:

```
// Vector function
boost::array<double, TWO> vectorFunc(double t)
{ // t --> (t^2, 1 - t), parametric representation
  // of a curve in an interval [a,b]

    boost::array<double, TWO> result;

    result[0] = t*t;
    result[1] = 1.0 - t;

    return result;
}
```

As before, we create the function and compute the curve which is then outputted to the console using a `print()` function:

```
// Working with vector functions
VectorFunction<double, TWO, double> myVecFunc(vectorFunc);
print(myVecFunc(-4.0));
```

1.9.3   Vector-valued Function

These are functions that represent mappings of n-dimensional space to m-dimensional space. We take an example of mapping a two-dimensional array to a three-dimensional array:

```
// Vector valued function
boost::array<double, THREE> vectorValuedFunc(
    const boost::array<double, TWO>& input)
{
    // Reduce to simple variables for readability
    double x1 = input[0];
    double x2 = input[1];

    double y1 = 2.0*x1 + x2;
    double y2 = -4.0*x1 - 2.0*x2;
    double y3 = -2.0*x1 - x2;

    boost::array<double, THREE> result = {y1, y2, y3};

    return result;
}
```

We use this code as follows:

```
// Working with vector valued functions
boost::array<double, TWO> input = {1, 1};
VectorValuedFunction<double, THREE, double, TWO>
    myVectorValFunc(vectorValuedFunc);
print(myVectorValFunc(input));
```

This class hierarchy can be extended to suit various kinds of applications. In this case we may need to define more member functions and we can also extend the functionality in a non-intrusive way using the *Visitor* pattern (GOF 1995). For example, we can apply the classes to define functions that are defined at discrete points in n-dimensional space using the Boost MultiArray library that we discuss in Chapter 14.

1.10 Conclusions and Summary

We have given an introduction to the Boost.Function library that generalises and extends the concept of function pointer. The syntax is straightforward and we have given a number of examples of use.

General guidelines on using Function are:
- Create the function definition.
- Create an instantiation of the function.
- Assign the function to the instantiation.
- Use the instantiation in client code.

We have discussed the most important functionality in the library. We have also given an indication of how useful it is when combined with design patterns and how natural it is when developing applications. It can be a viable alternative to other ways that model functions. As always, it is a choice between flexibility and efficiency. In particular, Boost.Function (as well as a number of other Boost libraries) enable developers to design and implement component-based software systems based on object connection architectures, interface connection architectures and plug and socket architectures (see Leavens 2000). This ability allows developers to create generic interface-based software systems.
We shall discuss some important applications of the library in Volume II.

2 Bind

2.1 Introduction and Objectives

In chapter 1 we discussed how to model functions using the Function library. We saw how to use functions as members of classes and as callbacks in event-notification applications. In this chapter we extend their capabilities by using them in combination with the Bind library. This library allows us to adapt functions so that they can be integrated with user code on the one hand and with other libraries (such as STL) on the other hand. We pay particular attention to function composition and creating functions from other functions.

A function can be identified by:
1. Its input arguments.
2. Its return type.
3. Its name.
4. The body of code that implements the function.

The first three elements refer to the *function prototype* and they correspond to an abstract specification of an infinite set of 'real' functions having a body that implements this specification.
C and C++ programmers know how to implement function pointers and use them in code. Their generalisations are called *functors* or *function objects*. In general, we prefer to use functors instead of function pointers for the following reasons:

- Reliability; functors are objects. It is not possible to supply a null functor as input argument in client code while with function pointers it is possible to have null pointers.
- Functionality: functors are 'smart functions' in the sense that their functionality is beyond what is possible with function pointers. For example, functors can have state and this can be used when we evaluate a function. It is also possible to create hierarchies of functors.
- Interoperability: many C++ libraries use functors rather than function pointers. This makes the resulting code more reusable.
- Efficiency: functors are faster than ordinary functions because they are defined at compile-time. Thus passing functors can result in improved performance; they can be inlined while function pointers cannot be inlined.

In general, function objects are useful as they allow algorithms to be customised.

The convenience header file when using Bind is:

```
#include <boost/bind.hpp>
```

2.2 An Introduction to Function Objects

A function object (or functor) is a C++ class that implements the function call operator (). The operator has zero or more input parameters and has a given return type. The corresponding body can use the member data of the class instance as well as the values of the input parameters. We take a first example to show how the technique works. In this case we define a class whose instances compute the weighted average of two numbers. This is a model problem and it can be generalised to cases in which the weights and input variables are vectors.

The weighting parameters are defined for each instance while the numbers to be averaged are input parameters:

```
class Combiner
{ // Calculates the linear combination a*x + b*y

private:
    // Weighting parameters
    double a; double b;

public:
    Combiner(double A, double B) { a = A; b = B; }

    // Using operator overloading
    double operator () (double x, double y) { return a*x + b*y; }

    // Modify weight parameters
    void modify(double A, double B) { a = A; b = B; }
};
```

In this example we have a clear separation between 'intrinsic' member data and data that is needed as arguments when calling the operator (), for example:

```
Combiner c1(0.5, 0.5);
Combiner c2(0.75, 0.25);
Combiner c3(0.0, 1.0);

double x = 10.0; double y = 20.0;

cout << "c1: " << c1(x, y) << endl;
cout << "c2: " << c2(x, y) << endl;
cout << "c3: " << c3(x, y) << endl;

// Change parameters
c1.modify(0.75, 0.25);
cout << "c1: " << c1(x, y) << endl;
```

We can create hierarchies of functor classes by defining a pure `virtual` version of the operator () in the base class and then overriding it in derived classes. To this end, consider the case of creating functors that model actions on a shared resource, in this case a vector. Thus, it should be possible to carry out various mathematical operations on the vector such as scalar multiplication and negating each element of the vector. This is in fact an implementation of the *Command* design pattern. The base class defines the interface and it stores the shared vector resource:

```
class Base
{// Emulating the Command Design pattern

protected:
    // Data store on which commands work
    vector<double>* vec;

public:
    Base(vector<double>& dataStore) { vec = &dataStore; }

    virtual void operator () () = 0;

    void print() const
    {
        cout << endl;
        for (unsigned j = 0; j < vec->size(); ++j)
        {
```

```
              cout << (*vec)[j] << ",";
        }
    }
};
```

Derived classes must implement the abstract operator ():

```
class Mirror: public Base
{ // All elements made negative

public:
    Mirror(vector<double>& dataStore) : Base(dataStore){}

    void operator () ()
    {
        for (unsigned j = 0; j < vec->size(); ++j)
        {
            (*vec)[j] = -(*vec)[j];
        }
    }
};

class Scale: public Base
{ // All elements scaled by a number

private:
    double a;

public:
    Scale(vector<double>& dataStore, double factor) : Base(dataStore)
    {
        a = factor;
    }

    void operator () ()
    {

        for (unsigned j = 0; j < vec->size(); ++j)
        {
            (*vec)[j] = a * (*vec)[j];
        }
    }

};
```

We achieve uniformity of usage by defining command-specific data in the corresponding constructors, as the following code shows:

```
// Commands using functors
vector<double> vec(10);
for (unsigned j = 0; j < vec.size(); ++j)
{
    vec[j] = double(j);
}

Mirror mirrorCommand(vec);
mirrorCommand();

Scale scaleCommand(vec, 0.5);
scaleCommand();
```

Thus, we implement the function objects as void functions with no input argument.

From these examples we can see a number of advantages when using functors; first, standardised interfaces that promote readability of the code and improved interoperability; second, functors promote reliability. This completes the introduction to function objects.

2.3   Predefined and User-defined Function Objects

STL provides a number of predefined function objects that you can use in applications. Many of them implement standard operators. These function objects allow us to compare object values and this feature is important when we use associative (sorted) containers such as set and map and when sorting criteria need to be defined. Some examples are:

- plus<type>()   // param1 + param2
- less<type>()   // param1<param2
- logical_not<type>()   // ! param

For more examples, see Josuttis 1999. Let us take an example to show how to use predefined function objects in combination with STL containers. In this case we create two sets where the elements of the first set are sorted in ascending order and the elements of the second set are sorted in descending order:

```
// Predefined function objects
set<long, less<long> > mySet;          // Sort elements with '<'
for (long j = 10; j <= 19; j += 2)
{
    mySet.insert(j);
}

// Descending order
set<long, greater<long> > mySet2;      // Sort elements with '>'
for (long j = 20; j <= 29; j += 2)
{
    mySet2.insert(j);
}
```

It is possible to define your own function objects. For example, let us define a function object that is a wrapper for the exponential function:

```
template <typename T> struct MyExp
{ // For illustrative purposes

    double operator () (T& t) { return exp(t); }
};
```

We now use this function object in combination with the STL transform() algorithm by applying it to the elements of a vector:

```
// Exponentiate each element of a vector
vector<double> vec(10); double start = 0.01;
for (long n = 0; n < vec.size(); ++n)
{
    vec[n] = start;
    start += 0.1;
}
transform(vec.begin(), vec.end(),   // source
          vec.begin(),              // destination
          MyExp<double>());         // 'my' operation
```

This technique can be used with the other algorithms in STL and in this way you can customise STL to suit your needs.

We conclude this section by examining a more extended example. In this case we create two sets of `Person` instances where `Person` is a class that models a person's name, date of birth and other attributes; the first set is sorted on the name of the person while the second set is sorted on the person's date of birth. In each case we create a function object to compare two `Person` instances:

```cpp
struct PersonSortOnName
{
    bool operator () (const Person& p1, const Person& p2)
    {
        return p1.nam < p2.nam;
    }
};

struct PersonSortOnDate
{
    bool operator () (const Person& p1, const Person& p2)
    {
        return p1.dob < p2.dob;
    }
};
```

We now create a number of `Person` instances and we insert them into the two sets called `personSet1` and `personSet2` as follows:

```cpp
DatasimDate myBirthday(29, 8, 1952);
string myName("Cuchulainn");
Person dd(myName, myBirthday);

DatasimDate bBirthday(06, 8, 1994);
string bName("Pokemon");
Person bd(bName, bBirthday);

DatasimDate bBirthday2(06, 8, 2);
string bName2("Zachary");
Person bd2(bName2, bBirthday2);

DatasimDate bBirthday3(06, 8, 1901);
string bName3("Zeelzeebub");
Person bd3(bName3, bBirthday3);

DatasimDate bBirthday4(06, 8, 1);
string bName4("Adam");
Person bd4(bName4, bBirthday4);
```

The sets are defined as follows:

```cpp
// Creating sets with various sorting criteria
set<Person, PersonSortOnName> personSet1;
personSet1.insert(dd);
personSet1.insert(bd);
personSet1.insert(bd2);
personSet1.insert(bd3);
personSet1.insert(bd4);

set<Person, PersonSortOnDate> personSet2;
personSet2.insert(dd);
personSet2.insert(bd);
personSet2.insert(bd2);
personSet2.insert(bd3);
personSet2.insert(bd4);
```

We define a function to print the elements of a set in conjunction with the `for_each()` algorithm:

```
for_each(personSet1.begin(), personSet1.end(), &Print<Person>);
```

where the function `Print()` is defined as:

```
template <typename T> void Print(const T& t) { cout << t << ", "; }
```

The output in the case when the set is ordered by name is:

```
Person: (Adam, 6/8/1)
   , Person: (Cuchulainn, 29/8/1952)
   , Person: (Pokemon, 6/8/1994)
   , Person: (Zachary, 6/8/2)
   , Person: (Zeelzeebub, 6/8/1901)
```

We now print the set that is ordered by date of birth:

```
for_each(personSet2.begin(), personSet2.end(), &Print<Person>);
```

The output in the case when the set is ordered by date of birth is:

```
Person: (Adam, 6/8/1)
   , Person: (Zachary, 6/8/2)
   , Person: (Zeelzeebub, 6/8/1901)
   , Person: (Cuchulainn, 29/8/1952)
   , Person: (Pokemon, 6/8/1994)
```

This technique can also be used with other associative containers.

2.4   The `for_each()` Algorithm

This algorithm iterates over the elements of a collection and it applies a modifier function to each element of the collection. Thus, the functions that operate on the element must accept a reference as input argument. We take an example in which we define a number of global functions:

```
// Global functions
template <typename T> void Square(T& t)
{
    t *= t;
}

template <typename T, long increment> void Add(T& t)
{
    t += T(increment);
}

template <typename T> void Print(const T& t)
{
    cout << t << ", ";
}
```

We also define a function object that we can then use with `for_each()`:

```
// Function Object in C++
template <typename T> struct PrintIt
{
    void operator () (const T& val) { cout << val << " "; }
};
```

Now we define a vector and we apply the above three global functions and the function object on its elements:

```
long Size = 10;
vector<double> vec(Size);
for (long n = 0; n < vec.size(); ++n)
{
    vec[n] = double(n);
}
```

We now call `for_each()` with these four functions:

```
for_each(vec.begin(), vec.end(), PrintIt<double>()); cout<<endl;
for_each(vec.begin(), vec.end(), &Square<double>);
for_each(vec.begin(), vec.end(), &Print<double>); cout<<endl;
const long myIncrement = 20;
for_each(vec.begin(), vec.end(), &Add<double, myIncrement>);
```

2.5 Function Adapters for Member Functions and Ordinary Functions

We conclude our discussion of STL function objects by introducing the concept of *function binding* and how STL realises it. In particular, we are interested in combining function objects with each other. We discuss:

- Predefined function adapters.
- Adapters for member functions.
- Adapters for ordinary functions.

We discuss two important predefined function adapters:

- `bind1st`: a template function that creates an adapter to convert a binary function object into a unary function object by binding the first argument of the binary function to a specified value.
- `bind2nd`: a template function that creates an adapter to convert a binary function object into a unary function object by binding the second argument of the binary function to a specified value.
- We can create function objects by deriving them from the `binary_function<Arg1, Arg2, Arg3>` template class (the last template parameter `Arg3` represents the return type of the function while the other parameters represent the input arguments taken from left to right):

```
template <typename Arg1, typename Arg2>
struct Multiply: public binary_function<Arg1, Arg2, Arg1>
{ // Compute base*exponent

    Arg1 operator () (Arg1 base, Arg2 exponent) const
    {
        return base * exponent;
    }
};
```

We now create and populate a set:

```
set<long, less<long> > mySet;    // Sort elements with '<'
for (long j = 1; j <= 4; ++j)
{
    mySet.insert(j);
}
```

Finally, we multiply each element in the set by a common exponent:

```
int exponent = 4;
transform(mySet.begin(), mySet.end(),                 // source
        ostream_iterator<long>(cout, ", "),            // destination
        bind1st(Multiply<long, int>(), exponent));    // operation
```

The output consists of the values 4, 8, 12, 16.

The next example computes the number of elements in a vector whose values are greater than a given threshold value:

```
// Simpler example of bind2nd
vector<int> vec(7);
for (int j = 0; j < vec.size(); ++j)
{
    vec[j] = double(j);
}

int threshold = 4;
int num = count_if(vec.begin(), vec.end(),
                    bind2nd(greater<int>(), threshold));
cout << "\nNumber above threshold: " << num << endl; // Ans. 2
```

STL provides some additional function objects that allow us to call a member function for each element of a collection. To this end, we return to the set personSet1 of Person instances that we introduced in section 2.3 and in this case we call the Person::print() member function by invoking the mem_fun_ref function object. This is the helper template function used to construct function object adapters for member functions when initialised with reference arguments:

```
// Function adapters for Member Functions
for_each(personSet1.begin(), personSet1.end(),
        mem_fun_ref(&Person::print));
```

Finally, we can define function objects for global functions. To this end, we create a queue with values 10, 20, 30, 40 and we find the first element in the queue that has the value 20.

```
// Define and populate the queue
deque<long> myQue;

// Copy data from 'mySet'
transform(mySet.begin(), mySet.end(),          // source
        back_inserter(myQue),                   // destination
        bind2nd(multiplies<long>(), 10));      // operation
```

We now search in the queue for the value 20 using the adapter ptr_fun():

```
deque<long>::iterator pos = find_if(myQue.begin(), myQue.end(),
                                    ptr_fun(check));
if (pos != myQue.end())
{
    cout << "Value is: " << (*pos) << endl;
}
else
{
    cout << "\nEnd of file reached, value not found" << endl;
}
```

where we have created a function adapter `check()` for the free function:

```
bool check(long i)
{
    return (i == 20);
}
```

We have completed the introduction to function objects in STL. We now discuss how to implement similar functionality in Boost.Bind.

2.6   Introducing Bind

The Boost.Bind library extends and improves the functionality that `bind1st` and `bind2nd` offer. As we saw in section 2.5, these functions can be difficult to understand and they are awkward to use. Boost.Bind resolves these problems by normalising the syntax and extending the functionality that STL offers by supporting the following features:

- Free functions and function pointers.
- Function objects.
- Pointers to member functions and to member data.
- Nested binds and functional composition.
- Overloaded operators.

This library avoids much of the difficult syntax in STL and in this way it is possible to write code that is easier to understand.

2.7   Placeholders and Arguments

In general, we associate the formal input parameters of a free (global) function or member function with specific values of those parameters. The way to do this is to employ the overloaded function `bind` in combination with *placeholders*. A placeholder is an index into the function and it tells us which specific value to use for a given formal argument. We take a simple example to motivate what we mean. Consider the scalar-valued free function with two input arguments:

```
double func(double a, double b)
{
    return a - b;
}
```

In this case the first placeholder (denoted by _1) will correspond to the variable a while the second placeholder (denoted by _2) will correspond to the variable b. We can now assign specific values to the placeholders when calling the `bind` function as the following code shows (you can check the return values):

```
// Bind params 1 and 2, answer = -1
double result = (boost::bind(&func, _1, _2))(1.0, 2.0);
cout << "_1, _2: " << result << endl;

// Bind params 2 and 1, answer = 1
result = (boost::bind(&func, _2, _1))(1.0, 2.0);
cout << "_2, _1: " << result << endl;
```

We can define the specific values at run-time:

```
// Binding to params chosen at run-time
cout << "Give a value 1: "; int v1; cin >> v1;
cout << "Give a value 2: "; int v2; cin >> v2;

result = (boost::bind(&func, _1, _2))(v1, v2);
cout << "_1, _2: " << result << endl;
```

We note that it is possible to use a placeholder more than once in a function call. In the following two examples the return value result will be zero:

```
// Using placeholders in more than one place in an expression
result = (boost::bind(&func, _1, _1))(v1, v2);
cout << "_1, _1: " << result << endl;

result = (boost::bind(&func, _2, _2))(v1, v2);
cout << "_2, _2: " << result << endl;
```

Summarising, the general bind syntax is:

```
boost::bind(f, vp1, vp2, …, vpN)(a1, a2, …, aN)
```

where f is the function to call, *vpn* a fixed input value for the bound function or a placeholder (_1 etc.) referring to one of the arguments that should be used as input to the bound function, $n = 1, \ldots, N$.

2.8   Calling a Member Function

It is possible to call a member function using Bind. To this end, consider the following class with several overloaded print() functions:

```
struct MyStruct
{
    MyStruct() { cout << "MyStruct() called" << endl; }

    MyStruct(const MyStruct& o2)
    {
        cout<< "MyStruct(const MyStruct& o2) called" << endl;
    }

    void print()
    {
        cout << "Member function 1, empty: " << endl;
    }

    void print(const string& s)
    {
        cout << "Member function 2: " << s << endl;
    }

    void print(const string& s1, const string& s2)
    {
        cout << "Member function 3: " << s1 << ", " << s2 << endl;
    }
};
```

We now show how to bind these functions to specific values. First, we create two strings and then we call the member functions:

```
string myString("Cuchulainn");
string myString2("Part 2");

MyStruct myS;
boost::bind(&MyStruct::print, _1)(myS);
boost::bind(&MyStruct::print, _1, _2)(myS, myString);
boost::bind(&MyStruct::print, _1, _2, _3)(myS, myString, myString2);
boost::bind(&MyStruct::print, _1, _3, _2)(myS, myString, myString2);
```

We see in these examples that the first argument to the bind function is the instance name while the other arguments are the values corresponding to the member function's input arguments.

The output from the above code is:

```
Member function 1, empty:
Member function 2: Cuchulainn
Member function 3: Cuchulainn, Part 2
Member function 3: Part 2, Cuchulainn
```

Instead of using a placeholder for the instance name, we can also pass the instance name directly:

```
boost::bind(&MyStruct::print, myS)();
boost::bind(&MyStruct::print, myS, _1)(myString);
boost::bind(&MyStruct::print, myS, _1, _2)(myString, myString2);
boost::bind(&MyStruct::print, myS, _2, _1)(myString, myString2);
```

Please note the relationship between placeholders and their associated values, in particular the values and their positions in the function argument list.

2.9   Using Bind with Function Objects

In addition to global functions and member functions, we see that Bind supports the binding of arbitrary function objects. We take an example:

```
struct MyFunctionObject
{
    int operator () (int a, int b) { return a - b; }
    double operator () (double a, double b) { return a + b; }
};
```

We have defined two operators, each of which accepting two parameters. We wish to bind to two, one or zero values. We take the case of binding to two parameters and we provide the return type of the function as template argument to bind:

```
MyFunctionObject fo;

// A. Binding with two values
int a = 10;
int b = 20;

cout << boost::bind<int>(fo, _1, _2)(a, b) << endl;

double x = -3.1415;
double y = 2.71;
cout << boost::bind<double>(fo, _1, _2)(x, y) << endl;
```

We now consider fixing one argument while allowing the other arguments to be variable:

```
// B. Binding with one value
// A 'semi-discretisation' by specifying the second parameter
double xnew = 0.0;
for (xnew = 0.0; xnew <= 1.0; xnew += 0.1)
{
    cout << boost::bind<double>(fo, _1, 0.5)(xnew) << endl;
}

// Specify first parameter while second parameter is variable
for (xnew = 0.0; xnew <= 1.0; xnew += 0.1)
{
    cout << boost::bind<double>(fo, 0.5, _1)(xnew) << endl;
}
```

Finally, we give specific values for all arguments which implies that no variable arguments need to be given:

```
// C. Binding with all variables fixed
cout << "No parameters\n";
cout << boost::bind<int>(fo, 1, 2)() << endl;
```

We note that the binding process makes copies of arguments passed to bind. This may be undesirable, for example if the object is noncopyable or is expensive to copy. Furthermore, when the function changes the state of the object it will be done to a copy instead of the original object. Thus, the changes are lost when bind is called. We then prefer to work with references and in that case we use boost::ref and boost::cref (reference and const reference, respectively) to store a reference to the object rather than a copy in order to improve performance. Here is an example to show three ways of binding to a member function; first, we use the default case (a copy of myII is made), secondly we create a reference to myII (note however, that the reference itself is copied) and finally another way to avoid copies of myII is to pass arguments by pointers:

```
cout << "The effects of object copies in Bind\n";
MyStruct myII; // MyStruct could contain non-negligible state
boost::bind(&MyStruct::print, myII, _1)("copied object");

cout << "The effects of when NO object copies are made in Bind\n";
boost::bind(&MyStruct::print, boost::ref(myII), _1)("using reference");
boost::bind(&MyStruct::print, &myII, _1)("passing arg by pointer");
```

The same conclusions hold when binding to a function object:

```
MyFunctionObject fo; int a=10; int b=20;

// Makes copy of "fo"
cout << boost::bind<int>(fo, _1, _2)(a, b) << endl;

// No copy of "fo"
cout << boost::bind<int>(boost::ref(fo), _1, _2)(a, b) << endl;
```

You can run this code and you will see that the copy constructor is called several times in the default case. For this reason it is important to use references in order to avoid copying large-grained objects. We see multiple calls to the default constructor and copy constructor of MyStruct and MyFunctionObject when we use the default binding.

2.10 Dynamic Sorting and Bind

We show how to sort collections in combination with Bind. For example, the STL `sort()` algorithm allows us to sort between two iterators in a collection and it also uses a *binary predicate* (returns a `bool`) to compare two arguments. To take an example, we first create an array of `Person` instances:

```
vector<Person> personSet22;
```

We now define the binary predicate for sorting (in descending order) based on age; notice the use of placeholders:

```
// Sort the vector on age using Boost Bind (bind to age member)
std::sort(personSet22.begin(), personSet22.end(),
        boost::bind(greater<int>(), boost::bind(&Person::age, _1),
        boost::bind(&Person::age, _2)));
```

We can also sort the array by binding to the person's name and again using the appropriate placeholders:

```
// Sort the vector on name using Boost Bind (bind to name member)
std::sort(personSet22.begin(), personSet22.end(),
        boost::bind(greater<string>(), boost::bind(&Person::name, _1),
        boost::bind(&Person::name, _2)));
```

2.11 Function Composition

The concept of function composition is closely related to mathematics. In general, a function maps a domain into a range. We can now 'combine' functions in such a way that the range of one function becomes the domain of another function. In other words, the output from an 'inner' function becomes the input to the 'outer' function when these two functions are composed. We give two examples to show how function composition works. Let us consider first of all two functions with the same signature:

```
double g(double x)
{
    return x*x;
}

double f(double x)
{
    return sqrt(x);
}
```

We can compose these functions in various ways as the following code shows:

```
x = 3.0;
cout << boost::bind(f, boost::bind(g, _1))(x) << endl;
cout << boost::bind(g, boost::bind(f, _1))(x) << endl;

cout << boost::bind(f, boost::bind(f, boost::bind(g, _1)))(x) << endl;
cout << boost::bind(g, boost::bind(g, boost::bind(f, _1)))(x) << endl;
```

Here we see that the function `g` and `f` are nested. The output from the above code is 3, 3, 1.73205, 9.

The following example is different because in this case we compose functions having different arities. In particular, we define a function having two input arguments:

```
double G(double x, double y)
{
    return x*x + y*y;
}
```

We can compose this function with the function f above if we 'project' G into a function that accepts one parameter:

```
x = 3.0;
double fixedValue = 4.0;
cout << boost::bind(f, boost::bind(G, _1, fixedValue))(x) << endl;
```

In this case the first argument of G is variable while the second parameter is fixed ('pinned down'), thus allowing function composition to take place.

2.12 Applications and Relationships with STL and Boost

As a first example, consider a scalar-valued function $f(t,x)$ of two variables. We pick an array xarr of x values and we use them in $f(t,x)$ to produce what is essentially a scalar-valued function $G(t)$ of the single variable t. We use two function objects, one of which models $f(t,x)$:

```
struct Coefficient
{ // The basic function of two (continuous) variables

    double operator () (double t, double x)
    {
        return t * x;
    }
};
```

The other function object Client depends only on the variable t. This class is able to produce an array of values for any value of t. Its interface is given by:

```
struct Client
{ // Models a discretised equation by using discrete values of x

    vector<double> xarr;
    Coefficient fo;    // Function object

    Client(const vector<double>& mesh, const Coefficient& function)
    { // Copy everything for convenience

        xarr = mesh;
        fo = function;
    }

    vector<double> operator () (double t)
    {
        vector<double> result(xarr.size());

        for (int j = 0; j < xarr.size(); ++j)
        {
            result[j] = boost::bind<double>(fo, _1, xarr[j])(t);
        }
        return result;
    }
};
```

Here we apply Bind to produce a class that uses a combination of discrete and continuous variables. We could have solved this problem in other ways (for example, directly evaluating fo) but the current solution shows the usefulness of Bind. A test program is:

```
int main()
{
    Coefficient fo; cout << fo(1.0, 2.0) << endl;

    vector<double> xarr(10);

    xarr[0] = 0.0;
    for (int j = 1; j < xarr.size(); ++j)
    {
        xarr[j] = xarr[j-1] + 0.1;
    }

    Client myDiscrete(xarr, fo);

    xarr = myDiscrete(2.0);

    for (int j = 1; j < xarr.size(); ++j)
    {
        cout << xarr[j] << endl;
    }

    return 0;
}
```

We conclude this section by generalising the above code. We create a template version of Client in which the template parameter is a function object representing the function under consideration:

```
template <typename FO>
struct GenericClient
{ // Models a discretised equation by using discrete values of x

    vector<double> xarr;
    FO fo;    // Generic function object

    GenericClient(const vector<double>& mesh, const FO& function)
    { // Copy everything for convenience

        xarr = mesh;
        fo = function;
    }

    vector<double> operator () (double t)
    {
        vector<double> result(xarr.size());

        for (int j = 0; j < xarr.size(); ++j)
        {
            result[j] = boost::bind<double>(fo, _1, xarr[j])(t);
        }
        return result;
    }
};
```

We can then use this class with a number of function objects:

```
Coefficient fo;
GenericClient<Coefficient> myDiscrete2(xarr, fo);
xarr = myDiscrete2(20.0);
```

```
Coefficient2 fo2; // Some other function object
GenericClient<Coefficient2> myDiscrete3(xarr, fo2);
xarr = myDiscrete3(26.0);
```

Were `Coefficient2` is defined as:

```
struct Coefficient2
{ // The basic function of two (continuous) variables

  double operator () (double t, double x)
  {
    return t + x;
  }
};
```

2.13 Summary and Conclusions

We have given an introduction to STL Bind and Boost.Bind. The main applications of Boost.Bind have to do with the ability to adapt functions and function objects so that they can be used with STL, support for function composition and creating new function objects from existing ones.

In general, we try not to use STL Bind because Boost.Bind is easier to learn (and to remember!). However, you may still need to understand STL Bind if your applications use it. In chapter 4 we introduce Boost.Phoenix, one of whose components is called Bind and that allows us to tie a function to some arguments for lazy evaluation.

3 Event Notification, Observer Pattern and Signals Library

3.1 Introduction and Objectives

In this chapter we introduce the Boost.Signals library that addresses the problem of keeping the data in object networks synchronised. The library can be seen as a specific implementation of an event notification pattern that has a variety of names, such as *Observer* (GOF 1995) and *Publisher-Subscriber* (POSA 1996). In general, this pattern ensures that the underlying data in an object-oriented software system remains consistent; in other words, when the data in an object (the *publisher* role) changes then all objects (the *subscriber* role) that depend on it must be updated. The main use cases are:

- U1: define publisher and subscribers.
- U2: connect (register) a subscriber with a publisher.
- U3: update a subscriber when an event takes place in the publisher.
- U4: disconnect a subscriber from a publisher.

We discuss these use cases and we show how to implement them using the Signals library. Before we go into the details of the library we first introduce some typical object dependency graphs that underlie event notification patterns and we also give an example of using the *Observer* pattern using the object-oriented approach. We then introduce the main concepts (namely *signals* and *slots*) in Boost.Signals and we show how they can be used to implement a template-based version of *Observer*. We show how to implement use cases U1 to U4 and we show how to extend this list by defining slot groups, explicit support for connections, default and user-defined strategies for combining the results when subscribers are updated. Finally, we introduce the thread-safe version of the Signals library.

The convenience header file when using Signals is:

```
#include <boost/signals.hpp>
```

3.2 Notification Patterns in Object-Oriented Systems

Object-oriented software is typically constructed as a network of inter-related and dependent objects. In general, an object *provides* services to other objects in the form of member functions and it *requires* services from other objects. A dependency between two objects A and B exists if A requires the services of B. We can then model this relationship as a directed graph between A and B by modelling the graph nodes as objects and the edges (or arcs) as directed lines between A and B. Different kinds of graphs can be defined and each one corresponds to some well-known design pattern. A number of common cases are shown in Figure 3.1 and they correspond to the notification patterns as described in GOF 1995 and POSA 1996. Thus, once we know which graph type is appropriate for a given problem we can then associate it with a solution using a design pattern which we then implement in C++ using the Signals library. The different topologies are:

- Type (a): this is the *Observer* pattern, namely one publisher and N subscribers. An object can only play one role; it is either a publisher or a subscriber, but not both. The data structure is a tree of depth one.
- Type (b): in this case an object can be a subscriber of a given publisher and a publisher for other objects. There is one object (called the *root*) that is a publisher only and objects (called *leaves*) that are subscribers only. The data structure in this case is a tree. The corresponding design pattern is called *Propagator*.

- Type (c): the data structure is a graph. There is no special root object as in cases (a) and (b). We remark that the Boost Graph Library (BGL) provides developers with ready-made graph classes.
- Type (d): this is an important notification pattern that models the *Mediator* pattern (GOF 1995). In this case we promote loose coupling by placing a mediator object M between the sender S and receiver R of an event.
- Type (e): this pattern models the *Layers* (POSA 1996) and *Chain of Responsibility* (GOF 1995) patterns. Each object plays the role of subscriber for the objects in a lower layer while an object plays the role of publisher for the objects in its upper layers.

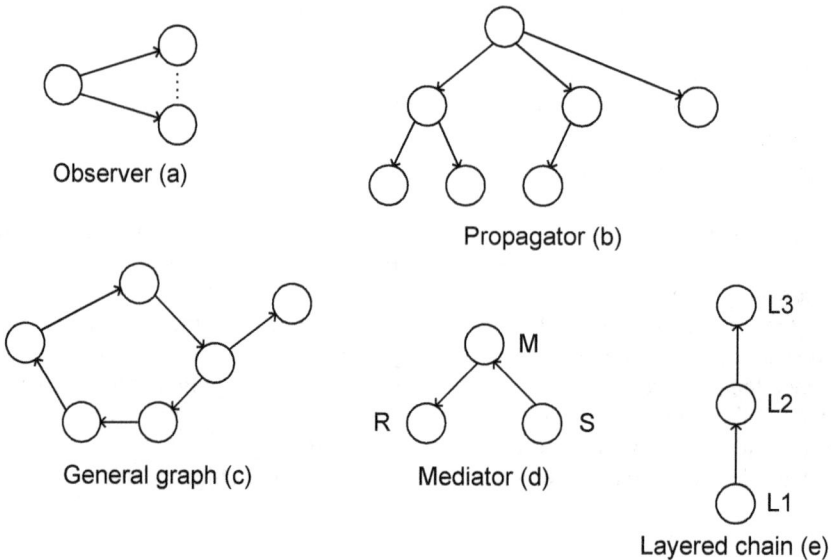

Observer (a)

Propagator (b)

General graph (c)

Mediator (d)

Layered chain (e)

Figure 3.1 Event notification scenarios

3.3 The GOF Observer Pattern: what is it and what are the Problems?

This pattern is popular because it satisfies a need, namely keeping the data in object networks consistent and synchronised. When data of interest changes in one object all other dependent objects are notified of the change and they can then determine what to do, for example by modifying their state.

In this section we review the *Observer* pattern. We take a specific example in order to remain focused and we implement it in the object-oriented way. Having done that, we discuss the advantages and disadvantages of this solution which will then lead us to a discussion on how to improve the design by incremental modification of the C++ code.

When implementing the *Observer* pattern we first create two base classes corresponding to the roles in the pattern. On the one hand, we have the *Observable* base class (also known as the *Publisher* or *Subject*) that contains changeable data and the *Observer* base class (also known as the *Subscriber*) whose instances are updated when changes occur in *Observable* instances.

The pattern describes how observers can be connected to and disconnected from observables. Synonyms for the connection are attachment and registration while synonyms for disconnection are detachment and deregistration. When an observer is connected to an observable it will be notified of changes in the latter object.

We take the case of an observable having an internal changeable counter and an observer that is notified each time the state changes. The UML class diagram is showed in Figure 3.2 and here we see that concrete observable and observer classes are derived from their respective base classes.

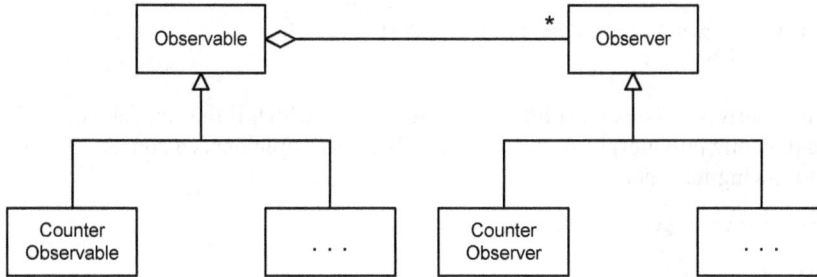

Figure 3.2 Observer Pattern: Object-Oriented version

We now describe the code that implements the classes in Figure 3.2. Class `Observable` contains a list of connected observers (hence the aggregation relationship in Figure 3.2) as well as member functions for connection and disconnection and finally a member function called `NotifyObservers` that notifies all connected observers when data changes:

```
class Observable
{
private:

    // Set of connected observers
    list<Observer*> Observers;

    Observable(const Observable& org);
    Observable& operator = (const Observable& org);

public:
    Observable();                           // Default constructor
    virtual ~Observable();                  // Destructor

    void AddObserver(Observer* obj);     // Add an observer to the list
    void DeleteObserver(Observer* obj); // Remove an observer from the list
    void NotifyObservers();                 // Notify the observers
};
```

The body of the member function to notify observers uses an iterator to visit each observer in the list and it calls the `Update()` member function:

```
void Observable::NotifyObservers()
{
    list<Observer*>::iterator it;
    list<Observer*>::iterator end = Observers.end();

    for(it = Observers.begin(); it != end; ++it)
    {
        (*it)->Update(*this);
    }
}
```

We now turn our attention to the `Observer` class:

```
class Observer
{
private:
    Observer(const Observer& orig);
    Observer& operator = (const Observer& orig);

public:
    Observer();
    virtual ~Observer();

    // Method is called when observable object has change in state
    virtual void Update(Observable& obj) = 0;
};
```

We see that derived classes must implement `Update()` which is the standard way of realising dynamic polymorphism in C++. The class that implements a counter abstraction has the following interface:

```
class Counter: public Observable
{
private:

    // Changeable state
    long CounterValue;

    Counter(const Counter& orig);
    Counter& operator = (const Counter& orig);

public:
    Counter();                  // Default constructor
    ~Counter();                 // Destructor

    long GetCounter() const;    // Return the counter value
    void operator ++ (int j);
    void operator -- (int j);
};
```

In this case the changeable data is a counter that is modified by the increment and decrement operations. The counter then triggers the connected observers:

```
// Increase the internal counter, use postfix ++
void Counter::operator ++ (int j)
{
    CounterValue++;
    NotifyObservers();
}

// Decrease the internal counter, use postfix -
void Counter::operator -- (int j)
{
    CounterValue--;
    NotifyObservers();
}
```

We now discuss the derived observer class that displays the current counter value:

```
class CounterObserver: public Observer
{
private:

    // ...
public:
```

```
    CounterObserver(Counter& obj);

    // Method called when the observable object has a change in state
    void Update(Observable& obj);
};
```

The code for this class is:

```
CounterObserver::CounterObserver(Counter& obj)
{
    obj.AddObserver(this);
}

// Method is called when the observable object changes its state
void CounterObserver::Update(Observable& obj)
{
    Counter* pCounter = dynamic_cast<Counter*>(&obj);

    // Check if a null object/wrong kind of object has sent signal
    if (pCounter != 0)
    {
        cout << "Observer address : " << this
             << " Counter has changed : " << pCounter->GetCounter();
    }
    else cout << "Unknown observable" <<endl;
}
```

Finally, we create code to show how the pattern works by instantiating a counter and two observers:

```
void main()
{
    // Create a counter object
    Counter cnt;

    // Just increase the counter without observing it
    cnt++; cnt++; cnt++;

    // Create an observer
    CounterObserver observer1(cnt);

    // Decrease the counter
    cnt--; cnt--; cnt--;

    // Create another observer
    CounterObserver observer2(cnt);

    // Increase the counter
    cnt++; cnt++; cnt++;

    // Remove the first observer
    cnt.DeleteObserver(&observer1);

    // Increase the counter
    cnt++; cnt++; cnt++;
}
```

This is the essence of the GOF *Observer* pattern. It is useful and we can create more concrete observable and observer classes by using inheritance.

3.3.1   The GOF Observer Pattern: Critique

The *Observer* pattern is popular and it has been used in a number of applications, namely those that have an object dependency graph as shown in Figure 3.1 (a). For more complex applications we need ad-hoc workarounds and additions to the pattern have been proposed. Some problems in the authors' experience are:

- Inflexible design: the *Publisher* and *Subscriber* classes are tightly coupled. If we wish to define a new subscriber class we must derive it from the `Observer` base class as well as implementing the `Update()` member function.
- Unexpected updates: observers have no knowledge of each other and we run the risk when a given observer updates publisher data that this may lead to a cascade of updates to other observers and their dependent objects.
- Dangling references: deleting a publisher should not produce dangling references in its observers. Memory management and object lifecycle is the responsibility of the developer.
- The *Observer* pattern is not thread-safe. It is possible to experience race conditions because two observers are simultaneously accessing a publisher.

We discuss and resolve these shortcomings in the rest of this chapter.

3.4   An Introduction to the Signals Library

The Signals library implements the *Observer* pattern and it also lays the foundation upon which other event notification patterns can be built, such as *Chain of Responsibility*, *Mediator*, *Layers*, *Model View Controller* (MVC), *Presentation-Abstraction-Control* (PAC) and *Blackboard* patterns (GOF 1995, POSA 1996, Jagannathan 1989). The library uses a number of concepts; first, *signals* are publishers of data and *slots* are the corresponding subscribers. Signals can be connected to and disconnected from slots. The multiplicity relationships is 1:N which means that one signal is connected to zero or more slots and the precise number can vary at run-time. One advantage of this library is that it allows developers to decouple the publisher of an event (a signal in this case) from the code that handles it, namely one or more slots. In this sense we reduce type dependencies due to the fact that there is an abstract connection between signals and slots. Slots can accept arguments of any type, thus making the library very flexible. Furthermore, we can implement slots using function pointers, function objects, binded functions and lambda expressions.

We give a summary of the functionality in the library:

- Connecting multiple slots to a signal; disconnecting a slot from a signal. It is possible to temporarily *block* a slot which implies that it is not disconnected but it will be ignored when the signal is invoked.
- Slot groups: the order of execution of slots is not deterministic in general; however, a given slot can be stored in a group where each group has a unique number. Then slots in groups are invoked in ascending order of their group number. For example, the slots in group 1 are executed before the slots in group 2. Within a group however, the order of invocation of slots is not specified.
- Merging the return values from slots by using *combiners*. A combiner is a parameterised type and it is responsible for combining returned values from individual slots. The Signals library offers a default combiner which returns the value for the last invoked slot. You can create your own combiners as we shall see in section 10.
- We can create slots using Bind and Lambda.

- Signals2 library: this is the thread-safe version of the Signals library. Signals2 also allows the user to specify the manner in which multiple return values are combined.

We now discuss each of these topics and we give examples on how to apply them in code.

3.5   Signals and Slots

We begin our discussion of slots and signals by an example. In this case we define a global function and a function object which will play the role of slots:

```
void mySlot()
{
    cout << "a first slot \n";
}

struct SecondSlot
{
    int data;

    SecondSlot() { data = 0; }
    SecondSlot(int val) { data = val; }

    void operator () () { cout << "a second slot " << data << endl; }
    void operator () (int n) {cout << "a second slot "<< data + n << endl;}
};
```

We now define a signal and we connect these two slots to it. We can also determine the number of connected slots by calling the member function num_slots():

```
boost::signal<void ()> signal;

// Connect slots
signal.connect(&mySlot);
signal.connect(SecondSlot());    // Default object

// Connect a non-default object
SecondSlot s2(99);
signal.connect(s2);

cout << "Number of slots: " << signal.num_slots() << endl;

// Emit the signal
signal();
```

In this case we have three slots connected to the signal. The syntax:

```
boost::signal<void ()> signal;
```

means that all slots must conform to this function signature and in this case the input argument of the signal (it is empty) is the same as that of the connected slots. We now take an example in which a signal has an int as input argument:

```
boost::signal<void (int)> signal2;
```

This means that slots must have the same signature, for example the function:

```
void mySlot2(int n)
{
    cout << "a first slot with value: " << n << endl;
}
```

We can now connect this function and the function object `slot2` as slot to `signal2`:

```
signal2.connect(&mySlot2);
SecondSlot slot2(10);
signal2.connect(slot2);

// Define the data in signal that slots will receive
int transferData = 10;
signal2(transferData);
```

This completes the basic examples.

3.6   Slot Groups

We now discuss how to disconnect a slot from a signal and how to specify the order in which slots are invoked. For example, the following code will produce 'World Hello' as output:

```
void Hello()
{
    cout << "Hello ";
}

void World()
{
    cout << "World ";
}

int main()
{
    boost::signal<void ()> signal;
    signal.connect(&World);
    signal.connect(&Hello);
    signal();   // Will print "World Hello"

    return 0;
}
```

If we wish to influence the order of slot invocation we place slots in groups; each group has an associated number and the default navigation order is ascending. For example, when the above `connect()` statements are replaced by the following `connect()` statements, the code will produce 'Hello World' as output:

```
// Place slots in groups
signal.connect(1, &World);
signal.connect(0, &Hello);
```

We note that the order of invocation of slots within a group is non-deterministic. Thus, if you wish to call slots in a certain order you should place each one in its own unique group.

We can disconnect all the slots in a given group by calling the member function `disconnect()` as the following example shows for group number 1:

```
signal.disconnect(1);
signal();
```

The output becomes 'Hello'.

Finally, here is an example where we have three groups and a slot that is not in any of them:

```
boost::signal<void ()> signalII;

// Define three groups and place some slots in them
int groupA = 0;
int groupB = 1;
int groupC = 2;

// Create slots
SecondSlot sA;
SecondSlot sB(10);
SecondSlot sC(20);
SecondSlot sC_1(-20);

cout << "Connecting three groups\n";
signalII.connect(groupA, sA);
signalII.connect(groupB, sB);
signalII.connect(groupC, sC);
signalII.connect(groupC, sC_1);
signalII.connect(&mySlot);          // mySlot defined in section 3.5

signalII();
```

When we run this code we get the following output:

```
Connecting three groups
a second slot 0
a second slot 10
a second slot 20
a second slot -20
a first slot
```

Notice the order in which the values are printed; this is determined by the group number. In other words, using groups allows you to define the order in which subscribers are updated. Finally, we can disconnect all the slots in a group as the following example shows:

```
cout << "Disconnecting two groups\n";
signalII.disconnect(groupA);
signalII.disconnect(groupB);
```

When an event occurs, the subscribers in these two groups will not be updated.

3.7   Objects playing Roles of Signals and Slots

The *Observer* pattern supports objects that play the role of either publisher or subscriber. It is not possible to let an object be a publisher for some events and subscriber for other events unless we modify the code in some way. If we examine the different dependency graphs in Figure 3.1 we see that objects play both roles in general. This scenario can be modelled using Signals. We take an example that is advanced enough to show how to implement most scenarios. We create a template class called PropagatorSlot that is a function object and hence can play the role of subscriber. It has a template parameter whose instantiation will be a function object which then plays the role of publisher.

We use Figure 3.3 to make the object relationships and code easier to visualise. Here we have one main signal (signalA), three ultimate subscribers (slotA, slotB, slotC) and three propagators (ps, ps2, ps3) that are subscribers for signalA and publishers for the slots slotA, slotB and slotC.

The new class that models propagators is:

```
template <typename FO>
struct PropagatorSlot
{ // This is a slot that also plays the role of signal

    int data;
    FO* slot; // FO is a function object that is a slot

    PropagatorSlot(FO& mySlot)
    {
        data = 0;
        slot = &mySlot;
    }

    PropagatorSlot(FO& mySlot, int val)
    {
        data = val;
        slot = &mySlot;
    }

    void operator () ()
    {
        cout << "Propagator slot " << data << endl;
        (*slot)();
    }

    void operator () (int n)
    {
        cout << "Propagator slot " << data + n << endl;
        (*slot)();
    }
};
```

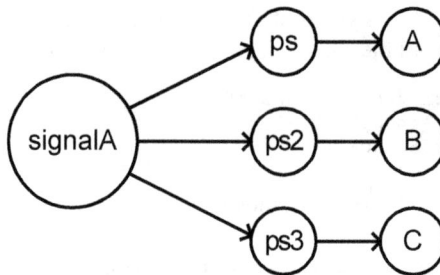

Figure 3.3 Extended Signals and Slots

For completeness, we give the definition of the classes SecondSlot and ThirdSlot:

```
struct SecondSlot
{
    int data;

    SecondSlot() { data = 0; }
    SecondSlot(int val) { data = val; }

    void operator () () { cout << "a second slot " << data << endl; }
    void operator () (int n) { cout << "a second slot " << data+n << endl;}
};
```

```
struct ThirdSlot
{
    int data;

    ThirdSlot() { data = 0; }
    ThirdSlot(int val) { data = val; }

    void operator () () { cout << "a third slot " << data << endl; }
    void operator () (int n) { cout << "a third slot " << data+n << endl; }
};
```

We now implement the tree in Figure 3.3 as follows:

```
cout << "Showing chain of responsibility...\n";
boost::signal<void ()> signalA;

SecondSlot slotA(10);
PropagatorSlot<SecondSlot> ps(slotA, 10);
SecondSlot slotB(20);
PropagatorSlot<SecondSlot> ps2(slotB, 20);
ThirdSlot slotC(30);
PropagatorSlot<ThirdSlot> ps3(slotC, 30);

signalA.connect(ps);
signalA.connect(ps2);
signalA.connect(ps3);

signalA();
```

You can check that the output is given by:

```
Showing chain of responsibility...
Propagator slot 10
a second slot 10
Propagator slot 20
a second slot 20
Propagator slot 30
a third slot 30
```

We see some advantages of this design philosophy. First, subscriber classes do not have to be derived from a single base class and all they need to do is to overload the function call operator (). Second, there is no artificial separation of publisher and subscriber roles; an object can play both roles.

3.8   Connection Management and the connection Class

In this section we introduce the connection class. This class has knowledge of all objects in a given connection. This is a useful feature because we can disconnect a slot from a signal and we can test if a slot is currently connected to a signal. Some other functions in connection are:

- Block and unblock a connection.
- Is a connection blocked?
- Is a connection connected?
- Comparing connections.
- Swap the signal/slot knowledge of two connections.

We show how to create instances of `connection`. First, we consider the following class:

```
struct SlotClass
{
    string data;

    SlotClass() { data = string("Default"); }
    SlotClass(const string& val) { data = val; }

    void operator () (const string& val)
    {
        cout << "A second slot: " << val+data << endl;
    }
};
```

We then define a signal:

```
// 1. Create signal
boost::signal<void (const string&)> mySignal;
```

Then we create the slot and connections:

```
// 2. Create slots
SlotClass sc1(string("sc1"));
SlotClass sc2(string("sc2"));

// 3. Create connection objects
boost::signals::connection c1 = mySignal.connect(sc1);
boost::signals::connection c2 = mySignal.connect(sc2);
```

We now query the status of the connections:

```
// 4. Some properties of the connection
cout << boolalpha;    // True and false will be 'literally' outputted
cout << "c1 == c2: " << (c1 == c2) << endl; // false
cout << "c1 < c2: " << (c2 < c2) << endl;    // false
cout << "c1 > c2: " << (c2 > c2) << endl;    // false
```

We note that slots can be blocked which implies that they will be ignored when the signal is invoked. We can unblock the slot and it is possible to query the blocked/connected status as the following code shows:

```
// 5. Blocking and unblocking a connection
cout << "c1 blocked: " << c1.blocked() << endl;        // false
c1.block();
cout << "c1 blocked: " << c1.blocked() << endl;        // true
c1.unblock();
cout << "c1 blocked: " << c1.blocked() << endl;        // false

cout << "c1 connected: " << c1.connected() << endl;  // true
c1.disconnect();
cout << "c1 connected: " << c1.connected() << endl;  // false
```

Connections are resources. We may wish to make sure that a connection is disconnected when it goes out of scope and to this end we use the `scoped_connection` class. We give an example by comparing `connection` and `scoped_connection`:

```
// 6. Using scoped connections
boost::signal<void (const string& val)> mySignal2;
```

```
// Normal connection
{
   boost::signals::connection c3 = mySignal2.connect(SlotClass("ZZ"));
   mySignal2("AA");      // Print AAZZ
}

mySignal2("BB");         // Prints BBZZ

// Scoped connection
boost::signal<void (const string& val)> mySignal3;
{
   boost::signals::scoped_connection c4 =
      mySignal3.connect(SlotClass("XX"));
   mySignal3("CC");                     // Print CCXX
} // c4 goes out of scope

mySignal3("DD");         // Prints 'nothing', no connection anymore
```

In the latter case we see that there is no output because the `scoped_connection` has already terminated the connection between the slot and the signal. Finally, we can use connections in combination with STL. For example, we can create named connections as follows:

```
// Connections and STL
map<string, boost::signals::connection*> Registry;
Registry["local"] = &c1;
Registry["remote"] = &c2;
```

This option can be useful in more advanced notification scenarios.

3.9 Creating Slots using Bind and Lambda

We now give a short discussion on how to make life easier when working with Boost.Signals. First, we show how to avoid creating many function objects by using *lambda* (unnamed) functions whose body can be defined *in place* that is, at the client site. Second, we can add an extra level of indirection to code by binding the code for the function call operator `()` to a function with a compatible signature.

3.9.1 Creating Slots 'on the fly' with Lambda

We give a preview of Boost.Lambda. Lambda functions avoid our having to create numerous small function objects. Lambda employs placeholders as delayed arguments to lambda expressions.

Let us take a simple example. In this case we define a signal that returns `void` and that has a (modifiable) reference to a `double` as input argument:

```
// A. using Lambda
#include <boost/lambda/lambda.hpp>
using namespace boost::lambda;

// 1. Create signal
boost::signal<void (double&)> mySignal;
```

We now define two lambda functions that modify their input arguments in some way and we connect them to the signal:

```
// 2. Use placeholder _1 for variable
int GroupA = 0;
```

```
int GroupB = 1;

// 3. Make connections
double x = 9.0;
mySignal.connect(GroupA, _1 += sqrt(x));
mySignal.connect(GroupB, _1 *= _1);
```

We note that the slot function is created *in place* and we do not need to create separate functions or function objects. The last step, namely event notification takes place and the value is computed:

```
// 4. Trigger event
double value = 2.0;       // the run-time value of placeholder_1
mySignal(value);
cout << "Value is: " << value << endl; // Value '25' printed
```

It is preferable to use Boost.Phoenix instead of Boost.Lambda in our opinion because it has more functionality. We discuss Boost.Phoenix in chapter 4.

3.9.2   Creating Slot Types with Bind

We know that slots implement the function call operator `()`; however, not all classes that we would like to use as slots implement this operator. For example, consider a class that implements two algorithms:

```
struct MultiAlgorithmClass
{ // A class that plays a slot role;
  // different algos are called from signal

    double setValue;

    MultiAlgorithmClass() { setValue = sqrt(2.0); }
    MultiAlgorithmClass(double val) { setValue = val; }

    double AlgoI(double parameter)
    {
       if (setValue > parameter)
       {
          return setValue;
       }
       return parameter;
    }

    double AlgoII(double parameter)
    {
       return 0.5 * (setValue + parameter);
    }
};
```

This class cannot be used in its present form with Signals because it does not support the function call operator. So, what can we do? The answer is that we employ a configurable function object which can then delegate to the appropriate member function in `MultiAlgorithmClass`. In general, this technique is useful when an object responds to different events where each event has the same slot signature. In other words, these objects need different member functions which are called for different events, for example:

```
boost::signal<double (double)> mySignal2;

MultiAlgorithmClass obj1;
MultiAlgorithmClass obj2(-3.0);
cout << "Which algorithm?: 1) I, 2) II"; int c; cin >> c;
```

```
if (c == 1)
{
   mySignal2.connect(bind(&MultiAlgorithmClass::AlgoI, &obj1, _1));
}
else
{
   mySignal2.connect(bind(&MultiAlgorithmClass::AlgoII, &obj2, _1));
}

cout << mySignal2(2.0) << endl; // Give return value of computation
```

In general, we apply this technique to create slots or binders as non-intrusive wrappers for existing classes so that they can be used with the Signals library.

3.10 Combiners

Many – but not all – applications involve slots which have `void` as return type. In some cases the return type could be a `bool`, a `double` or it could even be user-defined. Second, in a multi-slot application we may wish to know more about the values of the return types of individual slot functions. Some examples are:

- Stop iterating in connected slots when the first invoked slot returns `false`.
- Return the maximum, minimum or average of all values returned by invoked slots.

The way to achieve this functionality is through default (provided by Signals) and user-defined *combiners*. The default combiner is called `boost::last_one` and it returns the value of the last invoked slot.

We can create combiners. A combiner is a function object containing a special `typedef` and it implements the function call operator that is parametrised on the iterator type on which it will be invoked. We take an example in which we define a number of slots that simulate a process that bootstraps a number of components in a hardware application. The idea is that event notification should cease as soon as an invoked slot returns `false`. To this end, we create a custom combiner as follows:

```
struct BootstrapCheck
{ // Iterate in slots and return first 'false' value; otherwise, 'true'

   template <typename InputIterator>
   bool operator () (InputIterator first, InputIterator last) const
   {
      while (first != last)
      {
         if (!*first)
         {
            return false;
         }
         ++first;
      }

      return true;
   }
};
```

We now create a signal with the given `BootstrapCheck` combiner:

```
boost::signal<bool (), BootstrapCheck> sig;
```

Next, we define three slots and we connect them to the signal `sig`:

```
bool Phase1()
{
    cout << "Phase 1 OK\n";
    return true;
}

bool Phase2()
{
    cout << "Phase 2 fails\n";
    return false;
}

bool Phase3()
{
    cout << "Phase 3 OK, never reached\n";
    return true;
}

// Create slots
int group1 = 0;
int group2 = 1;
int group3 = 2;

// Connect slots
sig.connect(group1, &Phase1);
sig.connect(group2, &Phase2);
sig.connect(group3, &Phase3);

// Trigger event
sig();
```

When we run the program, we shall see that `Phase3()` is never called because iteration stops at `Phase2()`.

3.11 Thread-Safe Signals Library

The Signals library is not thread-safe which means that race conditions, silent data corruption and non-deterministic behaviour are possibilities during event updating. The Signals2 library resolves these problems by introducing mutexes and locks. The convenience header file for using Signals2 is:

```
#include <boost/signals2/signal.hpp>
```

The class `signal` (note the presence of a mutex as template parameter) is now defined as:

```
template <typename Signature,
        typename Combiner = optional_last_value
            <typename boost::function_traits<Signature>::result_type>,
        typename Group = int,
        typename GroupCompare = std::less<Group>,
        typename SlotFunction = function<Signature>,
        typename ExtendedSlotFunction =
            typename detail::extended_signature
            <function_traits<Signature>::arity, Signature>::function_type,
        typename Mutex = mutex >
```

```
class signal: public detail::signal<
              function_traits<Signature>::arity, Signature,
              Combiner, Group,
              GroupCompare, SlotFunction,
              ExtendedSlotFunction, Mutex>::type
{
};
```

Using Signals2 is easy, as the following code shows:

```
struct MyStruct
{
   double val;

   MyStruct(double v) { val = v; }

   void operator () (double newValue)
   {
      val = newValue;
   }
};

int main()
{

   // Signal with double argument and a void return value
   boost::signals2::signal<void (double)> sig;

   // Connect slots
   MyStruct mySlot(3.0);
   sig.connect(0, mySlot);

   MyStruct mySlot2(399.0);
   sig.connect(1, mySlot2);

   // Call all of the slots
   sig(39.0);

   return 0;
};
```

Since multi-core processors have become commodity products we shall probably see more multi-threaded desktop applications in the future and it is then advisable to use Signals2 library for these applications. We discuss multi-threading in chapter 18.

3.12 The GOF Observer Pattern revisited

In this section we use the functionality of Signals to create a more flexible version of the GOF Observer pattern that we discussed in section 3.3. The objective is to resolve some of the shortcomings that we mentioned in section 3.3.1. The new interface for Observable is:

```
#include <boost/signals.hpp>

class Observable
{
private:

   boost::signal<void ()> signal;

   // etc.
};
```

The code for adding and removing slots is achieved by the following template member functions:

```
// Template member functions
template <typename Observer> void AddObserver(const Observer& slot)
{
    signal.connect(slot);
}

template <typename Observer> void DeleteObserver(const Observer& slot)
{
    signal.disconnect(slot);
}

void NotifyObservers()
{
    signal();
}
```

Due to the combination of Signals and templates we do not need to create a hierarchy of observer classes. In fact, we can use a 'mix' of free functions and function objects as elements of an observer list:

```
Observable mySubject;
cout << "**First notification:\n";
mySubject.AddObserver(SecondSlot());   // Function object
mySubject.AddObserver(&mySlot);        // C function
mySubject.NotifyObservers();

cout << "**Second notification:\n";
mySubject.DeleteObserver(&mySlot);
mySubject.NotifyObservers();
```

where `SecondSlot` is a function object that we have already discussed in section 3.5 and `mySlot()` is a global function:

```
void mySlot()
{
    cout << "a first slot \n";
}
```

The output from the above code is:

```
**First notification:
a second slot 0
a first slot
**Second notification:
a second slot 0
```

This completes our discussion of the Signals-based *Observer* pattern. It would be possible to make it more general but this is outside the scope of the current book.

3.13 Summary and Conclusions

In this chapter we have introduced the Boost.Signals library and we discussed how it allows developers to create flexible and extendible code in event-driven applications. It can be used with the Boost.Function, Boost.Bind and Boost.Lambda libraries.

What's after Signals? In Volume II we shall apply it to create a number of patterns and software frameworks for event notification based on the design and system patterns in GOF 1995 and POSA 1996. We also show what the advantages are when compared to the way patterns are implemented using the object-oriented paradigm.

4 Phoenix

4.1 Introduction and Objectives

In this chapter we introduce the Boost.Phoenix library. This library has support for a number of features in the functional programming (FP) paradigm. The central concept in FP is the function. In contrast to C++ functions – which are evaluated as soon as their arguments are known – evaluation of Phoenix functions is deferred; we call this lazy function evaluation. In particular, we can compose functions into higher-order functions, we can define unnamed (lambda) functions and we can partially evaluate a function (to produce another function) by supplying only some of the arguments. Furthermore, functions may even return functions. The usefulness of Phoenix lies in the fact that it saves developers having to create specialised function objects that are used with standard algorithms.

We see functional programming as complementing the object-oriented and generic programming models. Popular functional programming languages are Haskell and F#.

We use the following files and namespaces:

```
#include <boost/spirit/home/phoenix/core.hpp>
#include <boost/spirit/home/phoenix/function.hpp>

using namespace boost::phoenix;
using namespace boost::phoenix::arg_names;
```

4.2 Motivating Phoenix: a Test Case

Before we discuss the architecture and modules in Phoenix we give examples to show how easy it is to write code and how much effort is saved when compared with the traditional approach of using function objects. The examples are to find the average value of a vector and to multiply all the elements of a vector by a number. The requirement is that we use the `for_each()` algorithm:

```
template <class InputIterator, class Function>
Function for_each(InputIterator _First, InputIterator _Last,
                  Function _Func);
```

This algorithm gives the function object as its return type. Function objects that are used by `for_each()` must implement the function call operator `()`.
We define two function objects:

```
class Average
{ // Function object to find the average of a collection

private:
    int num;        // The number of elements
    double sum;     // The sum of the elements

public:
    // Constructor initializes the value to multiply by
    Average() : num(0), sum(0.0)
    {
    }

    // The function call to process next element
    void operator () (double elem)
    {
        num++;
```

```
        sum += elem;
    }

    // Give final value using the cast to double operator
    operator double()
    {
        return sum/double(num);
    }
};

template <typename T>
class MultiplyByValue
{ // Multiply a value by a given factor

private:
    T factor;    // The value to multiply by

public:
    // Constructor initializes the value to multiply by
    MultiplyByValue(const T& value): factor (value) {}

    // The function call for the element to be multiplied
    void operator () (T& elem) const
    {
        elem *= factor;
    }
};
```

We can now create a vector and compute the vector average; we also multiply the elements of the vector by 2.0 using the above function objects:

```
// Create a vector with values
int size=4;
vector<double> v(size);
for (int i=0; i<size; ++i) v[i]=i*2.5;

cout<<"Vector: ";
for (int i=0; i<size; ++i) cout << v[i] << ", ";
cout<<endl;

// Finding the average with user-defined function object
// for_each returns the Average object so you can directly get the result
// from it because Average implements the "cast to double" operator.
double avg = for_each(v.begin(), v.end(), Average());
cout << "Average: " << avg << endl;

// Multiply elements of a vector by a double using function object
vector<double> v2(v);
for_each(v2.begin(), v2.end(), MultiplyByValue<double>(2.0));

// Print the resulting vector
cout<<"Vector multiplied by two: ";
for (int i = 0; i < v2.size(); ++i) cout<<v2[i]<<", ";
cout<<endl;
```

The code works as expected but we do have a number of comments; first, while it is not difficult to create function objects this process is tedious and second the amount of code to be maintained increases as more functionality is needed. In particular, client and function object code are normally defined in different files, thus making it more difficult to maintain the code. Fortunately, Phoenix allows us to create unnamed (lambda) functions at the point where they are needed, that is, the last argument in the for_each() algorithm. For the case in which we compute the average value of a vector, the code is:

```
// Finding the average with Phoenix
double avg = 0.0;
double N = v.size();
for_each(v.begin(), v.end(), ref(avg) += arg1/val(N));
cout << "Average: " << avg << endl;
```

In this code we initialise a variable `avg` to hold the result. The presence of the predefined placeholder `arg1` (which is the current element value in the vector) ensures that the expression `ref(avg) += arg1/val(N)` becomes a lambda function and hence can be lazily evaluated. The code for multiplying the elements of the vector by the value 2.0 is even easier:

```
for_each(v.begin(), v.end(), arg1 *= 2.0);
```

Easy! We shall discuss these and other issues in more detail in the following sections.

4.3   Introduction to Functional Programming

The functional programming model is based on the idea that a program consists of functions. The main program is itself a function which produces output from its input. In general, a main function is defined in terms of other functions which in their turn are defined in terms of other functions. The lowest-level functions are language primitives. Some of the advantages of functional programming languages are:

- Functional programs contain no *side effects*, in other words, a function call computes a result and has no further effect on its environment. This feature eliminates many sources of bugs in programs.
- The programmer does not need to prescribe the flow of control in functional programs.
- Some applications are suited to a solution using the functional programming model, leading to higher programmer productivity levels when compared to other programming models. In particular, the ability to glue simple functions together to produce more complex functions promotes modularisation.

In the current context, most concepts in Phoenix are functions that we evaluate as $f(x1, x2, x3, ..., xn)$ where n is the *function arity* and $x1, x2, ..., xn$ are the input arguments that the function expects. A function is a black box; it produces output from input. In contrast to normal functions – where we must provide all input arguments in order to compute them – Phoenix functions support partial function application. For example, let us consider a real-valued function of two variables:

```
double func(double x, double y)
{
    //...
}
```

What we would like to do now is to create a partially applied function having one input argument, the other argument being set to a value. The pseudo-code would now look like:

```
double func(double x, 2.0)
{
    //...
}
```

With Phoenix we can achieve this level of support.

4.3.1   Lambda Calculus and Lambda Functions

The lambda calculus is a mathematical abstraction for describing functions and their evaluation. This calculus forms the foundation for functional programming languages and was introduced by Alonzo Church as a means of formalising the concept of computability. It consists of a single transformation rule (variable substitution) and a single function definition scheme. One of the advantages of the Lambda calculus is that it enables the definition and use of *unnamed functions*. We take an example of a real-valued function that accepts two input parameters:

```
double SquareAdd(double x, double y)
{
    return x*x + y*y;
}
```

Looking at this function at a more abstract level we see that the function name is less important than how input is mapped to output. We represent the transformation as follows:

```
(x,y) -> x*x + y*y;
```

In the context of Boost libraries we can use this functionality in client code without having to call or even define `SquareAdd()` explicitly; instead, we use the above transformation directly at the client site.

We shall see in the following sections how to create lambda functions in Boost.Phoenix. Incidentally, Boost.Lambda (BLL) supports lambda functions but we do not discuss this library here because similar functionality is to be found in Boost.Phoenix. We do however, provide examples of Lambda code that accompanies the book.

The advantage of using lambda functions is that they lead to code that is easier to understand and to maintain than code that uses many small function objects scattered throughout an application.
A related topic is called *currying* and it is the technique of transforming a function that takes multiple arguments (or an n-tuple of arguments) in such a way that it can be called as a chain of functions each with a single argument.

Uncurrying is the dual transformation to currying, and can be seen as a form of defunctionalisation. It takes a function $f(x)$ which returns another function $g(y)$ as a result, and yields a new function $f'(x, y)$ which takes a number of additional parameters and applies them to the function returned by f.

4.4   The Architecture of Phoenix

Phoenix consists of a number of orthogonal modules arranged in a layered *'uses' hierarchy* as shown in Figure 4.1. There are three layers, with the 'Actor' module being the lowest layer and 'Algorithm' being the highest layer. There are no cyclic dependencies between layers because lower layers do not depend on higher layers.
We first give a short description of the modules in Figure 4.1 before discussing them in detail:

- Actor: this is the main concept in the library. Actors are function objects that accept a number of parameters in the closed range [0, PHOENIX_LIMIT]. The client passes arguments to the actor which then funnels them into a tuple for subsequent evaluation.

- Primitives: these are the building blocks in Phoenix and consist of primitives for function arguments (including predefined and user-defined arguments), values, references and their evaluation. For example, predefined arguments are called arg1, arg2, ..., argN (up to some limit N).
- Composite: these are actors consisting of zero or more actors. Composites are hierarchical, recursive actors and are similar to instances of the *Composite* design pattern (see GOF 1995). The added value is that we can combine functions, statements and expressions.
- Function: the class template function is the mechanism for the lazy evaluation of functions. A *lazy function* is not executed immediately because execution is delayed.
- Operator: this is similar to the Function module but in this case the Operator module provides a mechanism for the *lazy evaluation* of operators. A lazy operator looks like an ordinary prefix, infix or postfix operator at the syntax level but the execution is delayed.
- Statement: this module contains logic for building complex block structures. The stylised structures are similar to normal C++ structures such as `if/else`, `switch`, `while`, `for` and `try/catch`.
- Object: this module is concerned with object construction, destruction and conversion. It provides lazy versions of C++ native `new`, `delete` and the four major casting operators, for example `dynamic_cast`.
- Scope: using this module we can define and access local variables on the stack. This facility is of particular importance when using recursion. Another application of the module is when a lambda function is an input argument to another lambda function. We also consider lazy functions that accept one or more higher order functions.
- Bind: this module supports binding that allows us to tie a function to some arguments for lazy evaluation.
- Container/Intrinsic: this module contains a number of predefined lazy functions that operate on STL containers and sequences. In particular, this module provides a mechanism for the lazy evaluation of the public member functions of STL containers, for example `push_back()`.
- Algorithm: this module provides wrappers for the standard algorithms in `<algorithm>` and `<numeric>`; for example, we can use lambda functions in combination with iteration algorithms (such as `for_each()`), querying algorithms (such as `find_if()`) and transformation algorithms (such as `copy()`, `transform()` and `set_union()`).

Container			Algorithm		
Function	Operator	Statement	Object	Scope	Bind
Primitives			Composite		
Actor					

Figure 4.1 Phoenix and software layering

We now discuss each module in Figure 4.1.

4.5   Actors, Arguments and Fundamentals

We combine primitive actors to form composite actors. The primitive Phoenix functions are:
- Value function objects (`val()`).
- Reference function objects (`ref()`).
- Function arguments.

A *value function* object is a *nullary function* (that is, it has no input) that returns an immutable value. When the `val()` function is called an **actor<value<T> >** object is created. A *reference function* object is a nullary function that returns a reference to a value. The returned value can be changed and this is done using the assignment operator. The `ref()` function creates an **actor<reference<T> >** object. Finally, we can create constant reference function objects using `cref()` in order to avoid having to copy large objects as would be the case with `val()`. The `cref()` function creates an **actor<reference<const T&> >** object.

The following code shows how to use these primitives:

```
// Create value function objects and call it (the 2nd brackets).
// Then print the output.
cout<<val(3.14)()<<endl;            // Value FO returning 3.14
cout<<val("Hello World")()<<endl;   // Value FO returning "Hello World"

// Create reference function objects and call it.
// Result is reference so it can be changed.
double d = 3.14;
ref(d)() = 6.28;

string s2("Good morning");
ref(s2)() = string("Buon giorno");
```

To show how `const` references work, let us define a struct containing a large amount of data:

```
struct BigData
{
   boost::array<double, 1000> data;

   friend ostream& operator << (ostream& os, const BigData& data)
   {
      os << "Size of array is 1000:\n"; return os;
   }
};
```

In this case it is advisable to use a `const` reference:

```
// Constant reference
BigData myData;

cref(myData);       // My Data is not copied
val(myData);        // My Data is copied
```

We conclude this section by discussing argument function objects. An *argument function object* returns one of the arguments that were passed to it. The actor in this case is **actor<argument<N> >**. For example, some of its predefined instances that you can use in code are:

```
actor<argument<0> > arg1 = argument<0>();
actor<argument<1> > arg2 = argument<1>();
actor<argument<2> > arg3 = argument<2>();
```

It is possible to define your own argument names, for example:

```
actor<argument<0> > x;
actor<argument<1> > y;
```

How do we evaluate an argument? In this case the Nth argument is selected from the sequence of arguments given by the client. Here is an example:

```
// Create the values for the arguments.
double d = 3.14;
int i = 10;
char* s = "Hello World";
BigData myData;

// Use the pre-defined arguments function objects and print the result
cout<<"Argument 1: "<<arg1(d, i, s)<<endl;        // print d
cout<<"Argument 2: "<<arg2(d, i, s)<<endl;        // print i
cout<<"Argument 3: "<<arg3(d, i, s)<<endl;        // print s
cout<<"Argument 4: "<<arg4(d, i, s, myData)<<endl;// print myData
```

4.6   Composite

We can create recursive structures and their evaluation is handled by a composite specific evaluation policy. In particular, we can combine some of the primitives that we introduced in the previous section to create higher-level functionality. We take an example of searching for the first occurrence of an element in a vector whose value is between 9.5 and 15.0. To this end, we build the expression from simpler ones:

```
// Create a vector with values
int size=10;
vector<double> v(size);
for (int i=0; i<size; i++) v[i] = i*1.5;
```

We now call `find_if()` with the last parameter being a Phoenix composite function:

```
v[1] = 16.0;
cout<<"First number >= 9.5,<= 15.0: "
    << *find_if(v.begin(), v.end(),
              arg1 >= val(9.5) && arg1 <= val(15.0) )<<endl;
```

It is not difficult to write C++ code that can emulate this code but it would be less compact. Using Phoenix, the code is essentially a 'one-liner'.

4.7   Function and Operator

Phoenix provides a mechanism for implementing lazily evaluated functions. These functions look like normal C++ functions except that function execution is delayed.
We discuss the steps to create a lazy function:
1. Create a function object that implements the function call operator () and function logic.
2. Add a nested struct 'result' that defines a typedef 'type' to indicate the result type of the function object.
3. Wrap the function object in a Phoenix function that we can use in client code.

An example of this process is code to compute Fibonacci numbers. The code corresponding to steps 1 and 2 is given by:

```
#include <boost/spirit/home/phoenix/function.hpp>
```

```
struct FibonacciImpl
{
    // Metafunction 'result' that takes arguments and
    // returns the result type of the function
    template <typename Arg>
    struct result
    {
        typedef Arg type;
    };

    template <typename Arg>
    Arg operator () (Arg n) const
    {
        if (n == 0)
        {
            return 0;
        }

        if (n == 1)
        {
            return 1;
        }

        return this->operator()(n-1) + this->operator()(n-2);
    }
};
```

Step 3 entails creating a Phoenix function:

```
function<FibonacciImpl> myFibonacci;
```

Using this function in client code is given by:

```
int main()
{ // 0, 1, 1, 2, 3, 5, 8, 13, 21, 34, 55, 89, 144, 233, 377, 610,
  // 987, 1597, 2584, 4181, 6765 . . .

    int N = 15; // How many Fibonacci numbers to compute

    for (int n = 0; n < N; ++n)
    { // The actor now funnels the arguments passed by the client into a
      // tuple and calls the eval member function

        cout << myFibonacci(arg1)(n) << ",";
    }

    return 0;
}
```

It is also possible to lazily evaluate operators. A lazy operator looks like a normal operator. The following operators are supported:

```
prefix:   ~, !, -, +, ++, --, & (reference), * (dereference)
postfix:  ++, --
binary:   +, -, *, /, %, &, |, ^, <<, >>,  =, [], +=, *=, /=,
          %=, &=, |=, ^=, <<=, >>= ==, !=, <, >, <=, >=, &&, ||, ->*
ternary:  if_else(c, a, b) // The c?a:b operator can't be overloaded
```

It is possible to combine these operators as well as using them in combination with lazy functions and lazy statement. As an example, consider the problem of modifying the elements of a vector based on its values:

```
#include <boost/spirit/home/phoenix/core.hpp>
#include <boost/spirit/home/phoenix/operator.hpp>
```

```
// Create two source vectors with values
int size=8;
vector<double> v1(size); vector<double> v2(size);
for (int i=0; i<size; i++)
{
    v1[i]=i*1.5;
    v2[i]=i-4.0;
}
```

We now combine these two vectors using `transform()`:

```
transform(v1.begin(), v1.end(), v2.begin(), result.begin(),
          arg1*arg2 + val(10.0));
```

Finally, we give an example of the ternary `if_else` operator:

```
transform(v1.begin(), v1.end(), v2.begin(), result.begin(),
          if_else( arg2<=val(0), arg1*arg2, arg1/arg2) );
```

In this case we multiply the values in `v1` and `v2` if `arg2` is non-positive, otherwise we give their quotient.

4.8   Statement

It is possible to create lazy statements which are stylised versions of well-known C++ statements:

```
block statement
if_statement
if_else statement
switch_statement
while_statement
dowhile statement
for_statement
```

In order to avail of the above functionality, we include the following file:

```
#include <boost/spirit/home/phoenix/statement.hpp>
```

The block statement allows us to create a code block and place comma-separated statements within that block. The general syntax is:

```
statement,
(
    statement1,
    statement2,
    ...
    statementN
)
```

We take an example. In this case we iterate in a vector and we execute two simple print functions in a single block:

```
// Create two source vectors with values
int size=8;
vector<int> v(size);
for (int i=0; i<size; i++) v[i]=i;
```

```
// Block statement
for_each(v.begin(), v.end(),
    (
        cout << arg1 << endl,
        cout << arg1*2 << endl
    )
);
```

These are comma-separated statements. The next example prints the elements of a vector and checks if these elements are even or odd. The code is:

```
// Print each number as odd or even. Note the dot before the else
for_each(v.begin(), v.end(),
    if_(arg1%2)
    [
        cout<<arg1<<" is odd"<<endl
    ]
    .else_
    [
        cout<<arg1<<" is even"<<endl
    ]
);
```

A useful statement is the for_statement that we can use in applications with embedded loops:

```
// Use the "for_each" statement
int i;                          // Space for the counter
for_each(v.begin(), v.end(),
    ( // Round brackets because we have more than one statement
        for_(ref(i)=0, ref(i)<arg1, ref(i)++)
        [
            cout<<val("*")
        ],
        cout<<val("\n")// Print new line. Note, we must use val()
    )
);
```

The output of this code is the following pattern that is printed three times:

```
*
**
***
****
*****
******
*******
********
```

We conclude this section with some more examples using the switch statement and while loop:

```
// Use the "switch_" statement
for_each(v.begin(), v.end(),
    switch_(arg1)
    [
        case_<1>( cout<<arg1<<": one"<<endl ),
        case_<2>( cout<<arg1<<": two"<<endl ),
        case_<3>( cout<<arg1<<": three"<<endl ),
        default_( cout<<arg1<<": many"<<endl )
    ]
);

int i;          // Space for the counter
```

```
// Use the "while_" statement
for_each(v.begin(), v.end(),
    ( // Round brackets because we have more than one statement
        ref(i)=arg1,        // Store the input value in the counter
        while_(ref(i)--)  // As long as the counter is positive
        [
            cout<<val("*") // Print stars.
        ],
        cout<<val("\n")    // Print new line.
    )
);
```

4.9   Object

The Object module is concerned with object construction (on the stack or on the heap),
object destruction and object conversion operators in C++. The following lazy operations
are supported:

```
- construct<T>(arg1, ..., argN)          // Create an object on the stack
- new_<T>(arg1, ..., argN)               // Create an object on the heap
- delete_(arg)                           // Delete an object from the heap
- static_cast_<T>(lamda_expression)      // As static_cast<T>
- dynamic_cast_<T>(lamda_expression)     // As dynamic_cast<T>
- const_cast_<T>(lamda_expression)       // As const_cast<T>
- reinterpret_cast_<T>(lamda_expression) // As reinterpret_cast<T>
```

In order to use these operations we need an include file:

```
#include <boost/spirit/home/phoenix/object.hpp>
```

We now take some examples based on class `Point` and its base class `Shape`. We place their
instances in a vector. The first example uses a vector of points:

```
vector<Point> v(3);
```

The next step is to create a number of temporary points (on the stack) and we then assign
each one to a point in the vector v:

```
int counter=0;
for_each(v.begin(), v.end()
        arg1=construct<Point>(++ref(counter), ref(counter)) );
```

Please note that the constructor arguments are evaluated from right to left; the points in the
vector will now have the values (1, 0), (2, 1), (3, 2).
The next example creates a vector of pointers to the base class `Shape` and it initialises the
vector's elements with heap-based `Point` instances. In this case we use the operation `new_`:

```
vector<Shape*> vp(3);
counter=0;
for_each(vp.begin(), vp.end(),
        arg1=new_<Point>(++ref(counter), ref(counter)) );
```

When a Phoenix lambda fucntion get an object or object pointer as argument, you might
want to call a method on that object. However, you can't directly use the dot (`.`) operator or
arrow (`->`) operator on the Phoenix variable. Instead you need to used the `->*` operator with
the address of the member function to call. You use this on object pointers. For objects you
first need to take the address of the variable:

```
// Call the Print() function on each shape.
// It is not possible to use the -> operator directly on a
// Phoenix object pointer. So we need to use the ->* operator
// with the address of the function to call.
// Not possible: for_each(vp.begin(), vp.end(), arg1->Print() );
for_each(vp.begin(), vp.end(), (arg1->*&Shape::Print)() );

// Call the Print function on all Point objects.
// Can't directly use the dot operator on a Phoenix object,
// but we can take the address of the object and then use
// the ->* operator as with object pointers.
// Not possible: for_each(v.begin(), v.end(), arg1.Print() );
for_each(v.begin(), v.end(), (&arg1->*&Shape::Print)() );
```

Further you might need to down cast a base class pointer to a derived class pointer. This is possible using the Phoenix `dynamic_cast_<T>()` after which you can call a method on the derived class using the `->*` operator. Note that the `->*` operator only works for methods that are not overloaded:

```
// Cast the argument to a point and print X.
// We need the Phoenix dynamic_cast_<>() to cast the Shape* to a Point*.
// Note, the ->* operator only works if the function is not overloaded.
// So we need to use Point::GetX()/Point::SetX() instead of the
// overloaded Point::X() getter/setter.
for_each(vp.begin(), vp.end(), cout<<val("x: ")<<
        ((dynamic_cast_<Point*>(arg1))->*&Point::GetX)()<<endl );
```

Finally, we delete these objects from memory as follows:

```
for_each(vp.begin(), vp.end(), delete_(arg1) );
```

4.10 Scope and Local Variables

We now create and access local variables on the stack and use them in Phoenix expressions. This feature is especially important when we use recursion, for example when a lambda function is passed as an argument to another function. Normally, when we need a variable within a Phoenix expression we can pass a variable as a `ref(x)` but in the case of recursive functions we need a local variable. We define local variables using **actor<local_variable<Key> >**. Finally, the predefined local variables _a,..., _z are defined in the namespace `boost::phoenix::local_names`. We use the following:

```
#include <boost/spirit/home/phoenix/scope.hpp>
using namespace boost::phoenix::local_names;
```

We define local variables using the syntax:

```
let (<local-declarations>)
[
    <let-body>
]
```

It is possible to declare predefined or user-defined variables in the local declarations body and they can be assigned to lambda expressions.

The following example updates a vector v with a combination of values from vectors v1 and v2. In particular, it calculates the sum of squares of v1 and v2 using local variables as placeholders:

```
vector<double> v(3);
```

```
int counter=0;
vector<double> v1(3);
vector<double> v2(3);
v1[0]=3.45; v2[0]=5.34;
v1[1]=8.45; v2[1]=3.30;
v1[2]=1.50; v2[2]=2.84;

for_each(v.begin(), v.end(),
    let(_a=arg1, _b=0.0, _c=0.0, _d=0.0, _e=ref(counter))
    [
        _b=ref(v1)[_e],    // Get value from first vector
        _c=ref(v2)[_e],    // Get value from second vector
        _d=_b*_b + _c*_c, // Calculate final value
        _a=_d,             // Assign final value to output
        _e++               // Increment the counter
    ]
);
```

4.11 Bind

Binding refers to the process of tieing a function to a number of arguments for lazy
evaluation.

What can we bind?
- Global functions.
- Member functions.
- Member variables.

We need to create a function object to support named lazy functions (in contrast to unnamed
lambda functions). Using the overloaded bind template functions we can transform functions
and variables to a lambda expression. The bind functions generate a *binder object*, (which is
a composite).
When using the Bind module we include the following file:

```
#include <boost/spirit/home/phoenix/bind.hpp>
```

Our first example binds a member function. To this end, consider the following functor with
two member functions called Increment() and Decrement():

```
class BindingClass
{
public:
    double value;      // Public member variable that can be bound.

    BindingClass(): value(0.0) {}          // Default constructor.
    BindingClass(double v): value(v) {}    // Constructor with init value.
    double GetValue() { return value; }    // Return the value.
    void SetValue(double v) { value=v; }   // Set the value.

    // Increment the value and return the new value.
    double Increment(double v)
    {
        value+=v;
        return value;
    }

    // Decrement the value and return the new value.
    double Decrement(double v)
    {
        value-=v;
        return value;
```

```
    }
};
```

In order to show how binding works in this case we consider transforming one vector into another one by binding to `Increment()` with `arg1` as argument:

```
BindingClass bc(3.5);
std::transform(v.begin(), v.end(), result.begin(),
               bind(&BindingClass::Increment, bc, arg1) );
```

We also can bind to the public member data in `BindingClass`, for example:

```
BindingClass bc(3.5);
std::transform(v.begin(), v.end(), result.begin(),
               arg1+bind(&BindingClass::value, bc) );
```

A lazy member function expects the first argument to be a pointer or reference to an object. Both the object and the arguments can be lazily bound, for example:

```
MyClass obj;                          // A class with member function func()
bind(&MyClass::func, arg1, arg2);     // arg1.func(arg2)
bind(&MyClass::func, obj, arg1);      // obj.func(arg1)
bind(&MyClass::func, arg1, 100);      // arg1.func(100)
```

Finally, we can bind a global function such as:

```
void func(double d)
{
    cout << d << endl;
}
```

We now use this function with `bind`, in this case a somewhat long-winded way to print the elements of a vector:

```
int N = 5;
vector<int> v2(N);
for (int i=0; i < v2.size(); ++i) v2[i]= i;

for_each(v2.begin(), v2.end(), bind(&func, arg1));
```

4.12 Container

The Container module contains a set of lazy functions that operate on STL containers, in particular for the lazy evaluation of the public member functions of the following containers:

- `deque`
- `list`
- `map` and `multimap`
- `vector`

Lazy functions are provided for about 30 member functions such as `erase`, `resize`, `size` and many more. Please consult the Boost.Phoenix documentation for more details.

4.13 Algorithm

The Algorithm module delivers wrappers for the standard algorithms in the `<algorithm>` and `<numeric>` headers. There are three categories, namely iteration, transformation and querying. We include the following header file:

```
#include <boost/spirit/home/phoenix/algorithm.hpp>
```

Alternatively, you can include separate header files:

```
#include <boost/spirit/home/phoenix/stl/algorithm/iteration.hpp>
#include <boost/spirit/home/phoenix/stl/algorithm/querying.hpp>
#include <boost/spirit/home/phoenix/stl/algorithm/transformation.hpp>
```

We have already given some examples of the STL algorithms, namely `for_each()` and `transform()`. Here is a simple example of the Phoenix lazy copy. Note that the Phoenix algorithms accept a container instead of iterators:

```
int main()
{
    const int N = 3;
    int v1[] = {1, 2, 3};
    int v2[N];

    // Copy all arg1 values to arg2 (from v1 to v2)
    boost::phoenix::copy(arg1, arg2)(v1, v2);

    for (int j = 0; j < N; ++j)
    {
        cout << v2[j] << ",";
    }

    // Copy a vector to a list
    vector<double> vA(10);
    list<double> myList;
    boost::phoenix::copy(arg1, arg2)(vA, back_inserter(myList));

    return 0;
}
```

4.14 Summary and Conclusions

We have given an introduction to the Boost.Phoenix library that supports a number of features provided by functional programming languages. In particular, it allows us to create higher-order (composite) functions, unnamed (lambda) functions and it supports currying (partial function evaluation) as well as lazy function and operator evaluation. This library enhances the multi-paradigm capabilities of C++ and consists of a number of orthogonal modules. These are showed in Figure 4.1 and an overview of the responsibilities of each module was given in section 4.4.

There are many applications of Boost.Phoenix which we have not discussed in this chapter. For example, it is a component in Boost Spirit which is an object-oriented recursive-descent parser and output library in C++. It enables developers to write grammars and format descriptions using Extended Backus-Naur Form (EBNF) syntax directly in C++. A discussion of this library and its applications is outside the scope of this chapter. An immediate application of Boost.Phoenix is to use it to create lambda functions that we can apply in combination with STL containers and algorithms.

We wish to say that the C++0X standard supports for Lambda functions. These lambda functions provide functionality similar to Phoenix.

5 Smart Pointers and Serialisation

5.1 Introduction and Objectives

In this chapter we introduce the Smart Pointer library that makes object lifecycle management easier when compared to using the *new* and *delete* operators in C++. In particular, the responsibility for removing objects from memory is taken from the developer's shoulders. To this end, we discuss a number of template classes that improve the reliability of C++ code. The two most important classes in our experience are:

- *Scoped pointer*: ensures proper deletion of dynamically allocated objects. These are objects having a short lifetime (for example, *factory objects*) and that are typically created and deleted in a single function block. In other words, these objects are not needed outside the code block in which they are defined.
- *Shared pointer*: ensures that a dynamically allocated object is deleted only when no other objects are referencing it. The shared pointer class eliminates the need to write code to control the lifetime of objects. It enables *shared ownership* of objects.

The four other classes are:

- *Scoped array*: ensures proper deletion of dynamically allocated arrays in a function block.
- *Shared array*: enables shared ownership of arrays. It is similar to the shared pointer class except that it is used with arrays instead of with single objects.
- *Weak pointer*: this is an observer of a shared pointer. It does not interfere with the ownership of the object that the shared pointer shares. Its main use is to avoid dangling pointers because a weak pointer cannot hold a dangling pointer.
- *Intrusive pointer*: this is a special kind of smart pointer and is used in code that has already been written with an internal reference counter or when you are not happy with the performance of shared pointers. We do not discuss intrusive pointers in this book but we do provide some examples in the source code.

We introduce the syntax of smart pointers and we give some initial examples. Having done that, we examine advanced examples such as using smart pointers in combination with STL containers and avoiding memory problems when exceptions are thrown.

We give a short introduction to Boost.Serialization in this chapter. An application of Boost.Serialization to Computer Aided Design (CAD) will be given in chapter 17.

5.2 An Introduction to Memory Management

In this section we give an overview of object lifecycle. In particular, we are interested in heap-based memory allocation of single objects and arrays of objects. Heap memory allocation and deallocation in C++ is the responsibility of the developer. But knowing when memory is no longer needed is not easy to determine and this uncertainty leads to a number of problems:

- *Dangling pointers*: these occur when an object is deleted or deallocated without modifying the value of the pointer. In this case the pointer continues to point to the location of the deallocated memory.
- *Wild pointers*: these are pointers that are used before they are initialised.
- *Memory leak*: in this case the program is unable to release memory that it has acquired. This situation can be caused by a pointer when it goes out of scope. In other words, the dynamically allocated memory is unreachable.

- *Double free bugs*: this refers to when we try to delete memory that has already been deleted.

In order to resolve (or avoid) these problems we have a number of options open to us. We can surrender all responsibility and allow automatic memory management by using *garbage collection* (GC). The garbage collector attempts to reclaim memory used by objects that will never be accessed again in an application. Garbage collection is the opposite of manual memory management.

There are various kinds of garbage collectors, the most common being called *trace garbage collectors*. These first determine which objects are reachable (or potentially reachable) and they then proceed to discard the remaining 'dead' objects.

There is also the *reference counting* technique that stores the number of pointers or handles to a dynamically allocated object. When an object is no longer referenced it will be deleted from memory.
Reference counting is a form of garbage collection in which each object contains a count of the number of references to it that are held by other objects. Reference counting can entail frequent updates because the reference count needs to be incremented or decremented when an object is referenced or dereferenced.

Some of the advantages of reference counting are:
- Objects are reclaimed as soon as they are no longer referenced and then in an incremental fashion without incurring long waits on collection cycles.
- Reference counting is one of the simplest forms of garbage collection to implement.
- Reference counting is useful in real-time systems with limited memory and in applications that need to be responsive.
- It is a useful technique for the management of non-memory resource objects (such as file and database handles).

Some disadvantages of reference counting are:
- Frequent updates are a source of inefficiency because objects are being accessed continually. Furthermore, each memory-managed object must reserve space for a reference count.
- Some reference counting algorithms cannot resolve reference cycles (objects that refer directly or indirectly to themselves).

We now discuss how the smart pointer library addresses these issues. We note that garbage collection is not implemented in C++.

5.3   An Introduction to Smart Pointers

There is a need in C++ for some kind of automatic (or semi-automatic) memory management mechanism and to this end Boost provides template classes to help developers create reliable and robust code. In general, we use smart pointers in the following situations:
- Avoiding the errors that we discussed in section 5.2.
- Creating objects with well-defined lifecycles.
- Shared ownership of resources.
- Resolving a number of exception-unsafe problems when using raw pointers.

5.4   Scoped Pointers and Scoped Arrays

Scoped pointers are used in applications when we create objects whose lifetime is well-defined and bounded. In particular, we create an object whose lifetime is typically limited to the scope of a single function. It is possible to define scoped pointers for both user-defined and built-in types, as the following examples show. First, we create two objects on the heap using raw pointers:

```
{ // Block with raw pointer lifecycle

    double* d = new double(1.0);
    Point* pt = new Point(1.0, 2.0);      // 2d Point class

    // Dereference and call member functions
    *d = 2.0;
    (*pt).X(3.0);       // Modify x coordinate
    (*pt).Y(3.0);       // Modify y coordinate

    // Can use operators for pointer operations
    pt->X(3.0);         // Modify x coordinate
    pt->Y(3.0);         // Modify y coordinate

    // Explicitly clean up memory
    delete d;
    delete pt;
}
```

This code is correct because it allocates and deallocates memory. However, the developer may forget to include code to delete memory or an exception may be thrown before the delete operator can be executed. The scoped pointer class avoids these potential problems. To this end, we have modified the above code:

```
{ // Block using scoped pointers

    // Define scoped pointers instead of raw pointers
    boost::scoped_ptr<double> d(new double(1.0));
    boost::scoped_ptr<Point> pt(new Point(1.0, 2.0));

    // Dereference
    *d = 2.0;
    (*pt).X(3.0);       // Modify x coordinate
    (*pt).Y(3.0);       // Modify y coordinate

    // Can use operators for pointer operations
    pt->X(3.0);         // Modify x coordinate
    pt->Y(3.0);         // Modify y coordinate

    // Explicit clean up of memory not needed
}
```

We can see from this code that a scoped pointer is used in much the same way as we use ordinary pointers because the operators for pointer operations have been overloaded. It is not necessary to delete memory when the scoped pointer goes out of scope.

The scoped_ptr class has a number of other functions:
- reset(); delete the data that the scoped pointer already owns. It may be needed in the rare cases when a resource needs to be freed before the scoped pointer is destructed in the normal way. The use of reset() is a possible indication of a weak design.

- get(); returns the stored pointer; the added value is that it allows us to test if the stored pointer is null. Some functions in an application may need raw pointers.
- swap(); exchange the contents of two scoped pointers.

The following code creates a scoped pointer, resets the memory and casts it to a raw pointer. We also check if the pointer is a null pointer:

```
{ // Accessing the memory owned by the scoped pointer

    boost::scoped_ptr<double> d(new double(1.0));

    d.reset();

    double* dp = d.get();

    if (dp == 0)
    {
        cout << "Pointer is zero, yes\n";
    }
    else
    {
        cout << "Pointer is not zero, no\n";
    }
}
```

Summarising, scoped pointers are useful when:
- The lifetime of a dynamically allocated object is limited to a specific scope, for example, factory objects (GOF 1995).
- A pointer is used in a scope where an exception may be thrown; we use scoped pointers when exception safety is important.

We now discuss scoped arrays. In many cases we wish to create dynamically allocated arrays using the scoped_array class. This is useful in cases when the size of an array is constant. We cannot use the scoped_ptr class for dynamic arrays because arrays are deleted differently (delete versus delete[]). The following example shows how to create a dynamically allocated array using raw pointers and then using a scoped array:

```
{
    const int N = 4;
    Point* pointArray = new Point[N];

    for (int i = 0; i < N; ++i)
    {
        cout << pointArray[i] << endl;
    }

    delete[] pointArray;
}

{
    const int N = 4;
    boost::scoped_array<Point> scopedPointArray(new Point[N]);

    for (int i = 0; i < N; ++i)
    {
        scopedPointArray[i] = Point(double(i), double(i));
        cout << scopedPointArray[i] << endl;
    }
}
```

In both cases the memory is deleted but in the latter case this is automatically taken care of.

An alternative to scoped arrays is to use scoped pointers in combination with STL vectors, as the following example shows:

```
{ // STL vector and scoped pointer

    int n = 10;
    boost::scoped_ptr<vector<Point> >
        scopedPointArray(new vector<Point>(n));

    for (int i = 0; i < n; ++i)
    {
        (*scopedPointArray)[i] = Point(double(i), double(i));
        cout << (*scopedPointArray)[i] << endl;
    }
}
```

It is not clear without doing some tests whether it is preferable to use scoped arrays (of fixed size) or scoped pointers to vectors.

5.5   Shared Pointers and Shared Arrays

In larger applications we employ shared pointers for a number of reasons. For example, we need a mechanism whereby a dynamically allocated object is created once and subsequently shared by other objects. We use *reference counting*. When the reference count becomes zero this implies that the object is no longer needed and it can then be deleted. To this end, shared_ptr is a template class that non-intrusively references dynamically allocated objects. As a first example, we consider two classes C1 and C2 that shared common data d:

```
class C1
{
private:
    boost::shared_ptr<double> d;

public:
    C1(boost::shared_ptr<double>& value) : d(value) {}
    virtual ~C1() { cout << "\nC1 destructor\n"; }
    void print() const { cout << "Value " << *d; }
};

class C2
{
private:
    boost::shared_ptr<double> d;

public:
    C2(boost::shared_ptr<double>& value) : d(value) {}
    virtual ~C2() { cout << "\nC2 destructor\n"; }
    void print() const { cout << "Value " << *d; }
};
```

We now create instances of C1 and C2 by calling their constructors with the shared variable commonValue as argument:

```
boost::shared_ptr<double> commonValue(new double(3.1415));
```

and

```
C1 object1(commonValue); C2 object2(commonValue);
```

In this case the variable `commonValue` has a reference count of 3 because it is accessed by two objects and furthermore it has already been initialised in another part of the application (thus contributing to the total reference count). When both objects `object1` and `object2` go out of scope the reference count will drop by 2 and when the program ends the reference count will drop to zero. Then the shared memory will be deleted.

5.5.1   Functionality of `shared_ptr`

This class has an interface consisting of overloaded member functions belonging to the following categories:
- Constructors (using raw pointers, copy constructor, weak pointer, `auto_ptr`) and assignment operator.
- `reset()`; stop sharing ownership of a shared resource.
- Comparing shared pointers (operators ==, !=, <, >).
- Retrieving and manipulating the stored pointer (using overloaded operators).
- Determining the number of references to a shared resource.

The smart pointer library offers about ten functions to promote interoperability and integration with legacy code using `auto_ptr` and raw pointers. We do not discuss these issues here.

The first two constructors are concerned with the creation of a shared pointer from a raw pointer. In this case the shared pointer takes on ownership of the resource and the reference count is set to one. The difference between the two constructors has to do with how the resource is deallocated; in the default case the shared pointer deletes the raw pointer whereas it is also possible to delegate this to a function object which may execute other duties (such as closing a file, for example) before deleting the resource.

The following code shows how to create a shared pointer from a raw pointer:

```
boost::shared_ptr<Point> sp(new Point(0, 2.0));
```

Now consider the more complex case when we carry out some duties (just) before a resource is deleted. In this case we create the shared pointer with a raw pointer and a function object as input arguments, as the following code shows:

```
MyFinalizer myF;

// shared_ptr delegates delete stuff to myF
boost::shared_ptr<Point> sp2(new Point(1.0, 2.0), myF);
```

where the variable `myF` is an instance of the `MyFinalizer` class:

```
struct MyFinalizer
{
   MyFinalizer() {}
   MyFinalizer(const MyFinalizer& fin2) {}
   void operator () (Point* p)
   {
      // Carry out duties before deleting resources
      cout << "Finalizing..\n";

      delete p;
   }
};
```

We now discuss the copy constructor and assignment operator. The copy constructor results in the resource being shared by the newly created shared pointer and the reference count being incremented by one; you can determine the number of references to a resource by calling the member function `use_count()` (which is useful for debugging purposes):

```
boost::shared_ptr<Point> sp(new Point(1.0, 2.0));
boost::shared_ptr<Point> sp2(sp);
cout << "Number of references, copy constructor: "
     << sp2.use_count() << endl; // 2
```

The assignment operator is used to stop sharing a resource and start sharing another resource. Please note the function `unique()` that returns `true` if the shared pointer is the sole owner of the resource, otherwise it returns `false`:

```
// Assignment operator
Point* pt2 = new Point(-1.0, -2.0);
boost::shared_ptr<Point> sp4(pt2);
boost::shared_ptr<Point> sp5 = sp4;
cout << "Number of references: " << sp5.use_count() << endl;   // 2
boolalpha(cout);
cout << "Is sp5 the sole owner? " << sp5.unique() << endl;      // false
```

Next, we can create a shared pointer from an STL `auto_ptr`; in this case a copy of the resource is made and stored in the shared pointer while `release()` is called on the `auto_ptr`.

```
using std::auto_ptr;

// Define auto_ptr
auto_ptr<Point> ap(new Point(1.0, 2.0));
boost::shared_ptr<Point> sp6(ap);
```

5.5.2   Stop Sharing Ownership

In some cases we discontinue sharing ownership of a resource by using the overloaded member function `reset()`; calling it results in ownership being relinquished and the reference count being decremented by one:

```
// Default case, destructor called
cout << "Resetting\n";
Point* pt = new Point(-1.0, -2.0);
boost::shared_ptr<Point> sp(pt);
sp.reset();
cout << "Number of references: " << sp.use_count() << endl; // 0
```

5.5.3   Retrieving the Resource from Shared Data

The dereferencing and pointer operators are overloaded and they return a reference to the object being pointed to. An example of use is:

```
{ // Accessing the resource

    Point* pt = new Point(-1.0, -2.0);
    boost::shared_ptr<Point> sp(pt);

    Point pt2 = *sp;
    Point* pt3 = sp.get();

    // Now when sp is null
    sp.reset();
```

```
//pt2 = *sp; // Undefined behavior

// Preferred way of retrieving the stored pointer
Point* ptB = sp.get();
cout << (ptB == 0) << endl;
}
```

Finally, we can test for equality and inequality of shared pointers to determine if they refer to the same data:

```
{ // Comparing shared pointers

Point* pt = new Point(-1.0, -2.0);
boost::shared_ptr<Point> sp(pt);
boost::shared_ptr<Point> sp2(sp);
boost::shared_ptr<Point> sp3(new Point (0.5, 0.5));
boolalpha(cout); cout << (sp == sp2) << endl;      // true
boolalpha(cout); cout << (sp == sp3) << endl;      // false
}
```

5.5.4   Shared Arrays

The class shared_array is a smart pointer that enables shared ownership of arrays. It is similar to shared_ptr except that it works with arrays instead of single objects. Its interface is similar to that of shared_ptr with additional support for the indexing operator []. An example of use is:

```
const int N = 4;
boost::shared_array<Point> sharedPointArray(new Point[N]);

for (int i = 0; i < N; ++i)
{
    sharedPointArray[i] = Point(double(i), double(i));
    cout << sharedPointArray[i] << endl;
}
```

An alternative to this option is to use shared pointers and STL vectors, as in the example:

```
int n = 10;
boost::shared_ptr<vector<Point> > sharedPointArray(new vector<Point>(n));

for (int i = 0; i < n; ++i)
{
    (*sharedPointArray)[i] = Point(double(i), double(i));
    cout << (*sharedPointArray)[i] << endl;
}
```

Summarising the member functions in shared_array are concerned with:
- Constructors.
- The use count.
- Comparing shared arrays.

5.5.5   Custom Deleters

In some applications we wish to execute commands such as closing a file in addition to deleting memory when an object goes out of scope. We give an example in which we create a text file and populate it with data. We use a shared pointer and when it goes out of scope it calls a function object that subsequently closes the file. We see from this discussion that the term 'custom deleter' is somewhat of a misnomer but 'custom finaliser' might be a more fitting term.

We discuss the implementation of the above custom finaliser. The main steps are:
- Decide which resource to use (in this case a FILE object).
- Decide what should happen to the resource when it goes out of scope.
- Show the robustness of the solution that uses the custom finaliser.

The example involves a file for writing. We encapsulate the file object in a shared pointer constructor and we define a finaliser that does the main postprocessing task, namely closing the file:

```
FILE* myFile = fopen("Test.dat", "w");
if (myFile == 0)
{
    cout << "Unable to open file\n";
}
else
{
    cout << "Opening file...\n";
}

boost::shared_ptr<FILE> mySharedFile(myFile, FileFinalizer());
```

In this case the finaliser class is:

```
struct FileFinalizer
{
    void operator () (FILE* f)
    {
        cout << "Closing file\n";
        if (f != 0)
        {
            fclose(f);
        }
        cout << "Closed file\n";
    }
};
```

We are ready to add records to the file. We simulate a disastrous event by placing a throw statement in the code before the file has been closed:

```
// Write some data to file
fprintf(mySharedFile.get(), "1\n");

// etc.

fprintf(mySharedFile.get(), "2\n");

// Simulate a disaster!
try
{
    cout << "When something goes wrong\n";
    throw string("exception thrown\n");
    fprintf(mySharedFile.get(), "3\n");
}
catch(string& s)
{
    cout << "exception caught " << s << endl;
}
```

After this code has been executed the finaliser will be called and the file closed. We can subsequently open it again and read its contents:

```
FILE* myFile = fopen("Test.dat", "r");

if (myFile == 0)
{
    cout << "Unable to open file for reading\n";
}
else
{
    cout << "Opening file for reading...\n";
}

// Read contents of file
char c;
while ((c = getc(myFile)) != EOF)
{
    cout << c;
}
fclose(myFile);
```

The console output when we run this code is:

```
Opening file...
When something goes wrong
exception caught exception thrown

Closing file
Closed file
Opening file for reading...
1
2
```

We note that shared arrays do not support custom deleters.

5.6   Weak Pointers

A weak pointer is an observer of a shared pointer. It does not allow direct access to a resource (this is done by the shared pointer) nor is it owner of the resource. Its main uses are: 1) when we use a shared resource without assuming ownership (for example, breaking cyclic dependencies) and 2) avoiding dangling pointers. It is possible to create a weak pointer from a shared pointer and vice versa and it is also possible to create a weak pointer from another weak pointer. Furthermore, a weak pointer does not affect the reference counter of the shared resource that it observes.

We now discuss constructors for weak pointers. First, we create a default weak pointer and we can use the member function `expired()` to determine whether it is attached to any resource:

```
// Create a default weak pointer
boost::weak_ptr<double> w;

if (w.expired()) // true
{
    cout << "No associated resource, OK " << endl;
}
else
{
    cout << "Has associated resource, not OK " << endl;
}
```

We can also create a weak pointer from a shared pointer:

```
// Create a weak pointer from a shared pointer
boost::shared_ptr<double> sp(new double(3.1415));
cout << "Ref count: " << sp.use_count() << endl;          // 1

// Assign shared pointer to weak pointer
w = sp;
cout << "Reference count: " << sp.use_count() << endl;     // 1
if (w.expired())
{
    cout << "No associated resource, not OK " << endl;
}
else
{
    cout << "Has associated resource, OK " << endl;
}
```

The advantage here is that the resource referenced by the shared pointer may be deleted independently of the existence of the weak pointer. Alternatively, we can create a shared pointer from a weak pointer as follows:

```
boost::shared_ptr<double> sp2(w);
cout << "Ref count, sp2: " << sp2.use_count() << endl;     // 2
```

Finally, we can return the shared pointer that a weak pointer observes (if any) by calling the lock() member function. A null pointer is returned if the weak pointer is not attached to any shared pointer. We note that the reference count is incremented when this function is called:

```
boost::shared_ptr<double> sp3 = w.lock();
cout << "Ref count: " << sp3.use_count() << endl;     // 3
cout << "Ref count: " << sp.use_count() << endl;      // 3
```

Weak pointers can be useful when keeping track of the current variables being referenced in an application.

5.7   Smart Pointers and Exception Handling

All the smart pointer template classes contain member functions which can never throw exceptions, because they neither throw exceptions themselves nor call other functions which may throw exceptions. These members are indicated by a comment:

```
// never throws in the boost source code.
```

5.8   Using Smart Pointers with STL Containers

In some applications we need to create STL containers whose elements are pointers to a base class. Each pointer is usually assigned to an address of an instance of some derived class. If the memory to which the pointer points is deleted we will then be left with a dangling pointer. Our goal in this section is to show how to store objects in STL containers using shared pointers. The advantage here is that client software does not need to get involved with maintaining the integrity of the elements (which are pointers) in the container. In particular, we do not have to manually delete the pointers. Consider the simple class hierarchy consisting of one base class and one derived class:

```
class Base
{ // Base class
private:

public:
    Base() {}
    virtual void print() const = 0;

protected:
    virtual ~Base() { cout << "Base destructor\n\n"; }
};

class Derived : public Base
{ // Derived class

private:

public:
    Derived() : Base() {}
    ~Derived() { cout << "Derived destructor\n"; }
    virtual void print() const { cout << "derived object\n"; }
};
```

We now create a vector of shared pointers to Base. For convenience we have created a convenience factory function that creates a shared pointer whose contents is an instance of Derived:

```
// Simple creator (FACTORY) function
boost::shared_ptr<Base> createBase()
{
    // Later versions we could also return other derived types
    boost::shared_ptr<Base> result(new Derived());

    return result;
}
```

We are now ready to create the container of shared pointers and populate it. We use typedefs to make the code more readable:

```
// Using STL containers
typedef vector<boost::shared_ptr<Base> > ContainerType;
typedef ContainerType::iterator iterator;
```

The following code populates the container:

```
// Create a vector of objects
ContainerType con;
const int NElements = 4;
for (int j = 0; j < NElements; ++j)
{
    con.push_back(createBase());
}
```

We can convince ourselves that the code is polymorphic by printing the elements of the container:

```
// Now iterate and print
iterator myIter;
for (myIter = con.begin(); myIter != con.end(); ++myIter)
{

    (*myIter) -> print();
}
```

Our final remark is that deletion is automatic; when the container instance `con` is destroyed all reference counters are set to zero and the elements are deleted.

5.9   Test Case: creating smart Composite Objects

Consider the following base class (including the interface for the *Prototype* design pattern using both raw pointers and shared pointers in order to support forward and backward compatibility) is:

```
class Shape
{
public:
// ..

    virtual Shape* Clone() const = 0;   // Prototype pattern
    boost::shared_ptr<Shape> SmartClone() const = 0;
};
```

We now discuss how we implemented composite objects with raw pointers as implementation. Its interface is:

```
class ShapeComposite: public Shape
{
private:
    // The shapelist using the STL list
    list<Shape*> sl;

    void Copy(const ShapeComposite& source);
    void RemoveAll();

public:
    // Constructors and destructor
    ShapeComposite();
    ShapeComposite(const ShapeComposite& source);
    virtual ~ShapeComposite();

    int Count() const;
    void AddFront(Shape* s);
    void RemoveFromFront();

    // Implement the Prototype pattern
    Shape* Clone() const;             // Create a copy of the shape
    boost::shared_ptr<Shape> SmartClone() const;
};
```

We see that the interface works primarily with pointers. All memory management issues are taken care of in `ShapeComposite` (please examine the code accompanying the book). For example, the destructor calls the following function:

```
void ShapeComposite::RemoveAll()
{ // Remove all shapes from the list

    // Create STL list iterator
    list<Shape*>::iterator it;

    for (it=sl.begin(); it!=sl.end(); it++)
    { // Delete every shape in the list

        delete (*it); // Delete shape
    }
```

```
    // Remove the shape pointers from the list (just to be sure)
    sl.clear();
}
```

We now turn our attention to reengineering the class **ShapeComposite**. The internal data structure now becomes:

```
list<boost::shared_ptr<Shape> > sl;
```

The modified member function is:

```
void AddFront(boost::shared_ptr<Shape> s);
```

In the new class SmartShapeComposite there is no need to manage memory explicitly because it is taken care of by the reference counting mechanism.
We now show how to use the new shape composite class. This may take some getting used to because we define both boost::shared_ptr<Shape> and boost::shared_ptr<SmartShapeComposite> in the code:

In order to make this code more readable we define two typedefs as follows:

```
typedef boost::shared_ptr<Shape> MyShape;
typedef boost::shared_ptr<SmartShapeComposite> MyShapeComposite;

SmartShapeComposite* c1 = new SmartShapeComposite;

MyShapeComposite c11(new SmartShapeComposite);
c11->AddFront(MyShape(new Circle(Point(0.0, 0.0), 1.0)));
c11->AddFront(MyShape(new Circle(Point(0.0, 0.0), 10.0)));

MyShapeComposite c12(new SmartShapeComposite);
c12->AddFront(MyShape(new Point(0.0, 0.0)));
c12->AddFront(MyShape(new Point(2.0, 2.0)));

c1->AddFront(c11);
c1->AddFront(c12);

delete c1;
```

We discuss *Generic Smart Composites* in chapter 17 in more detail.

5.10 Serialisation and Object Persistence

In this section we give an overview of Boost.Serialization. We use this library to save objects and data structures to persistent store and it is possible to reconstruct the original object structure from its persistent representation. These two processes are sometimes called *serialisation* and *deserialisation*, respectively. We use the term 'archive' to refer to some specific rendering of a stream of bytes, for example files consisting of binary data, text data or XML.

Some of the goals of the Serialization library are:
1. Code portability (all code depends on ANSI C++ only) and code economy.
2. Independent versioning for each class definition. In other words, when a class undergoes structural change (for example, acquires new member data or its position in a class hierarchy changes) then it should still be possible to reconstruct instances of the class from old persistent data. This facility is related to *schema evolution* in object-oriented

database technology and refers to the problem of evolving a database schema and adapting it when structure changes.

3. Proper deserialisation of pointers to shared data as well as serialisation of STL containers and other commonly used templates.
4. Data portability; the streams of data that represent persistent objects on one platform should be readable on another platform.
5. Non-intrusive property; it should be possible to apply serialisation to classes without having to alter their interface, in other words without having to write special member functions for serialisation and deserialisation. It should also be possible to write intrusive code to achieve the same ends.
6. Orthogonal specification of class serialisation and archive format. This means that the clients are independent of device-dependent file formats.
7. It should be possible to create new kinds of archivers.
8. The archive interface must be rich enough to allow creation of archives to present serialised data in XML format, for example.

The functionality and syntax in Boost.Serialization is roughly similar to that found in the Microsoft Foundation Class (MFC) library. In chapter 17 we discuss an application of Serialization. We now discuss the library in some more detail by giving an overview of the library and providing some examples.

There are various include files needed when using Serialization. The relevant ones can be found in the source code files accompanying this book.

5.10.1 Main Concepts and Initial Examples

We define functions that allow us to save state and to load this state in the same sequence in which it was saved. There are two distinct approaches to implementing serialisation. First, the *intrusive approach* requires that classes whose instances are to be serialised must be modified by creating a template member function called `serialize()` whose template parameter is an *Archive* class. The second formulation is to define the serialisation functionality outside the class scope. This is the *non-intrusive approach* and the main advantage is that it supports serialisation without our having to change the class definition. Of course, in this case we need to provide enough information in the class interface so that the class state can be saved. This is ensured by creating the appropriate `get()` functions (or in some cases we may allow the data to be public). In the non-intrusive case we create a global function `serialize()` in the namespace **boost::serialization**. Both the intrusive and the non-intrusive formulations function in the same way.

The template *Archive* type defines the operator '`&`'. The two special archive types are *input* and *output archives*. An output archive is similar to an output data stream. An input archive is similar to an input data stream.

We take an example of a record structure that we wish to serialise using both formulations. We take a three-dimensional point. First, we use the following headers:

```
// Include headers that implement a archive in simple text format
#include <boost/archive/text_oarchive.hpp>
#include <boost/archive/text_iarchive.hpp>
```

The class interface for `Point` (including the template serialise/deserialise member function) is:

```
class Point
{ // 3d point
```

```
public: // for convenience, only
   double x, y, z;

   Point() : x(0.0), y(0.0), z(99.99)
   { // Each serializable class needs a default constructor
   }

   // Template member function for serialisation (intrusive)
   template <typename Archive>
   void serialize(Archive& arc, const unsigned int version)
   { // Classes implements this function for intrusive case

      arc & x; arc & y; arc & z;
   }
};
```

The serialisation/deserialisation code in the non-intrusive case is (notice the nested namespace):

```
// Non-intrusive option; add to namespace
namespace boost
{
   namespace serialization
   {
      // Free template function for serialisation (non-intrusive)
      template <typename Archive>
      void serialize(Archive& arc, Point& pt, const unsigned int version)
      {
         arc & pt.x; arc & pt.y; arc & pt.z;
      }
   }
}
```

We now give an example of using the above functionality. In particular, we serialise and deserialise a point. The client code is the same for both the intrusive and non-intrusive versions of the serialize function:

```
// Create point
Point pt;
pt.x = 1.0; pt.y = 0.04; pt.z = 0.0;

// Save data to archive
{
   // Create and open a character archive for output
   std::ofstream ofs("Point.dat");
   boost::archive::text_oarchive oa(ofs);

   // Change some data
   pt.x = 0.20;

   // Write class instance to archive
   oa << pt;
}

// ... Some time later, restore the class
{
   Point newData;

   // Create and open an archive for input
   std::ifstream ifs("Point.dat", std::ios::binary);
   boost::archive::text_iarchive ia(ifs);

   // Read class state from archive
```

```
    ia >> newData;

    // Just checking
    cout << "(" << newData.x << "," << newData.y
        << "," << newData.z << ")" << endl;
}
```

This completes the discussion of initial examples of Boost.Serialization.

5.10.2   STL Containers and Serialisation of more Complex Objects

The library has support for the serialisation of STL containers. This means that you do not have to write your own code to do this. Instead, you can employ intrusive or non-intrusive options to serialise instances of classes with embedded STL containers as members. We take an example of a class called `Polyline` that models lists of `Point` instances and that uses `std::list<T>` as implementation.

The following header file is included:

```
// When using STL containers, you must include these headers
#include "boost/serialization/list.hpp"
// etc.
```

The class interface is:

```
class Polyline
{ // A collection of points

    list<Point*> coll;

public:

    Polyline() { coll = list<Point*>(); }

    void add(Point* pt) { coll.push_back(pt); }

    // Template member function
    template <typename Archive>
    void serialize(Archive& arc, const unsigned int version)
    { // Classes must implement this function

        arc & coll;
    }

    void print() const
    {
        if (coll.size() == 0)
        {
            cout << "List is empty..\n";
            return;
        }

        list<Point*>::const_iterator it;

        for (it = coll.begin(); it != coll.end(); ++it)
        {
        // print coordinates
            cout << (*it)->x << ", " << (*it)->y << ", "
                << (*it)->z << endl;
        }
    }
};
```

We see that serialisation is intrusive in this case. It is easy to create the code because it is a question of delegating to the serialising functions in `std::list<T>`. We take an example of a polyline that we serialise and deserialise:

```
// Saving composite data
Polyline myPolyline;
Point* hdata = new Point;

// Create a polyline with three points
myPolyline.add(hdata); myPolyline.add(hdata); myPolyline.add(hdata);

Point* h2data = new Point;
h2data->x = 10.0; myPolyline.add(h2data);
myPolyline.print();

std::ofstream ofsII("Polyline.dat");

// Save data to archive
{
    boost::archive::text_oarchive oaII(ofsII);

    // Write class instance to archive
    oaII << myPolyline;
}

delete hdata;
delete h2data;

// Recreate the polyline
// Create and open an archive for input
std::ifstream ifsII("Polyline.dat", std::ios::binary);
boost::archive::text_iarchive iaII(ifsII);

// Read class state from archive
Polyline myPolylineII;
try
{
    iaII >>  myPolylineII;
}
catch(exception& e)
{
    cout << "** " << e.what() << endl;
}

cout << "Print polyline\n";
myPolylineII.print();
```

5.10.3 XML Serialisation and Deserialisation

We now discuss how to serialise data in XML. The header files to be included are:

```
#include <boost/archive/xml_oarchive.hpp>
#include <boost/archive/xml_iarchive.hpp>
```

We take an example of a map whose key parameter is of type `string` and whose values are `double`:

```
// Serialising maps
map<string, double> option;
```

```
// Using indexing to define the keys in the map
option["r"]   = 0.10;        // Interest rate
option["sig"] = 0.28;        // Volatility
option["K"]   = 19.0;        // Strike price
option["T"]   = 0.75;        // Expiry dat
option["S"]   = 19.0;        // Underlying asset

cout << "Size of map: " << option.size() << endl;
```

As in previous examples, we create output and input archives for XML serialisation and deserialisation:

```
// Save and retrieve XML
std::ofstream ofsIV("OptionData.xml");

// Save data to archive
try
{
   boost::archive::xml_oarchive oaIV(ofsIV);
// BOOST_SERIALIZATION_NVP is a macro to create a name-value pair
// for XML serialisation
   oaIV & BOOST_SERIALIZATION_NVP(option);

}
catch(exception& e)
{
   cout << "** " << e.what() << endl;
}

map<string, double> myMap;
std::ifstream ifsIV("OptionData.xml");
boost::archive::xml_iarchive iaIV(ifsIV);

// Read class state from archive
try
{
   iaIV >> BOOST_SERIALIZATION_NVP(myMap);
}
catch(exception& e)
{
   cout << "** " << e.what() << endl;
}
cout << "Size of map: " << myMap.size() << endl;
```

You can check that the correct data is in the XML file by printing the elements of the map that was created from it:

```
map<string, double>::const_iterator it;

for (it = myMap.begin(); it != myMap.end(); ++it)
{
   cout << it->first << ", " << it->second << endl;
}
```

5.10.4 An Example from Boost Documentation: Serialization Tutorial

We conclude the introduction to Boost.Serialization by discussing the 'Serialization Tutorial' example code from the official Boost site. It is a routing problem for buses in a city. The UML diagram is shown in Figure 5.1. The main classes are:

- *GPS*: this class represents three-dimensional positions (degrees, minutes and seconds).
- *BusStop*: models the position of a bus stop that contains a latitude and a longitude (both are gps positions).

- *BusStopCorner*: a specialisation of a *BusStop* (derived class); it has two extra member data representing the names of the intersecting street.
- *BusStopDestination*: this is a *BusStop* with a name.
- *BusRoute*: a collection of *BusStop* instances.
- *BusSchedule*: a collection of bus routes, each one having a starting time.

This example contains many of the essential attention points when serialising objects in an object network:
- Raw pointers and shared pointers.
- Serialising instances of derived classes.
- Serialising aggregate objects (already discussed in the previous section).
- Splitting serialise into separate save and load operations.

We elaborate these issues by discussing how the classes in Figure 5.1 have been implemented in Boost. We use the same names for classes as in the Boost documentation.

The class that models gps position is:

```cpp
class gps_position
{
    friend class boost::serialization::access;

    int degrees;
    int minutes;
    float seconds;

    template <class Archive>
    void serialize(Archive& ar, const unsigned int /* file_version */)
    {
        ar & degrees & minutes & seconds;
    }
public:
    gps_position() {}
    gps_position(int _d, int _m, float _s) :
        degrees(_d), minutes(_m), seconds(_s)
    {}
};
```

A bus stop has the following structure:

```cpp
class bus_stop
{
    friend class boost::serialization::access;

protected:
    bus_stop(const gps_position& _lat, const gps_position& _long) :
        latitude(_lat), longitude(_long) {}

public:
    bus_stop() {}
    virtual ~bus_stop() {}
    virtual string description() const = 0;

    // Composition
    gps_position latitude;
    gps_position longitude;

    template <class Archive>
    void serialize(Archive& ar, const unsigned int version)
```

```
    {
        ar & latitude;
        ar & longitude;
    }
};
```

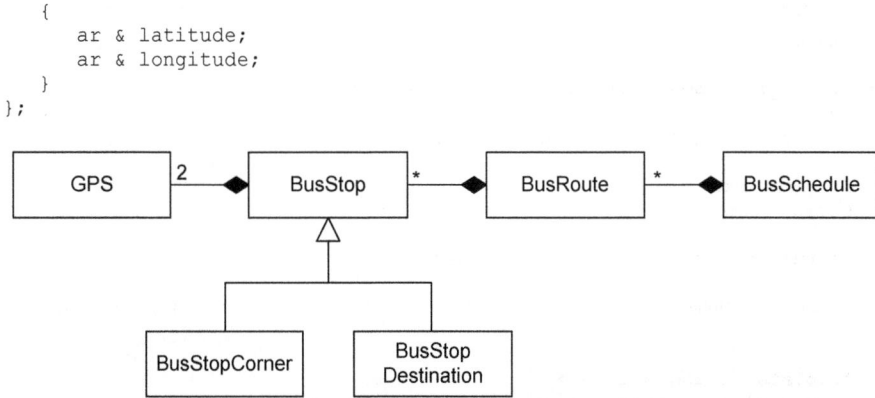

GPS — 2 — BusStop — * — BusRoute — * — BusSchedule

BusStopCorner BusStop Destination

Figure 5.1 UML class model

In the above code we see that serialising a bus stop entails serialising its two gps components.

```
class bus_stop_corner: public bus_stop
{
    friend class boost::serialization::access;

    // Member data
    string street1;
    string street2;

    virtual string description() const
    {
        return street1 + " and " + street2;
    }

    template <class Archive>
    void serialize(Archive& ar, const unsigned int version)
    {
        // save/load base class information
        ar & boost::serialization::base_object<bus_stop>(*this);
        ar & street1 & street2;
    }
public:
    bus_stop_corner() {}
    bus_stop_corner(const gps_position& _lat, const gps_position& _long,
        const string& _s1, const string& _s2) :
            bus_stop(_lat, _long), street1(_s1), street2(_s2)
    {}
};
```

Serialising an instance of a derived class involves first serialising its base class data and then the member data in the derived class itself. Note that we should not call serialising functions from the base class directly but instead we use the special function:

```
ar & boost::serialization::base_object<bus_stop>(*this);
```

Furthermore, we declare the friend function:

```
friend class boost::serialization::access;
```

that grants access to the private members of a given class to the serialisation library. This is needed because the serialise function is private. The next class models a bus stop:

```
class bus_stop_destination : public bus_stop
{
    friend class boost::serialization::access;

    // Member data
    string name;

    virtual string description() const
    {
        return name;
    }

    template <class Archive>
    void serialize(Archive& ar, const unsigned int version)
    {
        ar & boost::serialization::base_object<bus_stop>(*this) & name;
    }
public:
    bus_stop_destination(){}
    bus_stop_destination(const gps_position& _lat,
        const gps_position& _long, const string& _name) :
            bus_stop(_lat, _long), name(_name) {}
};
```

A bus route contains a list of polymorphic pointers. This means that each element in the list can point to a derived bus stop. Thus, we need some kind of *class identifier* when the pointer is saved. When the pointer is subsequently loaded the class identifier must be read and an instance of the appropriate derived class will be constructed. Finally, the data can be loaded into the newly created instance of the correct type. The process whereby base class pointers require explicit enumeration is called *registration* or *export* of derived classes and its realisation is given by the following code:

```
class bus_route
{
    friend class boost::serialization::access;
    friend ostream& operator << (ostream &os, const bus_route& br);

    // Member data
    typedef bus_stop* bus_stop_pointer;
    list<bus_stop_pointer> stops;

    template <class Archive>
    void serialize(Archive& ar, const unsigned int version)
    {
        ar.register_type(static_cast<bus_stop_corner*>(NULL));
        ar.register_type(static_cast<bus_stop_destination*>(NULL));

        ar & stops;
    }
public:
    bus_route() {}

    void append(bus_stop* _bs)
    {
        stops.insert(stops.end(), _bs);
    }
};
```

Finally, the interface for the bus schedule class is:

```cpp
class bus_schedule
{
public:
    // note: this structure was made public because the friend declarations
    // didn't seem to work as expected.

    struct trip_info
    {
        template <class Archive>
        void serialize(Archive& ar, const unsigned int file_version)
        {
            // in versions 2 or later
            if (file_version >= 2) ar & driver;    // read the drivers name

            // all versions have the follwing info
            ar & hour & minute;
        }

        // starting time
        int hour;
        int minute;

        // only after system shipped was the driver's name
        // added to the class
        string driver;

        trip_info() {}
        trip_info(int _h, int _m, const string& _d) :
            hour(_h), minute(_m), driver(_d) {}
    };

private:
    friend class boost::serialization::access;

    // Member data
    list<pair<trip_info, bus_route*> > schedule;

    template <class Archive>
    void serialize(Archive& ar, const unsigned int version)
    {
        ar & schedule;
    }

public:
    void append(const string& _d, int _h, int _m, bus_route* _br)
    {
        schedule.insert(schedule.end(),
            std::make_pair(trip_info(_h, _m, _d), _br) );
    }

    bus_schedule() {}
};
```

We conclude this section with a discussion of *class versioning* (*schema evolution*) and what to do when the save and load operations are dissimilar. Versioning is important when you modify class structure and when customers' data need to be compatible with multiple versions of the software. In general, the library stores a *version number* in the archive for each class serialised (the default version number is 0). The version number that is read is the one that was saved. Thus, we can make use of this fact as we shall see in the example below. The current serialisation version is specified by BOOST_CLASS_VERSION.

In some applications we make a distinction between the save and load operations. This is in contrast to the `serialize()` function which treats save and load operations uniformly. To split `serialize()` into a `load()` and `save()` function, we need to add `BOOST_SERIALIZATION_SPLIT_MEMBER()` for intrusive serialisation or `BOOST_SERIALIZATION_SPLIT_FREE()` for non-intrusive serialisation.
We take an example in which we load data into an object based on a check of the version number. The headers files are:

```
#include <boost/serialization/version.hpp>
#include <boost/serialization/split_member.hpp>
```

The function is replaced by:

```
// Separate save and load operations
template <class Archive>
void save(Archive& ar, const unsigned int version)
{
    ar & boost::serialization::base_object<bus_stop>(*this) & name;
}

template <class Archive>
void load(Archive& ar, const unsigned int version)
{
    if (version > 0)
    {
        ar & name;
    }

    ar & boost::serialization::base_object<bus_stop>(*this);
}

BOOST_SERIALIZATION_SPLIT_MEMBER()
```

We also add the current serialisation version number:

```
// The current version
BOOST_CLASS_VERSION(bus_route, 1)
```

In chapter 17 we discuss how to integrate Boost.Serialization with legacy applications.

5.11 Summary and Conclusions

In this chapter we have introduced a number of template classes that resolve problems that can occur in C++ applications using raw pointers or STL `auto_ptr`. The Smart Pointer library uses non-intrusive reference counting techniques and there is also support for creating user-defined reference counted classes. We also gave a short introduction to Boost.Serialization that allows us to save data to disk and to recreate objects from disk.

Which type of memory management type (raw, smart) to use in applications depends on a number of factors. Each choice has its own advantages and disadvantages. Finally, we note that the new C++ standard (C++0X) has support for automatic garbage collection; in particular, it supports shared and weak pointers.

6 Tuple

6.1 Introduction and Objectives

In this chapter we introduce the Boost.Tuple library that allows developers to group a fixed collection of heterogeneous data types into a single entity. We use such entities as input arguments to functions or as return types of functions. In the latter case we say that we provide support for *multiple return values*. We see this library as an extension of the `std::pair<>` which is a *2-tuple* consisting of a first element and a second element. Boost.Tuple supports *n-tuples* which are sequences of n variables, each of which is called a *component* of the n-tuple.

We discuss the following topics in this chapter:
- The background to n-tuples; what they are and why we need them.
- The basic `tuple` class and its member functions.
- The different ways to construct a tuple.
- Associating C++ variables with tuple components (*tieing*).
- Accessing the elements of a tuple; comparing tuples.
- Streaming of tuples and input-output issues.

Finally, we discuss the relationships with STL and we sketch some application areas for Boost.Tuple.

6.2 An Introduction to n-Tuples

A tuple is a sequence of values. The components in the sequence can be of any type. We call a tuple with n components an *n-tuple*. Tuples are used in many applications, for example:
- Complex numbers can be represented as 2-tuples.
- Quaternions can be represented as 4-tuples.
- Rows of database tables are n-tuples.
- A structure representing a DATE is a 3-tuple (it consists of a day, month and year).

We use tuples to model a group of related data items. Each item has a type and we can instantiate the tuple by assigning values to each of its components.

In general, given a collection $T_1, T_2, \ldots, T_n$ of data types we define a relation R on these types to be a set of ordered n-tuples $(t_1, t_2, \ldots, t_n), t_j \in T_j, j = 1, \ldots, n$. The sets $T_1, T_2, \ldots, T_n$ are the *domains* of R and the value n is called the *degree* of R.

We take an example (Date 1981). In this case we model manufactured items. We model the components as follows:
- Part number (integer type).
- Part name (string type).
- Colour (character type); we use codes, thus 'R' for 'red', for example.
- Weight (double type).
- City (string type).

An instance of this 5-tuple is a screw with values (1254, '10 mm screw', 'W', 1.42, 'London'). We can create more instances of this 5-tuple and they could be stored in a database. The data types of the components in the above example are built-in C++ types but we note that a tuple's components can also be user-defined types. Relational databases need to define the components as built-in types but we can create user-defined components since we are working in an object-oriented framework.

6.3   The `tuple` Class: Fundamental Properties

We now discuss the core library and class for creating tuples. In your code, you need to include the following file:

```
#include <boost/tuple/tuple.hpp>
```

and use the following namespace:

```
using boost::tuple;
```

The corresponding class has constructors for creating tuple instances. Our first example is a 2-tuple consisting of a `string` and a `double`. We create an instance using a constructor. The second example is a 2-tuple consisting of a `string` and an `int` and we create an instance using the function `boost::make_tuple()`:

```
#include <boost/tuple/tuple.hpp>
#include <string>

int main()
{
    // Using declaration, for readability purposes using boost::tuple;

    // Creating tuples, using ctor and free function 'make_tuple'
    tuple<string, double> myTuple(string("Hello"), 3.1415);
    tuple<string, int> myTuple2 = boost::make_tuple(string("101"), 0);

    return 0;
}
```

There are a number of ways to create a tuple:
- Default constructor.
- A constructor that initialises the types in the tuple.
- Copy constructor.
- Assignment operator.
- Using the free function `boost::make_tuple()`.

We discuss each of these options. In general, the number of arguments in a constructor is less than or equal to the number of components in the tuple. Any arguments corresponding to 'missing' elements are default initialised. Here is an example that shows how to create a parts object with varying numbers of arguments:

```
// Constructors for a n-tuple with k values, k in [0,n]
tuple<long, string, char, double, string>
    myPartI(1345, string("10 mm screw"), 'R', 0.12, string("Amsterdam"));

tuple<long, string, char, double, string>
    myPartII(1345, string("10 mm screw"), 'R', 0.12);

tuple<long, string, char, double, string>
    myPartIII(1345, string("10 mm screw"),'R');

tuple<long, string, char, double, string>
    myPartIV(1345, string("10 mm screw"));
```

```
tuple<long, string, char, double, string>
   myPartV(1345);

// Default constructor
tuple<long, string, char, double, string> myPartVI;
```

We can create instances by use of the assignment operator and the copy constructor; first, we create an object and we then clone tuples from it:

```
tuple<long, string, char, double, string>
   myPart(1345, string("10 mm screw"), 'R', 0.12, string("London"));

// Default parts, components are default-constructible
tuple<long, string, char, double, string> defaultPart;

// Now assign and copy construct
defaultPart = myPart;
tuple<long, string, char, double, string> myPartB(defaultPart);
```

The above example uses built-in data types as elements of the tuple. It is possible to define tuples whose elements are user-defined types. The first example models a person and has a Boost date to model the person's date of birth:

```
// for Dates using namespace boost::gregorian;
#include <boost/date_time/gregorian/gregorian.hpp>

// ISO 8601 extended format CCYY-MM-DD
string s("1952-08-29");                    // 29 August 1952
date myDate(from_simple_string(s));
tuple<string, string, date>
   person(string("Daniel"), string("London"), myDate);
```

Another example is a tuple that models 'named' two-dimensional points:

```
// User-defined types
Point pt(1.0, 2.0);
tuple<string, Point> namedPoint(string("#1"), pt);
```

Finally, we discuss how to instantiate tuples by invoking boost::make_tuple(). This free function is useful because it allows us to create a tuple with less effort than calling a constructor. To this end, here is an example that computes the sum and product of two numbers and that uses this free function to create the return type:

```
boost::tuple<double, double> Arithmetic(double f, double s)
{ // Simple 101 example

   // Create an anonymous object
   return boost::make_tuple(f+s, f*s);
}
```

6.4   Accessing Tuple Elements

Having created a tuple, it may then be necessary to access (read and modify) its elements. We have a choice between the member function get() and the free function get(). We use indexing (starting at 0) to access the individual elements of a tuple. As an example, we first give a function that prints the elements of a tuple representing manufactured parts:

```
void print(const boost::tuple<long, string, char, double, string>& part)
{ // Print a tuple
```

```
    // Retrieving values from a tuple, using a member function get()
    long ID = part.get<0>();
    string name = part.get<1>();
    char colour = part.get<2>();
    double weight = part.get<3>();
    string city = part.get<4>();

    cout << "Elements part: (" << ID << ", " << name << ", "
         << colour << ", " << weight << ", " << city << ")" << endl;
}
```

We can also use the `get()` member function to modify the values in a tuple using an index, for example:

```
double a = 2.0; double b = 3.0;
tuple<double, double> calc = Arithmetic(a, b);
// Modifying the tuple's element values using get<>() member function
calc.get<0>() = 3.0;
calc.get<1>() = 2.0;
cout << "Arithmetic: " << calc.get<0>() << ", " << calc.get<1>() << endl;
```

Finally we show how to use the free function `get<>()`.

```
// Modification using free function get<>(), notice the namespace
boost::tuples::get<0>(calc) = 5.0;
boost::tuples::get<1>(calc) = 5.0;
cout << "Arithmetic: " << calc.get<0>() << ", " << calc.get<1>() << endl;
```

6.5   Comparing Tuples

It is possible to compare tuple instances using overloaded relational operators. This saves the developer having to carry out the tests on each individual element:

```
#include <boost/tuple/tuple_comparison.hpp>

// Creating tuples
tuple<long, string, char, double, string> t1(1345, string("10 mm screw"),
                                              'R', 0.12, string("London"));
tuple<long, string, char, double, string> t2;

cout << boolalpha;

// Comparison operators, ==, !=, <, > etc.
cout << "t1 == t2 " << (t1 == t2) << endl;
cout << "t1 != t2 " << (t1 != t2) << endl;
cout << "t1 < t2 " << (t1 < t2) << endl;
cout << "t1 > t2 " << (t1 > t2) << endl;
cout << "t1 <= t2 " << (t1 <= t2) << endl;
cout << "t1 >= t2 " << (t1 >= t2) << endl << endl << endl;
```

In general, two tuples are equal if all the element pairs of these tuples are equal. Most of the relational operators perform lexicographical comparisons. In general, a *lexicographical comparison* of two sequences s1 and s2 entails comparing them element-by-element as discussed in Josuttis 1999.

Tuples can be sorted and thus can be stored in associative containers. To be able to do this, we define a function object that compares two tuples at a given position:

```
// Need a sorting criterion
template <int index> struct TupleLess
{
```

```
template <typename Tuple>
bool operator () (const Tuple& left, const Tuple& right) const
{ // Lexicographical comparison with respect to 'index'

    return boost::get<index>(left) < boost::get<index>(right);
  }
};
```

We now create a number of tuples, place them in a vector, sort the vector (using the second tuple component as key) using the above criterion; finally we display the elements of the vector:

```
tuple<int, string> tA(1, string("string with 1"));
tuple<int, string> tB(2, string("string with 2"));
tuple<int, string> tC(-3, string("string with -3"));

vector< tuple<int, string> > myVec;
myVec.push_back(tB);
myVec.push_back(tC);
myVec.push_back(tA);

sort(myVec.begin(), myVec.end(), TupleLess<1>()); // After sorting
cout << "Sorted vector: " << myVec[0].get<1>() << ", "
     << myVec[1].get<1>() << ", " << myVec[2].get<1>() << endl;

sort(myVec.begin(), myVec.end(), TupleLess<0>()); // After sorting
cout << "Sorted vector: " << myVec[0].get<1>() << ", "
     << myVec[1].get<1>() << ", " << myVec[2].get<1>() << endl;
```

6.6   Tuples and Streaming

The Boost.Tuple library supports both input and output streaming. For example, displaying the elements of a tuple is easy:

```
#include <boost/tuple/tuple_io.hpp>

tuple<int, string> tA(1, string("string with 1"));
tuple<int, string> tB(2, string("string with 2"));
tuple<int, string> tC(-3, string("string with -3"));

cout << tA; cout << endl;
cout << tB; cout << endl;
cout << tC; cout << endl;
```

We now discuss how to create a tuple instance based on console input. To this end, we need to define opening and closing delimiters as well as inter-element delimiters (the defaults are ')', ')' and ' ' for the three kinds of delimiters). For example, this code allows us to input the elements of a tuple and create the tuple:

```
// I/O of tuples
tuple<long, double> t3;
cout << "Enter a tuple in form (long double), e.g. (1 2.2): "; cin >> t3;
cout << t3 << endl;
```

We can change the delimiters by using *manipulators* (Stroustrup 2000), for example:

```
// Now change the default delimiters
cout << "Enter a tuple in form [long, double], e.g. [1, 2.2]: ";
cin >> boost::tuples::set_open('[') >> boost::tuples::set_close(']')
    >> boost::tuples::set_delimiter(',') >> t3;
cout << t3 << endl;
```

6.7 Applications of Tuple

In this section we discuss how to use the library with the objective of improving the efficiency, maintainability and reliability of code. In general, the advantage of using tuples is that we can manage related groups of data as one entity. Let us take an example that computes the sum and inner product of two vectors. Before using tuples, we had programmed separate functions for the sum and product:

```
template <typename V, typename I> V Sum(const Vector<V, I>& x)
{ // Sum of elements using the Datasim Vector class

    V ans = x[x.MinIndex()];

    for (I j = x.MinIndex()+1; j <= x.MaxIndex(); ++j)
    {
        ans += x[j];
    }

    return ans;
}

template <typename V, typename I> V Product(const Vector<V, I>& x)
{ // Product of elements

    V ans = x[x.MinIndex()];

    for (I j = x.MinIndex() + 1; j <= x.MaxIndex(); ++j)
    {
        ans *= x[j];
    }

    return ans;
}
```

While this code is correct, we see duplication of effort and we also need to iterate twice in a vector if we wish to compute both the sum and product of a vector, as the following example shows:

```
// Create a vector v1
Vector<double, long> v1(4);
for (long k = v1.MinIndex(); k <= v1.MaxIndex(); ++k)
{
    v1[k] = double(k);
}

// Without using tuples
cout << "V0: " << Sum(v1) << ", " << Product(v1) << endl;
```

Using tuples allows us to perform a form of *loop fusion* on the code:

```
template <typename V, typename I>
boost::tuple<V, V> SumAndProductVersionII(const Vector<V, I>& x)
{
    // Sum and product of a vector
    V sum = x[x.MinIndex()];
    V prod = x[x.MinIndex()];

    for (I j = x.MinIndex() + 1; j <= x.MaxIndex(); j++)
    {
        sum += x[j];
        prod *= x[j];
    }
```

```
      return boost::make_tuple(sum, prod);
   }
```

The code for this function is:

```
int main()
{
   // Using declaration, for readability purposes
   using boost::tuple;

   Vector<double, long> v1(4);
   for (long k = v1.MinIndex(); k <= v1.MaxIndex(); ++k)
   {
      v1[k] = double(k);
   }

   tuple<double, double> t2 = SumAndProductVersionII(v1);
   cout << "V2: " << t2 << endl;

   return 0;
}
```

We conclude this section by discussing how to relate C++ variables with the elements of a tuple. This technique promotes code readability and improves reliability because we can use these variables directly without having to access the tuple's elements. We thus 'tie' tuples to variables. We again take the example of computing the sum and product of a vector; the difference now is that the computed values are stored in variables:

```
// We tie tuple element to variables
double sum; double product;

boost::tie(sum, product) = SumAndProductVersionII(v1);
cout << "Sum: " << sum << ", Product: " << product << endl;
```

Finally, we may not always be interested in all the components of a tuple. In these cases we use a special object to discard or *ignore* a tuple element's value. For example, if we are only interested in the sum and not the product, we could proceed as follows:

```
// Ignoring some tuple elements
double sum2;
boost::tie(sum2, boost::tuples::ignore) = SumAndProductVersionII(v1);
cout << "Sum2: " << sum << endl;
```

6.8   Summary and Conclusions

We have discussed the Boost.Tuple library and the functionality that it offers. Its added value lies in its support for the mathematical concept of an n-tuple. Tuples can be used as input arguments to functions and as return values from functions. They make code easy to understand and their use leads to efficient code.

Appendix C contains exercises on applying tuples, for example in combination with Boost.MultiArray.

7 Any

7.1 Introduction and Objectives

In this chapter we discuss type-safe storage and retrieval of data using the Boost.Any library. This library can be considered as an object-oriented and robust alternative to `void*`. Instances of `any` class can hold heterogeneous data and this data can be extracted and converted to its original type. In other words, retrieval is type-safe.

In this chapter we discuss the following topics:
- The `any` class and its member functions.
- Casting and the corresponding exception handling issues.
- Using `any` with smart pointers (in particular `shared_ptr`).
- Heterogeneous data in STL containers.
- Applications of `any`.

7.2 The `any` Class: Fundamental Properties

When instantiating template classes we can replace the template type by a specific type. For example, the STL `list<T>` can be instantiated to `list<Shape*>` for example and this means that any derived class of `Shape` can be added to the list. It is not possible to add objects to the list whose classes are not derived from `Shape`. We would sometimes like to define truly heterogeneous data types so that we can add them to the list. In fact, we wish to define *indiscriminate types* that can refer to arbitrary data types. To this end, we introduce the `any` class. We take a simple example to show how to use this class. We define three built-in variables and a variable of type `any`. In the example you can see that this latter variable can be assigned to any other variable:

```
#include <boost/any.hpp>

// Initial example
int n = 0; double d = 1.0; string myString("my first");

any a = n;      cout << "any 1 " << n << endl;
a = d;          cout << "any 2 " << d << endl;
a = myString;   cout << "any 3 " << myString << endl;
```

The output from this code is `0`, `1.0`, `my first`. The next step is to determine the actual type residing in an `any` variable and then to cast it to this actual type. The first problem is resolved using RTTI:

```
// Now cast the any type back to the correct actual type
if (typeid(string) == a.type())
{
    cout << "It's a string.. \n";
}
else if (typeid(int) == a.type())
{
    cout << "An int\n";
}
else if (typeid(double) == a.type())
{
    cout << "A double\n";
}
else
{
    cout << "Oops, Something else\n";
}
```

Having determined that we have a string on our hands we can use the (overloaded) any_cast function:

```
// Now cast the any to a string
try
{
    string s1 = any_cast<string>(a);
    cout << "String value is: " << s1 << endl;
}
catch(bad_any_cast& error)
{
    cout << "Error: " << error.what() << endl;
}
```

If the cast was not successful a bad_any_cast exception will be thrown. This now completes our first example. To conclude, we show all the possibilities with any_cast:

```
namespace boost
{
    class bad_any_cast;
    class any;
    template <typename T> T any_cast(any&);
    template <typename T> T any_cast(const any&);
    template <typename ValueType> const ValueType* any_cast(const any*);
    template <typename ValueType> ValueType* any_cast(any*);
}
```

A ValueType is one that typically lives within objects or blocks, in other words on the stack. We manipulate value types directly as variables (or through references) and not as pointers. The focus of a value type lies in its state and not its identity. Value types should be *CopyConstructible* and *Assignable* (see Appendix C for a definition of these terms) and a destructor upholds the no-throw exception-safety guarantee.

The next example considers creating pointers to any, assigning them to an address of an any variable and finally casting the pointer to the actual type that it contains. The code is:

```
vector<string> vec2(4);
any anyOne = vec2;

// Create any* and assign it to address(any)
any* myAny = &anyOne;
int myInt = 10;
anyOne = myInt;

myAny = &anyOne;

// Now cast
try
{
    // Cast any* to valueType*
    int* i1 = any_cast<int>(myAny);
    cout << "Integer value is: " << *i1 << endl;
}
catch(bad_any_cast& error)
{
    cout << "Error: " << error.what() << endl;
}
```

7.3   Using `any` with Smart Pointers

We introduced smart pointers in chapter 5. In particular, we discussed the potential dangers of using raw pointers and why it is advisable to use `scoped_ptr` and `shared_ptr`. The question now is to examine how `any` and smart pointers can be used together. This is possible as the following example shows:

```
any A1(shared_ptr<Derived>(new Derived)); // derived class here
```

This code compiles because smart pointers can be the actual value for an `any` instance. We continue with another example in which we create a number of objects that depend directly or indirectly on a shared pointer (note the values of the reference count):

```
shared_ptr<Derived> sp(new Derived);
cout << "Use count: " << sp.use_count() << endl;                        // 1
any A3(sp); cout << "Use count: " << sp.use_count() << endl;   // 2
any A4(sp); cout << "Use count: " << sp.use_count() << endl;   // 3
any A5(A4); cout << "Use count: " << sp.use_count() << endl;   // 4
```

Finally, we wish to make explicit the deep copy aspect when creating instances of `any`. The first example creates two objects using a copy constructor:

```
cout << "Testing copying stuff\n";
int n2 = 10;
double d2 = 3.1415;

any One(n2);
any Two(One);

One = d2;
cout << "One: " << any_cast<double>(One) << endl;
cout << "Two: " << any_cast<int>(Two) << endl;

any Three = Two;
Three = complex<double>(1.0, 2.0);
cout << "Three, I: " << any_cast<complex<double> >(Three) << endl;
Three = Two;
cout << "Three, II: " << any_cast<int>(Three) << endl;
```

The output from this code is:

```
Testing copying stuff
One: 3.1415
Two: 10
Three, I: (1,2)
Three, II: 10
```

7.4   STL Containers whose Elements are of Type `any`

Having the ability to define objects containing heterogeneous data allows us to create STL containers (such as vectors, lists, maps and sets) whose elements can be of `any` type. To take an example, we create a number of objects that we add to a list:

```
string s("Hello");
vector<double> vec(10);

any A1 = s;
any A2 = vec;
any A4 = A1;

any A3(A1); // Copy constructor
```

We also create an object without assigning it to any specific data:

```
any A5;      // Contains no value
```

It is possible to test if such an object has been assigned by calling `empty()`:

```
if (A5.empty() == true)
{
    cout << "A5 is empty: OK\n";
}
else
{
    cout << "A5 is NOT empty: NOT OK\n";
}
```

We are now ready to add the above objects to a list:

```
list<any> myList;
myList.push_back(A1);
myList.push_back(A2);
myList.push_back(A3);
myList.push_back(A4);
myList.push_back(A5);
myList.push_back(make_pair<bool, double>(true, 3.1415));
```

7.5 Property Sets with heterogeneous Elements

In many applications we model named values (name-value pairs) where both the name and the value are generic types. To this end, we have defined classes called `Property<K,V>` and `SimplePropertySet<K,V>` in Duffy 2004 and Duffy 2009 that model name-value pairs and collections of name-value pairs, respectively. In the latter case we note that the template parameter `K` represents a set of unique keys. A discussion of properties and property sets (we called them *psets* in the sequel) is given in the Object Management Group (OMG) Property Service specification (see OMG 2000). Some scenarios are:

- S1: Operations for defining, deleting, enumerating and checking.
- S2: Operations for retrieving constraints on psets (for example, a property value is positive) and setting property modes (for example, read-only properties).
- S3: Operations to allow clients fine-grained control of properties. For example, we would like to iterate over the properties in a pset on the one hand and over the names of the properties only on the other hand.
- S4: Factories for creating properties and psets.

In this section we discuss the implementation in C++ of classes for properties and property sets. In this case the keys will be generic while the values will be stored as `boost::any` variables. The interface for the property class is:

```
template <typename Name = string> class Property:
    public PropertyThing<Name>
{
private:

    Name nam;
    boost::any con;

public:
    // Constructors and destructor
    Property();
    Property(const Name& name);
```

```
    Property(const Name& name, const boost::any& t);
    Property(const Property<Name>& source);
    virtual ~Property();

    // Accessing function operators
    // Get and set the value of the Property
    virtual boost::any operator () () const;
    virtual void operator () (const boost::any& t);

    // Get the name of the property
    virtual Name name() const;

    Property<Name>& operator = (const Property<Name>& source);
    PropertyThing<Name>* Copy() const;

    // True if names are the same
    bool operator == (const Property<Name>& prop2); // Keys the same
    bool operator != (const Property<Name>& prop2);

    void print() const;
};
```

This class has member data representing the name and value of the property. It also has constructors and member functions for accessing the member data. It is derived from the class `ProperyThing<N>` that has the interface:

```
template <typename Name> class PropertyThing
{
public:
    PropertyThing() {}
    virtual ~PropertyThing() {}
    virtual PropertyThing<Name>* Copy() const = 0; // Prototype
    virtual void print() const {}                  // FOR CONVENIENCE

    PropertyThing<Name>& operator = (const PropertyThing<Name>& source)
    { return *this; }
};
```

We have created this class because it is a base class for all future specialisations. We now discuss the derived class `SimplePropertySet<N>` that models a collection of properties and in which the keys are unique. The class offers the following functionality:
- Create a pset using a variety of constructors.
- Adding to, and removing properties from a pset.
- Navigating in psets using STL-compatible iterators.
- Selector functions (for example, give the value corresponding to a given key).

The key type is generic and the value type is `boost::any`. The relevant UML class diagram is Figure 7.1 where we see that the property set is an aggregation of properties; also it has a redundant set containing the keys of the property set:

```
template <typename N = string> class SimplePropertySet:
    public PropertyThing<N>
{
private:

    N nam;    // The name of the set

    // The SimplePropertySet list using the STL map
    map<N, boost::any> sl;
    Set<N> keys;
};
```

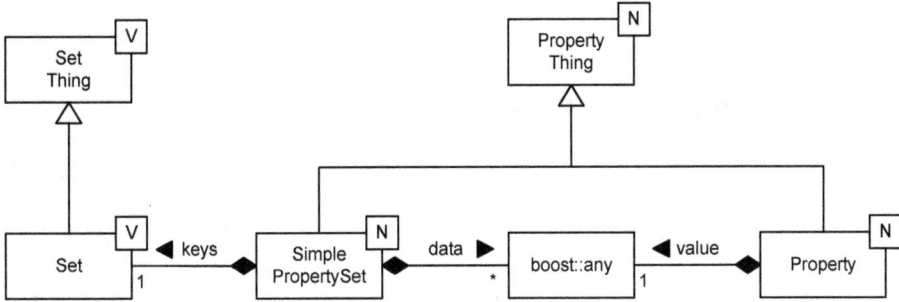

Figure 7.1 Properties and Property sets

How do we use `SimplePropertySet`? The main use case is to define a number of properties and add them to a property set, as the following example shows:

```
SimplePropertySet<string> MyDefaultSet;
boost::any val;
val = 1.0;

Property<string> r = Property<string>("Interest rate", val);
Property<string> sig = Property<string>("Volatility", val);
Property<string> K = Property<string>("Strike Price", val);
Property<string> T = Property<string>("Expiry date", val);
Property<string> U = Property<string>("Underlying Asset", val);
Property<string> b = Property<string>("Cost of carry rate", val);

// Add these properties to the set
myDefaultSet.add(r); myDefaultSet.add(sig);
myDefaultSet.add(K); myDefaultSet.add(T);
myDefaultSet.add(U); myDefaultSet.add(b);
```

We now discuss creating property sets by giving another example, namely psets whose values are arbitrary built-in or user-defined types. To this end, we create a simple class hierarchy. In practice these classes are more extensive and they contain non-trivial pricing and risk management code:

```
class Instrument
{ // Base class for all derivative products
public:

    virtual void print() const = 0;

};

class Option: public Instrument
{
public:

    void print() const
    {
        cout << "An option\n";
    }
};

class Bond: public Instrument
{
public:

    void print() const
    {
```

```
         cout << "A bond\n";
     }
};

class Swap: public Instrument
{
public:

    void print() const
    {
        cout << "A swap\n";
    }
};
```

and a separate class to model dates:

```
struct Date
{ // A simple date class

    int m;
    int d;
    int y;

    // etc.
};
```

The following code creates a pset containing properties from various classes and built-in types:

```
SimplePropertySet<string> myPortfolio;

// Create a number of specific instruments and add to portfolio
Option myOpt;
Bond myBond;
Swap mySwap;
Date myDate = {1, 7, 2010};

boost::any a1(myOpt);   boost::any a2(myBond);
boost::any a3(mySwap);  boost::any a4(myDate);

boost::any name(string("BB1A"));
int revision(1);

// Now add components to PSet
myPortfolio.add(string("Option"), a1);
myPortfolio.add(string("Bond"), a2);
myPortfolio.add(string("Swap"), a3);
myPortfolio.add(string("Date"), a4);
myPortfolio.add(string("Name"), name);
myPortfolio.add(string("Revision"), revision);
```

We now need to know how to extract the actual data from a pset. To do this, we create a function to compare boost::any with a predefined list of types:

```
void Classify(const boost::any& myAny)
{
    // Try to cast to a type
    if (typeid(Option) == myAny.type())
    {
        cout << "It's an option \n";
    }
    else if (typeid(Bond) == myAny.type())
    {
```

```
      cout << "It's a Bond\n";
   }
   else if (typeid(Swap) == myAny.type())
   {
      cout << "It's a swap\n";
   }
   else if (typeid(Date) == myAny.type())
   {
      cout << "It's a date\n";
   }
   else if (typeid(string) == myAny.type())
   {
      cout << "It's a string\n";
   }
   else
   {
      cout << "It's something else\n";
   }
}
```

The following code iterates in a pset and determines what the data is in each record of the set:

```
Set<string>::const_iterator itKey;
Set<string> keys = myPortfolio.definingSet(); // Gives the key set

boost::any tmp;

for (itKey = keys.begin(); itKey != keys.end(); itKey++)
{
   tmp = myPortfolio.GetValue(*itKey); // this is a boost::any
   Classify(tmp); // Hard-coded switch on the values in the pset
}
```

In future work, we prefer to use the libraries Boost.Property Map and Boost.Proptery Tree. A discussion of these libraries is outside the scope of this book.

7.6   Initialisation of Data with Assign Library

In this section we introduce functionality that reduces the amount of code that is needed in order to initialise STL (and Boost) container data. In particular, the Boost.Assign library makes it easy to fill containers by overloading certain operators. The library has predefined operators for the containers in the standard library and it is possible to initialise the data in these containers using comma-separated lists of data. The main use is in testing and prototyping applications when we create container data.

We take a simple example; we fill a vector with some data. The traditional (long-winded) way would be:

```
vector<int> myVec(6);
myVec[0] = 10; myVec[1] = 11; myVec[2] = 45;
myVec[3] = 80; myVec[4] = 23; myVec[5] = 99;
```

In order to avoid code pasting and general drudgery we can use the library to initialise the vector as follows:

```
vector<int> myVec;
myVec += 10,11,45,80,23,99;
```

This is much easier! Continuing, we now give an overview of the functionality in Boost.Assign and code that you can use as exemplars in your own applications. The library is very easy to use.

We distinguish between the functionality for adding elements to a container after it has been created (as in the example just given) and functionality that we need when initialising a container. The two function operators are:

- Function `operator += ()`

This fills a vector or any standard container with values, for example:

```
vector<pair<double, double> > myVec2;
myVec2 += (make_pair(3.1415, 2.71));
BOOST_ASSERT(myVec2.size() == 1);
```

The header `<boost/assert.hpp>` defines the macro `BOOST_ASSERT`, which is similar to the standard assert macro defined in `<cassert>`. The macro is intended to be used in Boost libraries.

By default, `BOOST_ASSERT(expr)` is equivalent to `assert(expr)`.

- Function `operator () ()`

This operator is useful when we construct objects that need several parameters. The following example shows how to add a list of pairs to a vector:

```
// Adding several arguments after having created a container
vector<pair<double, double> > myVec3;
push_back(myVec3)(3.1415, 2.71)(3.1415, 2.71)(3.1415, 2.71)(3.1415, 2.71);
BOOST_ASSERT(myVec3.size() == 4);

for (int n = 0; n < myVec3.size(); ++n)
{
    cout << myVec3[n].first << "," << myVec3[n].second << endl;
}
```

The same technique can be used to add a list of user-defined objects to a deque. This is a useful feature for prototyping, for example because we can then execute the commands in the deque:

```
// Command pipeline, defined below
Command c1("Open"), c2("Read"), c3("Close"); // Command defined shortly
deque<Command> myQue;
push_back(myQue) = c1, c2, c3;

deque<Command>::const_iterator it;
for (it = myQue.begin(); it != myQue.end(); ++it)
{
    it->execute();
}
```

Equivalently, we can access each element in the deque using operator overloading:

```
for (int n = 0; n < myQue.size(); ++n)
{
    myQue[n].execute();
}
```

Here we define the user-defined type `Command`:

```
struct Command
{
   string cmdType;

   Command(const string& command) { cmdType = command; }
   void execute() const { cout << cmdType << endl; }
};
```

We now discuss the issue of initialising a container. We discuss this in relation to maps, lists and tuples. The following code shows what we mean:

```
// Initialising a map
map<int, string> myMap = map_list_of (10,"3.14") (11,"hi")
                                       (45,"what?") (80,"123");

// Some checks
BOOST_ASSERT(myMap.size() == 4);
BOOST_ASSERT(myMap[80] == "123");

// Other data structures
list<int> myList = list_of (10) (11) (45) (80) (23) (-99);
BOOST_ASSERT(myList.size() == 6);

// Tuple list
typedef boost::tuple<int, Command, double> CommandTuple;
vector<CommandTuple> myTuple = tuple_list_of (1, c1, 3.1415)
                                             (2, c2, 2.71);

BOOST_ASSERT(myTuple.size() == 2);
```

Finally, we can add elements with the same values to a container, for example:

```
// Repeating the same value a number of times
vector<int> myVec4;
myVec4 += 1,2,repeat(10,45),repeat(12,99);
BOOST_ASSERT(myVec4.size() == 2+10+12);
```

In this case `repeat(n,m)` means that we add n elements to the container with each element having the value m.

The Assign library has more advanced functionality beyond what we have discussed here, and a discussion is outside the scope of the current book. Please see the Boost documentation.

For completeness, we give a list of header files to include for the examples in this section:

```
#include <boost/assign/list_of.hpp>        // for map_list_of etc.
#include <boost/assign/list_inserter.hpp>  // for insert()
#include <boost/assign/std/vector.hpp>     // for +=
#include <boost/assert.hpp>
#include <map>
#include <list>
#include <vector>
#include <string>
#include <iostream>
#include <boost/tuple/tuple.hpp>
#include <boost/any.hpp>
```

7.7   Summary and Conclusions

We have given an introduction to Boost.Any. This library contains the class `any` that can
hold heterogeneous data. It can be used in combination with STL containers and smart
pointers. The library allows us to create a type-safe alternative to `void*`.

The Boost.Any library is useful for applications that need to process heterogeneous data and
to applications that are extended to support new data types. The C solution to this problem is
to use `void*` but this leads to code that is not type-safe. Another approach is to create a
type-safe version using templates in computational finance applications (Duffy 2009). The
downside is that we had to write and support the code. Instead, we now use the Any library.
Exercise 2 in Appendix C deals with the problem of migrating legacy code to code that uses
Any.

8 Variant

8.1 Introduction and Objectives

In this relativily short chapter we discuss how to store and retrieve data taken from a user-defined set of types. In other words, we operate on a bounded set of types (in contrast to Boost.Any which operates on an unbounded set of data types). The Variant can be seen as the type-safe and object-oriented version of *unions* in C. Some of the advantages of using Boost variants are:

- Compile-time checked access to the values in a variant.
- Storing heterogeneous data in STL containers.
- The ability to model user-defined data types in a uniform manner.
- Efficient (stack-based) storage for variants.
- Safe operations on variants using the *Visitor* pattern.

We see that there is a need for variants in C++. In order to use Boost.Variant we include the following header file:

```
#include <boost/variant.hpp>
```

We also use the following namespace:

```
// Using declaration, for readability purposes
using boost::variant;
```

8.2 What is a Discriminated Union?

In C, a union is a variable that can hold objects of different types and sizes at different times. We do not have to keep track of the size and alignment requirements and hence we can manipulate different kinds of data in a single area of storage (Kernighan and Ritchie 1988). We take an example of a union that can hold any one of three types:

```
union NumericDataType
{
    int      i;
    float    f;
    double   d;
};
```

We define a variable Values that is large enough to hold the largest of the above types:

```
NumericDataType Values;
```

This variable can hold int, float or double and can subsequently be used in expressions. Some examples are:

```
Values.i = 10;
cout << "Integer: " << Values.i << endl; // Prints 10

Values.f = 1.098f;
cout << "Float: " << Values.f << endl;    // Prints 1.098
```

An important feature is that we can only retrieve the type that was most recently stored. For example, if we assign a double to Values, the values in the members fields i and f will be corrupted, as the following example shows:

```
Values.d = 3.1415;
cout << "Double: " << Values.d << endl;
```

```
// The variables i and f will not have correct values
cout << "Float: " << Values.f << endl;
cout << "Integer: " << Values.i << endl;
```

It is the responsibility of the programmer to keep track of which type is currently stored in the union.

A union is called *discriminated* in the sense that is contains a bounded set of members with each member having a certain type. We are interested in type-safe storage and retrieval of a bounded set of types and this is where Boost.Variant is needed.

8.3   The `variant` Class: Hello World Example

The variant class is a type-safe object-oriented version of a C `union`. It is templated and the number of template parameters is variable. For example, to create the equivalent of the union `NumericDataType` in section 8.2 we declare a variant with three parameters as follows:

```
// Equivalent of C union
typedef variant<int, float, double> NumericDataType;
```

We can create an instance of `NumericDataType` and assign it to an `int`, `float` or `double`:

```
NumericDataType myType = 3.142;
cout << myType << endl;
myType = 1.98f;
cout << myType << endl;
myType = static_cast<double>(3.14);
cout << myType << endl;
```

However, assigning the variant to a string or some other type that is not one of the three types above will result in an error:

```
myType = string("dddd");
```

8.4   Member Functions in `variant`

We now discuss the functionality in `variant`:
- Constructors: default constructor, copy constructor, constructor based on one operand, constructor for a variant as copy of another variant .
- Assignment operator.
- Destructor.
- `which()`: zero-based index of the current value's type in the set of bounded types.
- `type()`: return the `type_info` for the current value.
- Comparison operator `==` that returns `true` if the two operands are equal based on the equality operator of the current value's type.
- Inequality operator `var1 < var2` that returns true if `var1.which() < var2.which()`. If the indices are equal then it returns the result of calling the operator `<` on the current values of `var1` and `var2`.

We give some examples using constructors. To make things more exciting we let one of the parameters be a user-defined type, in this case `Point`.

The following code shows a number of ways to create and modify the variant:

```
// Some ways to construct a variant
variant<long, string, Point> myVariant;   // default long
variant<long, string, Point> myVariant2(myVariant);

Point pt(1.0, 2.0);
variant<long, string, Point> myVariant3(pt);

long val = 100;
variant<long, string, Point> myVariant4(val);

variant<long, string, Point> myVariant5 = myVariant4;

variant<long, string, Point> myVariant6 = val;

// Give some values
myVariant = 24;

myVariant = string("It's amazing");
myVariant = Point(3.0, 4.0);
```

Having created variants we may wish to extract the current data from them. To this end, we use the **boost::get<T>** free function. If we try to get the current member that is of the wrong type a run-time error will occur. For this reason we define a try/catch block:

```
myVariant = Point(3.0, 4.0);

// Try to get the value out of the variant
Point ptA;
string stA;
try
{
    ptA = boost::get<Point>(myVariant);
    stA = boost::get<string>(myVariant); // Wrong type, throws exception
}
catch(boost::bad_get& err)
{
    cout << "Error: " << err.what() << endl;
}

cout << "Value got from Variant: " << ptA << endl;
```

8.5   Type-safe Visitation of Variants

The situation with regard to the code in the previous section to access the members in a variant is not ideal. In some cases we would like to define new functionality that does the deciding for us in the sense that the correct function is called for the appropriate current type in the variant. To this end, we use the *Visitor* pattern (GOF 1995) and it is supported in the form of the abstract class **boost::static_visitor** from we can derive concrete visitor classes. We then use the apply_visitor function that allows compile-time checked type-safe application of the given visitor to the content of the variant, ensuring that all types are handled by the visitor.

We return to the union variant<long, string, Point> and we give it more functionality, for example creating type-safe print functions. The standard approach is to use a *Visitor* pattern and we use the function call operator () instead of the more usual Visitor::visit() function. We first define the namespaces:

```
// Using declaration, for readability purposes
using boost::variant;
using boost::apply_visitor;
```

All user-defined visitor classes are derived from `static_visitor`. The first example is a visitor that prints integers and strings:

```
class Variant_Visitor: public boost::static_visitor<void>
{
public:
};

class Print_Visitor : public Variant_Visitor
{ // A visitor with function object 'look-alike'

public:
    void operator () (long val) const { cout << "Long: " << val << endl; }
    void operator () (string& val) { cout << "String: " << val << endl; }
    void operator () (Point& val) { cout << "Point: " << val << endl; }
};
```

In order to use this functionality we create a variant and call `boost::apply_visitor` that associates this variant with a specific visitor:

```
variant<long, string, Point> myVariant;

Print_Visitor vis;

myVariant = Point(1, 3);
cout << "Using the visitor:\n";
boost::apply_visitor(vis, myVariant);
```

We create another visitor class that is a direct descendent of `static_visitor`:

```
class SimpleVisitor : public boost::static_visitor<int>
{
public:
    int operator () (long val) const { return val; }
    int operator () (string& val) const { return val.length(); }
};
```

In this case the return type of `SimpleVisitor` is an `int` which clients can use:

```
variant<long, string> myFirst("Hello you all");    // Variant with string
int result = boost::apply_visitor(SimpleVisitor(), myFirst);
cout << "Result of visitor: " << result << endl;
```

Finally, we remark that visitor classes can contain state. This state is normally computed when the function call `operator ()` executes. We shall give more examples of the *Visitor* pattern in chapter 17.

8.6   Summary and Conclusions

We have introduced Boost.Variant that offers type-safe discriminated union functionality, in particular type-safe storage and retrieval. The library supports bounded variant types, that is variants whose members belong to a fixed set of types.

The Variant library is useful when we wish to create code and applications that operate with a range of data structures.

In Exercise 3 (Appendix C) we discuss how to create a class that is able to operate with both fixed-sized and dynamic arrays. We recommend that you do this exercise because the design rationale underlying it is applicable to a range of problems.

9 Number Systems

9.1 Introduction and Objectives

In this chapter we introduce a number of data structures and classes that model number systems in mathematics. We concentrate on C++ classes for complex numbers and rational numbers. Complex numbers have many applications in engineering and mathematical physics while rational numbers allow us to define and use fractions (for example, 1/3) without loss of accuracy. We also introduce the boost GCD library that has functions to compute the *greatest common divisor* (gcd) and *least common multiple* (lcm) of two integral types.

9.2 A Review of STL `complex<T>`

We discuss how STL has implemented complex numbers in C++ (for an introduction to the mathematics of complex numbers, see Spiegel 1999). A complex number z is a pair of the form $z = a + bi$ where a and b are real numbers and i is the square root of -1 ($i^2 = -1$). The fundamental operations on complex numbers are:

- Addition:

$$z_1 = a + bi, \quad z_2 = c + di$$
$$z_1 + z_2 = (a + c) + (b + d)i.$$

- Subtraction:

$$z_1 - z_2 = (a - c) + (b - d)i.$$

- Multiplication:

$$z_1 * z_2 = (ac - bd) + (ad + bc)i.$$

- Division:

$$z_1 / z_2 = e + fi, \text{ where}$$

$$e = \frac{ac + bd}{c^2 + d^2}, \quad f = \frac{bc - ad}{c^2 + d^2}.$$

Some simple code examples are based on operator overloading:

```
complex<double> z1(-23.0, 5.3);
complex<double> z2(2.0, 3.0);

// Addition and subtraction
complex<double> z3 = z1 + z2;
complex<double> z4 = 2.0 + z3;
complex<double> z5 = z4 + 10.93;

// Multiplication and division
complex<double> z6 = z2 * 2.0;
complex<double> z7 = 2.0 * z2;
complex<double> z8 = z2 / 2.0;
complex<double> z9 = z6 / z7;
```

Other functionality that STL supports is:

- Properties of complex numbers (polar form, absolute value, real and imaginary parts).
- Trigonometric functions (sin, cos, tan).
- Hyperbolic functions (sinh, cosh, tanh).
- Other functions (exponential, square root, natural log and log to base 10).

The C++ code for these functions is easy to use. As an example, here is a generic function to use some trigonometric and hyperbolic functions:

```
template <typename T> void display(const complex<T>& c)
{
    // Standard functions
    cout << "sin; " << std::sin(c) << endl;
    cout << "cos; " << std::cos(c) << endl;
    cout << "tan; " << std::tan(c) << endl;

    cout << "sinh; " << std::sinh(c) << endl;
    cout << "cosh; " << std::cosh(c) << endl;
    cout << "tanh; " << std::tanh(c) << endl;
}
```

9.2.1 Application: Discrete Fourier Transform (DFT)

In this section we use complex numbers to compute the Fourier coefficients of a function. A discussion can be found in Press 2002 and Hsu 1995. Our interest lies in showing how to implement the algorithm that computes Fourier coefficients in C++. In particular, let f be real-valued function of a real variable and consider computing the Fourier coefficients $\{c_n\}_{n=0}^{N-1}$ for some integer $N > 1$:

$$f(x) = \sum_{n=0}^{N-1} c_n \exp(inx).$$

We specialise this equation by examining the known values of the function f at N discrete points, namely $\{f_n\}_{n=0}^{N-1}$.

Then the *Discrete Fourier Transform* (DFT) produces an array defined by:

$$F_k = \sum_{n=0}^{N-1} f_n W_N^{kn}, \tag{9.1}$$

where $W_N = e^{-i2\pi/N}$, $W_N^k = e^{-i2\pi k/N}$, $W_N^{kn} = e^{-i2\pi kn/N}$ for $k = 0, \ldots, N-1$.

We implement this algorithm in C++:

```
vector<complex<double> > DFT(const vector<double>& carr)
{ // Compute the discret Fourier transform using a double loop

    int N = carr.size();

    vector<complex<double> > result(N);

    complex<double> tmp;

    for (int k = 0; k < result.size(); ++k)
    {
```

```
        tmp = complex<double>(0.0, 0.0);
        for (int n = 0; n < carr.size(); ++n)
        {
            tmp += carr[n] * omega(N, n, k);
        }
        result[k] = tmp;
    }
    return result;
}
```

and the function `omega()` is given by:

```
complex<double> omega(int N, int n, int k, int factor = 1)
{
    double theta = (twoPi * double (k*n))/double(N);
    return complex<double>(cos(theta), -sin(theta));
}
```

In practice this solution is not used because there is a more efficient one. This is the famous *Fast Fourier Transform* (FFT) which is based on the observation that equation (9.1) can be written as a sum of two terms:

$$F_k = \sum_{n \ even} f_n W_N^{kn} + \sum_{n \ odd} f_n W_N^{kn}$$

$$= \sum_{n=0}^{N/2-1} f_{2n} W_{N/2}^{kn} + W_N^k \sum_{n=0}^{N/2-1} f_{2n+1} W_{N/2}^{kn}, \quad k = 0, \ldots, N-1.$$

The C++ code for this representation is:

```
vector<complex<double> > FFT(const vector<double>& carr)
{
    int N = carr.size();

    vector<complex<double> > result(N);

    complex<double> tmp;

    for (int k = 0; k < result.size(); ++k)
    {
        result[k] = FFTFactor(carr, k);
    }

    return result;
}
```

where the function `FFTFactor()` is defined by:

```
complex<double> FFTFactor(const vector<double>& carr,
                          int k, int FFTfactor = 1)
{ // Calculates kth factor in the FFT formula (even,odd sums)

    // factor = 1, FT, -1 inverse FT

    int N = carr.size();
    int NHalf = N / 2;                       // N is even
    complex<double> tmp;
    complex<double> factor = omega(N, 1, k);
    complex<double> result(0.0, 0.0);
```

```
    for (int n = 0 ; n < NHalf; ++n)    // upper limit (N/2) - 1
    {
        tmp = omega(NHalf, n, k, FFTfactor);
        result += carr[2*n]*tmp + (factor*carr[2*n + 1]*tmp);
    }

    return result;
}
```

It is possible to define the *inverse DFT* that maps an array of complex numbers back into the original array of real numbers:

$$f_n = \frac{1}{N} \sum_{k=0}^{N-1} F_k W_N^{-kn}, \quad n = 0, \ldots, N - 1.$$

The code for this algorithm is:

```
vector<double> FFTInverse(const vector<complex<double> >& carr)
{
    int N = carr.size();

    vector<double> result(N);

    double tmp;

    for (int k = 0; k < result.size(); ++k)
    {
        result[k] = FFTInverseFactor(carr, k, -1)/double(N);
    }

    return result;
}
```

where the function `FFTInverseFactor()` is defined by:

```
double FFTInverseFactor(const vector<complex<double> >& carr,
                        int k, int FFTfactor = 1)
{ // Calculates kth factor in Inverse FFT formula (even,odd sums)

    // factor = 1, FT, -1 inverse FT

    int N = carr.size();
    int NHalf = N / 2;                 // N is even
    complex<double> tmp;
    complex<double> factor = omega(N, 1, k);

    double result= 0.0;

    for (int n = 0 ; n < NHalf; ++n)    // upper limit (N/2) - 1
    {
        tmp = omega(NHalf, n, k, FFTfactor);
        result += (carr[2*n] * tmp + (factor * carr[2*n + 1] * tmp)).real();
    }

    return result;
}
```

Finally, we take an example to show how to use the algorithm. To this end, we create a vector, apply the DFT to it to produce a complex vector and then we apply the inverse DFT to the second vector to recover the original real vector:

```
const int M3 = 8;
vector<double> arrayC(M3);
for (int n = 0; n < arrayC.size(); ++n)
{
    arrayC[n] = 1.0;
}

arrayC[2] = -1.0;
arrayC[3] = -1.0;
arrayC[4] = -1.0;
arrayC[7] = -1.0;

vector<complex<double> > DFTArrayC = DFT(arrayC); print(DFTArrayC);

vector<complex<double> > FFTArrayC = FFT(arrayC); print(FFTArrayC);

vector<double> ArrayD = FFTInverse(FFTArrayC); print(ArrayD);
```

The field of Fourier analysis and its applications is vast and it is not possible to discuss it in any detail beyond what we have described here. The example in this section was chosen mainly for didactic reasons.

9.3   Complex Numbers Algorithms

We discuss a number of functions of a complex variable for inverse trigonometric and inverse hyperbolic functions that are supported in Boost. The six functions are:

$$\sin^{-1} z = \tfrac{1}{i} \ln(iz + \sqrt{1 - z^2})$$

$$\cos^{-1} z = \tfrac{1}{i} \ln(z + \sqrt{z^2 - 1})$$

$$\tan^{-1} z = \tfrac{1}{2i} \ln\left(\tfrac{1+iz}{1-iz}\right), \quad z \neq -i$$

$$\sinh^{-1} z = \ln\left(z + \sqrt{z^2 + 1}\right)$$

$$\cosh^{-1} z = \ln\left(z + \sqrt{z^2 - 1}\right)$$

$$\tanh^{-1} z = \tfrac{1}{2} \ln\left(\tfrac{1+z}{1-z}\right), \quad z \neq -1$$

where $ln(z)$ is the natural logarithm of z.

A simple example on how to use the above formulae in C++ is:

```
#include <complex>

#include <boost/math/complex/asin.hpp>
#include <boost/math/complex/acos.hpp>
#include <boost/math/complex/atan.hpp>
#include <boost/math/complex/asinh.hpp>
#include <boost/math/complex/acosh.hpp>
#include <boost/math/complex/atanh.hpp>

template <typename T> void display (const complex<T>& c)
```

```
    {
        cout << endl << "**complex number: " << c << endl;

        cout << "asin; " << boost::math::asin(c) << endl;
        cout << "acos; " << boost::math::acos(c) << endl;
        cout << "atan; " << boost::math::atan(c) << endl;

        cout << "asinh; " << boost::math::asinh(c) << endl;
        cout << "acosh; " << boost::math::acosh(c) << endl;
        cout << "atanh; " << boost::math::atanh(c) << endl;
    }

    int main()
    {
        // Two 'extreme' complex numbers
        complex<double> c1 (1.0, 0.0);
        complex<double> c2 (0.0, 1.0); // atan not defined when z = i

        display(c1);
        display(c2);

        complex<float> c3(1.0, 1.0);
        display(c3);

        return 0;
    }
```

These functions can be used in applications such as those discussed in Spiegel 1999.

9.4   Rational Numbers

In mathematics, a rational number is a set of ordered pairs of integers (Ayers 1965). For example, the fractions are examples of rational numbers. A rational number q can be written in the form $q = a/b$ where a and b are integers and b is non-zero. It is possible to define arithmetic operations on rational numbers as follows:

$$q_1 = \frac{a}{b}, \quad q_2 = \frac{c}{d}, \quad b \neq 0, d \neq 0$$

$$q_1 \pm q_2 = \frac{ad \pm bc}{bd} \text{ (addition, substraction)}$$

$$q_1 * q_2 = \frac{ac}{bd} \text{ (multiplication)}$$

$$q_1 / q_2 = \frac{ad}{bc} \text{ (division).}$$

The Boost Rational library supports rational numbers in the form of a template class **rational<I>** where I is of integral type. The above arithmetic operations translate to the following code:

```
    #include <boost/rational.hpp>
    rational<long> R1(1, 2);        // 1/2
    rational<long> R2(1, 4);        // 1/4


    // Arithmetic operations
    rational<long> R3 = R1 + R2;    // 3/4
    rational<long> R4 = R1 * R2;    // 1/8
    rational<long> R5 = R1 / R2;    // 2/1
```

Let $q = a/b$ be a rational number. Then a is called the *numerator* of q and b is called the *denominator* of q. To avoid run-time errors we can use the exception class `boost::bad_rational` as the following example shows:

```
try
{
    rational<int> R6(1, 0);    // denominator == 0
    R6 = 1/R6;                 // divison by zero
}
catch(const boost::bad_rational &e)
{
    cout << "Division by zero leads to " << e.what() << endl;
}
catch(...)
{
    cout << "Wrong exception raised!" << endl;
}
```

Calculations with rational numbers are exact if the numerator and denominator are within the value range of the underlying data type. In general, the numerator and denominator are stored in normalised form with no common factor. For example, in the following code snippet the rational numbers R7 and R8 have the same values and in fact R7 is normalised to R8:

```
rational<long> R7(1000, 2000);
rational<long> R8(1, 2);

if (R7 == R8) cout << "Normalisation " << endl;

cout << R7 << endl; // will give 1/2
```

A performance improvement is the use of *in-place assignment* instead of the standard assignment operator because we avoid the construction of a temporary object:

```
// Assignment, 2 types
rational<long> R9 = rational<long>(2, 5); // Classic

rational<long> R10;
R10.assign(2,5);                           // In-place assignment
```

Finally, we remark that normalisation costs two divisions and one gcd (greatest common divisor) operation, a topic that we now introduce.

9.5 Greatest Common Divisor (gcd) and Least Common Multiple (lcm)

In this section we discuss a number of topics that are related to the *divisibility* and *factorisation of integers*. Let a and b be integers with a being non-zero. Suppose $b = ac$ for some integer c. Then we say that a divides b (or b is dividable by a) and we use the notation $a|b$ to denote this relationship. We sometimes say that a is a *divisor* (factor) of b or that b is a multiple of a. We say that a positive integer $p > 1$ is a *prime number* (or prime for short) if its only divisors are ± 1 and $\pm p$, in other words that p has only trivial divisors. A number that is not a prime is called a *composite* because it can be written as a product of two integers. Examples of primes are 2, 3, 5, 7, 11, 13, 17, 19, ... Finally, any divisor of an integer n that is a prime is called a *prime divisor* of n. For example, 7 is a prime divisor of 42 because 7 is a prime and 42/7 = 6.

Let a and b be integers, not both zero. We say that the integer d is a *common divisor of* a and b if d divides both a and b, that is if $d|a$ and $d|b$. We note that 1 is a common divisor of a and b and that any common divisor of a and b cannot be greater than $|a|$ or $|b|$ where $|n|$ is the absolute value of the integer n. We conclude that there is a largest (greatest) common divisor of a and b that we denote by $gcd(a,b)$. Some examples are:

$$gcd(12, 18) = 6, \quad gcd(29, 15) = 1, \quad gcd(527, 765) = 17.$$

Now let a and b be nonzero integers. We note that $|ab|$ is a positive common multiple of both a and b and hence we know that there exists a smallest positive common multiple of a and b that we denote by $lcm(a, b)$. Some examples are:

$$lcm(2, 3) = 6, \quad lcm(4, 6) = 12, \quad lcm(27, 81) = 81.$$

The *Math Common Factor library* has support for computing gcd and lcm in the form of template function objects, function templates and functions. They are parameterised by a numeric type representing integers. Here is code that shows the use of each option:

```
#include <boost/math/common_factor_rt.hpp> // for gcd and lcm, run time
#include <boost/math/common_factor_ct.hpp> // compile time version

int main ()
{
    int n1 = 42;
    int n2 = 56;

    // Using function templates
    int g = boost::math::gcd<int>(n1, n2);
    cout << "gcd: " << g << endl;

    int least = boost::math::lcm<int>(n1, n2);
    cout << "lcm: " << least << endl;

    // Using function objects
    boost::math::gcd_evaluator<int> gcdVal;
    cout << gcdVal(n1, n2) << endl;

    boost::math::lcm_evaluator<int> lcmVal;
    cout << lcmVal(n1, n2) << endl;

    // Using unsigned long (compile time)
    cout << "GCD and LCM of " << n1 << " and " << n2 << " are "
         << boost::math::static_gcd<42, 56>::value << " and "
         << boost::math::static_lcm<42, 56>::value << endl;

    return 0;
}
```

You can run this code and check the output. In particular, the library supports run-time and compile-time evaluation of the greatest common divisor and least common multiple of two integers.

The mathematical foundations for the results in this section are discussed in Andrews 1971 and Hunter 1964. In particular, computing the greatest common divisor is realised by the *Euclidean algorithm* which in its turn is based on repeated application of the *Division Algorithm*:

Let a and b be integers with b being non-zero. Then there exist integers q and r such that $a = bq + r$ and $0 \leq r < |b|$.

Furthermore, the integers q and r are unique.

9.5.1   More general Cases

We can compute the greatest common divisor and least common multiple of an array of integers by repeated application of the formulae for two integers. In other words, we wish to compute the following:

$$gcd\,(a_1, a_2, \ldots, a_n)$$
$$lcm\,(a_1, a_2, \ldots, a_n).$$

How would we design this problem in C++? One solution that we take here is to first copy the array to a stack. We then create a loop in which we pop two elements $n1$ and $n2$ from the stack, push the value $gcd(n1, n2)$ onto the stack and proceed until there is only one element remaining on the stack. This value will then be the greatest common divisor of the array. This algorithm can be modified to compute the least common multiple of an array. The code that computes the desired number is:

```
double gcdList(const vector<int>& elements)
{
    stack<int> myStack;
    vector<int>::const_iterator it;

    // Stacks have no iterators, so we must push each element
    for (it = elements.begin(); it != elements.end(); ++it)
    {
        myStack.push(*it);
    }

    // Now pop 2 elements at a time,
    // do the gcd and push it back on until stack size == 1
    int n1, n2, g;
    while (myStack.size() != 1)
    {
        n1 = myStack.top();        // This code can be optimised
        myStack.pop();

        n2 = myStack.top();
        myStack.pop();

        g = boost::math::gcd<int>(n1, n2);
        myStack.push(g);
    }

    return myStack.top();
}
```

An example of use is:

```
vector<int> varr(3);
varr[0] = 4; varr[1] = 6; varr[2] = 20;
cout << "gcd of list: " << gcdList(varr) << endl;
```

Finally, we can use the Boost.Function library (that we introduced in Chapter 1) to create a generic function that can be used for both gcd and lcm. To this end, we define a function that has `int` as return value and two `int`s as input. The code is similar to above and we include only what is different:

```
int Compute(const boost::function<int (int, int) >& func,
            const vector<int>& elements)
{

    // ...

    g = func(n1, n2); // previously gcd<int>(n1, n2);

    // ...

}
```

We include exercises in Appendix C that discuss these issues.

An example of use is:

```
boost::math::lcm_evaluator<int> lcmVal2;
cout << "lcm of list, version II: " << Compute(lcmVal2, varr);

boost::math::gcd_evaluator<int> gcdVal2;
cout << "gcd of list, version II: " << Compute(gcdVal2, varr);
```

Using Function leads to generic and reusable code, as this example shows.

The rationale for the Math Common Factor library is summarised in the official documentation as follows: 'The greatest common divisor and least common multiple functions are used in some numeric contexts, including some of the other Boost libraries. Centralizing these functions to one header improves code factoring and eases maintenance.'

9.6   Quaternions and Octonians

We give a short overview of the data structures in the Math Quaternion and Math Octonion libraries that have applications in theoretical physics and computer graphics.

Quaternions define a four-dimensional space and were discovered by Sir William Rowan Hamilton. A quaternion q has a representation of the form:

$$q = a + bi + cj + dk$$
where

$$i^2 = j^2 = k^2 = -1$$
$$ij = k = -ji$$
$$jk = i = -kj$$
$$ki = j = -ik.$$

We can add, subtract, multiply and divide quaternions in much the same way as we do with complex numbers. We show how this is done in C++:

```
using boost::math::quaternion;
```

```
std::complex<float> c(1.0, -1.3);
quaternion<float> q(c);

// Basic operations
quaternion<float> q1(1.0, 2.0, 3.0, 4.0);
quaternion<float> q2(4.0, 3.0, 2.0, 1.0);

quaternion<float> q3 = q1 + q2;
quaternion<float> q4 = q1 - q2;
quaternion<float> q5 = q1 * q2;
quaternion<float> q6 = q1 / q2;

cout << q3 << endl;
cout << q4 << endl;
cout << q5 << endl;
cout << q6 << endl;
```

The output from this code fragment is:

```
(5,5,5,5)
(-3,-1,1,3)
(-12,6,24,12)
(0.666667,0.333333,0,0.666667)
```

We mention other functionality that the quaternion class offers:
- Creating quaternions from spherical, cylindrical and multi-polar representations.
- The exponential of a quaternion.
- Trigonometric and hyperbolic functions.

Quaternions are used in a number of computer graphics applications because they are an effective tool for rotating three-dimensional objects.

Finally, we introduce octonians that represent objects in eight-dimensional space. An octonion 0 has the representation:

$$0 = a + bi + cj + dk + ee' + \xi i' + \eta j' + \theta k'$$

where we need to define a matrix table for the unit octonions i, j, k, e' and so on. For example, one entry from the table is:

$$ii' = -e', \quad ij' = -k', \quad ik' = j'.$$

The matrix table is discussed in the Boost documentation.

An example of use is:

```
using boost::math::octonion;

// Basic operations
octonion<float> o1(1.0, 2.0, 3.0, 4.0, 5.0, 6.0, 7.0);
octonion<float> o2(8.0, 7.0, 6.0, 5.0, 4.0, 3.0, 2.0, 1.0);

octonion<float> o3 = o1 + o2;
octonion<float> o4 = o1 - o2;
octonion<float> o5 = o1 * o2;
octonion<float> o6 = o1 / o2;
```

We can create both quaternions and octonians from complex numbers and octonions from quaternions:

```
// Conversions Complex --> Quaternion --> Octonion
std::complex<float> c2(1.0, -1.3);

quaternion<float> q2(c2);
octonion<float> o3(c2);

quaternion<float> q3(1.0, 2.0, 3.0, 4.0);
octonion<float> o4(q3);

cout << "Conversions\n";
cout << "q2 " << q2 << endl;
cout << "o3 " << o3 << endl;
cout << "q3 " << q3 << endl;
cout << "o4 " << o4 << endl;
```

The output is:

```
Conversions
q2  (1,-1.3,0,0)
o3  (1,-1.3,0,0,0,0,0,0)
q3  (1,2,3,4)
o4  (1,2,3,4,0,0,0,0)
```

For an overview of octonions, see Baez 2001.

9.7   Conversions

We conclude this chapter with a discussion of a number of issues:
- Polymorphic conversions.
- Numeric casts.
- Lexical casting.

To this end, the Conversion library consists of four functions for numeric conversions, type promotions and demotions and various kinds of string conversions:
- `polymorphic_cast`: a type-safe competitor to `dynamic_cast`.
- `polymorphic_downcast`: efficient, type-safe cast between base class and derived class.
- `numeric_cast`: conversion between integral types.
- `lexical_cast`: casting between strings and numeric values (and vice versa).

The function `polymorphic_cast` is similar to `dynamic_cast`. It casts between pointers in a class hierarchy but the main difference is what happens when the cast is not successful; in the latter case a null pointer is returned and no exception is thrown while in the former case an exception is thrown. In some cases we do not care if the conversion has succeeded while in other cases we cannot ignore the fact that the cast has failed and in this case we define `try`/`catch` blocks. As an example, we consider classes that represent two-dimensional shapes:

```
Point base(1.0, 1.0);
double width = 10.0;
double height = 20.0;
Shape* s = new Rectangle(base, width, height);

/////////////// good cast
```

```
Rectangle* r;
try
{
    r = boost::polymorphic_cast<Rectangle*>(s);
    r->Print();
}
catch(std::bad_cast& error)
{
    cout << error.what() << endl;
}
```

In this case the cast is successful because we are casting a rectangle object to another rectangle object (they have the same type). If we now try to cast a rectangle to a square (they look similar but they are distinct C++ classes) an exception will be thrown and then caught:

```
Square* square;
try
{
    square = boost::polymorphic_cast<Square*>(s);
    square->Print();
}
catch(std::bad_cast& error)
{
    cout << error.what() << endl;
}
```

The function `polymorphic_downcast` is similar in intent to `polymorphic_cast` but we use it when we know that the conversion is safe. It is used when we downcast and need the speed of `static_cast` in release builds.

We conclude this section with a discussion of `lexical_cast`. In many cases we wish to convert numeric types to strings and vice versa without having to rewrite the conversion code each time. The usefulness of `lexical_cast` lies in the fact that it makes conversion look like other type-converting casts.

We show how to convert numeric types to strings and back again. In order to avoid code duplication and to have generic functions we define two templated conversion functions:

```
// Excapsulate lexical_cast functionality for convenience
template <typename T> string ToString(const T& t)
{ // Attempt to convert a T object to a string

    string result;

    try
    {
        result = boost::lexical_cast<string>(t);
    }
    catch(boost::bad_lexical_cast& error)
    {
        cout << error.what() << endl;
    }

    return result;
}


template <typename T> T ToType(const string& s)
{ // Attempt to convert a string to a T object
```

```
    T result;

    try
    {
        result = boost::lexical_cast<T>(s);
    }
    catch(boost::bad_lexical_cast& error)
    {
        cout << error.what() << endl;
    }

    return result;
}
```

The following code shows some examples of how to apply lexical casting:

```
// Some conversions to strings
double d = 1.2;     string s1 = ToString(d);
int n = 340;        string s2 = ToString(n);
char c = 'A';       string s3 = ToString(c);
complex<double> myComplex(0.0, 1.0); string s4 = ToString(myComplex);

cout << s1 << ", " << s2 << ", " << s3 << ", " << s4 << endl;

// Now convert back to original types
double d1 = ToType<double>(s1);
int n2 = ToType<int>(s2);
char c3 = ToType<char>(s3);
complex<double> myComplex4 = ToType<complex<double> >(s4);

cout << d1 << ", " << n2 << ", " << c3 << ", " << myComplex4 << endl;
```

Finally, we can modify user-defined types so that they can be lexically cast. To this end, we overload the operators << and >>. More information can be found in the Boost documentation.

9.8   Summary and Conclusions

We have introduced classes for complex numbers and rational numbers and we have discussed their properties and some simple applications on how to use them. In particular, complex numbers are used in engineering applications such as time series and signal analysis. We also gave a short overview of the quaternion and octonion classes in Boost. Finally, we discussed polymorphic casting.

The rationale for chapter 9 is that we wished to assemble functionality relating to complex numbers, rational numbers and related mathematical functionality in one place. We shall use this functionality in Volume II when we discuss statistical distributions and special functions in the Math library.

10 String Algorithm

10.1 Introduction and Objectives

In this chapter we introduce the String Algo library. It has functionality for string and text processing, in particular functions for modifying text and searching for substrings and patterns in a string, in particular:

- Converting strings from upper case to lower case (and vice versa).
- Removing leading and trailing characters from a string.
- Finding one substring (or its multiple occurrences) in a string.
- Substituting a matching substring in a string by another string.
- Splitting a string into its components.
- Using finders and formatters.

In general, we use the functions in this library rather than attempting to write our own home-grown versions. There are several function categories in the String Algo library and we devote a section to each one.
We use the following convenience files in our code:

```
#include <boost/algorithm/string.hpp>
#include <boost/algorithm/string_regex.hpp>
```

The functionality in this library is extensive and it should satisfy the needs of many applications that involve string and text processing. In the past developers needed to create this functionality in C or C++ but this time-consuming activity is no longer necessary, thanks to String Algo.

10.2 Case Conversion, Trimming and Predicates

Strings can contain a combination of lower-case and upper-case characters. We can convert a string's characters to upper case or lower case. Furthermore, we can choose to modify the original string or return to a copy, for example:

```
// Conversions
using namespace std;
string myLower("cuchulainn");
string myUpper("CUCHULAINN");

// Convert with copies of the input string
string sU = to_upper_copy(myLower);
string sL = to_lower_copy(myUpper);
cout << sU << ", " << sL << endl;

// Convert and modify the input string
to_upper(myLower); to_lower(myUpper);
cout << myLower << ", " << myUpper << endl;
```

Trimming is the process of removing spaces from the beginning or end of a string (or both). In this case we can choose to return a copy of the original string or we can modify it. We note that the trimming functions do not remove spaces that are embedded in interior of the string. Some examples are:

```
// Trimming
string s1("    AAAA   ");

// Make copies of s1 for use with modified functions
string s2(s1);
```

```
string s3(s1);

// Trimmed copies
string s4 = trim_copy(s1);            // remove lead/trail blanks
string s5 = trim_left_copy(s1);       // remove leading blanks
string s6 = trim_right_copy(s1);      // remove trailing blanks
cout << s4 << "," << s5 << "," << s6 << endl;

// Modifiers
trim(s1);                             // remove leading+trailing blanks
trim_left(s2);                        // remove leading blanks
trim_right(s3);                       // remove trailing blanks
cout << s1 << "," << s2 << "," << s3 << endl;
```

It is possible to define what we mean by 'space' when trimming strings; for example, we can trim strings in which space is interpreted as decimal digits. We shall discuss these *unary predicates* (functions with no input arguments that return a `bool`) in more detail in a later section. Here is an example that trims a string by removing leading and trailing decimal digits:

```
// Trim with different predicates
string sA("123AAA987");
trim_if(sA, is_digit());
cout << sA << endl;        // Output: AAA
```

It is also possible to use unary predicates that allow us to trim strings by removing the characters '/' and '*' from the input string, for example:

```
// Trim off any of a set of user-defined 'spaces'
string sY("*/**ABC/***/");
trim_if(sY, is_any_of("/*"));
cout << sY << endl;        // Output: ABC
```

Finally, logical operations (such as OR and AND) can be applied. For example, we extend the previous code by trimming digits from a string in combination with the characters '/' and '*'. Here is an example:

```
// Using logical operations
string sZ("*/9*6*ABC/2***/7");
trim_if(sZ, is_any_of("/*") || is_digit());
cout << sZ << endl;        // Output: ABC
```

We now discuss predicates that are concerned with the comparison of two strings:
- Is a string a prefix or suffix of another string?
- Does a string contain another string?
- Are two strings equal?
- Lexicographical string comparison.
- Do the elements of a string satisfy a given predicate?

The functions that implement these features have case-sensitive and case-insensitive variants and we concentrate mainly on the former category because the syntax is essentially the same in the latter case.

To determine whether a string contains another string as prefix or suffix, we use the functions **starts_with()** and **ends_with()**, respectively:

```
// Predicates
cout << "*** Predicates ***\n";
```

```
string sB("AAAwhat is this?.exe");
cout << starts_with(sB, "AAA") << endl;        // true
cout << starts_with(sB, "aaa") << endl;        // false
cout << istarts_with(sB, "aaa") << endl;       // true

cout << ends_with(sB, ".exe") << endl;         // true
cout << ends_with(sB, ".EXE") << endl;         // false
cout << iends_with(sB, ".EXE") << endl;        // true
```

Please note that these functions have case-insensitive versions. You can identify these functions because they begin with the letter 'i'.
We now determine if a string contains another string. To this end, the function contains() has two arguments; the first argument is the string we search in to determine if the second argument is contained in it. An example is:

```
// String containment
cout << "\nContainment\n";
string sC("AAAwhat is BBB this?.exe");

cout << contains(sC, "BBB") << endl;           // true
cout << contains(sC, "bbb") << endl;           // false
cout << icontains(sC, "bbb") << endl;          // true
cout << contains(sC, "XXL") << endl;           // false
```

and equality of strings:

```
// String equality
cout << "\nEquality\n";
string sD("AAAwhat is BBB this?.exe");
string sE("AAAwhat is bbb this?.exe");

cout << equals(sD, sE) << endl;                // false
cout << iequals(sD, sE) << endl;               // true
```

Finally, we can check if a string is lexicographically less than another string and we can also check if all elements of a string satisfy a given predicate (for example, if all elements are decimal digits):

```
// Lexicographical compare
cout << "\nlexicographical compare\n";
cout << lexicographical_compare(sD, sE) << endl;   // true
cout << lexicographical_compare(sE, sD) << endl;   // false

// Do all string elements satisfy a given predicate?
boolalpha(cout);            // print 'true' or 'false' in output
string sW("1245W789");
cout << "Contains only digits (false)? " << all(sW, is_digit()) << endl;
string sW2("ABCDEF");
cout << "Is upper case (true)? " << all(sW2, is_upper()) << endl;
```

Summarising, the functions in this category tell us about the presence (or otherwise) of a string in another string. We can also compare strings. However, the functions do not give information on the exact position of a substring within another string. We now address this topic.

10.3 Find Algorithms

The functions in this category are concerned with finding information in (input) strings.

The return type is an `iterator_range` (that we discuss in section 10.10) instance:
- Find the first and last occurrence of a string in the input string.
- Retrieve the tail and head of a string.

As before, there are case-sensitive and case-insensitive versions of these functions. Before we discuss these functions, we define a simple function to print an `iterator_range` object (see section 10.10 for a discussion of Boost.Range) (the `iterator_range` class encapsulates two iterators that satisfy the *ForwardRange* concept):

```
void print(const iterator_range<string::iterator>& iter)
{ // Simple function to print elements in an iterator range

    // The found range could be empty
    if (iter.size() == 0)
    {
        cout << "Empty range\n";
        return;
    }

    string::iterator it;
    for (it = iter.begin(); it != iter.end(); ++it)
    {
        cout << *it;
    }
    cout << endl;
}
```

We give an example that finds the first and last occurrence of a string in an input string. We then print the resulting `iterator_range` instance:

```
string sA("abc___cde___efg__cde");
string sB("abc");

// Find "cde" substring
iterator_range<string::iterator> rangeA=find_first(sA, string("cde"));
iterator_range<string::iterator> rangeB=find_last(sA, string("cde"));
iterator_range<string::iterator> rangeC=find_last(sB, string("cde"));

print(rangeA);    // output is "cde"
print(rangeB);    // output is "cde"
print(rangeC);    // output is "Empty range"
```

The next two functions allow us to extract a given number of elements from the head (start) and tail (end) of a string:

```
// Get the head of the string
string sD("1234567890");
int N = 5;  // Extract N elements from sD
iterator_range<string::iterator> head=find_head(sD, N); // "12345"
cout << "head(5) of sD: " << string(head.begin(), head.end()) << endl;

// Get the tail
N = 3;
head = find_tail(sD, N);    // "890"
cout << "tail(3) of sD: " << string(head.begin(), head.end()) << endl;
```

These two functions are useful when we truncate strings. We discuss more advanced find algorithms in section 10.6.

10.4 Erase and Replace

The functions in this category allow us to replace occurrences of a string in an input string by another string and they also allow us to erase occurrences of a string in an input string. Case-sensitive and case-insensitive versions exist as do versions that modify the input string. For example, the functions for erasing the first occurrence of a string in the input string are:

```
erase_first()
erase_first_copy()
ierase_first()
ierase_first_copy()
```

In the rest of this chapter we discuss those functions resembling the first function prototype `erase_first()`; in other words, the input is modified and element processing is case-sensitive. The other cases are similar and we do not discuss them for this reason.

The main functions in this category are the following:
- Replace/erase the first/last occurrence of a string in the input string.
- Replace/erase the nth occurrence of a string in the input string.
- Replace/erase all occurrences of a string in the input string.
- Replace/erase the head/tail of the input string.
- Generic replace algorithm.

We now describe how each function is used. In the next block of code we show some examples of replacing single or multiple occurrences of a string by some other string in the input string:

```
// Simpler replace
string sA("abc___cde___efg__cde");
replace_first(sA, "abc", "cde");        cout << sA << endl;
replace_last(sA, "cde", "abc");         cout << sA << endl;

int n = 0;  // 1st occurrence
replace_nth(sA, "abc", n, "XYZ");       cout << sA << endl;
replace_all(sA, "cde", "CDE");          cout << sA << endl;
```

The output from this code is:

```
cde___cde___efg__cde
cde___cde___efg__abc
cde___cde___efg__XYZ
CDE___CDE___efg__XYZ
```

There are two functions that replace/erase substrings that match a given regular expression and we shall discuss them in chapter 12.

10.5 Split and Join

Split functions extract information from a string while join functions merge information from some source (for example, an STL container) to produce a single string. The functionality is:
- Find/extract all matching substrings in the input string.
- Split the input string into parts.
- Use a *finder* to find all matching substrings in the input string.

- Use a finder to find all matching substrings in the input string and use them as separators to split the input into parts.
- Join all elements in a container into a single string.
- Join all elements in a container that satisfy a given condition into a single string.

As an example, we consider a string in comma-separated format. We extract the elements between the commas and produce a vector of strings:

```
string sA("1,2,3,4/5/9*56");
vector<string> splitArray;
split(splitArray, sA, is_any_of(",/*"));

for (int j = 0; j < splitArray.size(); ++j)
{ // Prints all the vector elements
    cout << splitArray[j] << ",";
}
```

The output from this code is the vector containing the numbers 1, 2, 3, 4, 5, 9 and 56. In the other direction, we create a string from a string vector:

```
// Join operations
string myJoin = boost::algorithm::join(splitArray, "/");
cout << "joined: " << myJoin << endl;
```

The generated string is now "1/2/3/4/5/9/56".

10.6 Finders and Formatters

A *finder* is a functor that knows what to look for in an input string and what the classification predicate is for actually finding what it is searching for. The supported finders in the String Algo library are:

- Search for the first/last match of a string in the input string.
- Search for the nth (zero-indexed) match of a string in the input string.
- Retrieve the head/tail of an input string.
- Search for a matching token in a given range.

The first example is concerned with the first and last matches of a string in an input string. The output is a modifiable range in the input string; for example, we could decide to convert its elements to upper case:

```
// First and last finders example
string str="the quick fox jumps over the lazy dog.";

// The iterator range used for the result of the algorithms.
iterator_range<string::iterator> r;

// Find a range in an input string and then do something with it
r=find(str, first_finder("o", is_equal()) );
to_upper(r);
cout<<endl<<"First 'o' (case sensitive) converted to upper case:"
    <<endl<<str<<endl;

r=find(str, last_finder("the", is_equal()) );
to_upper(r);
cout<<endl<<"Last 'the' (case sensitive) converted to upper case:"
    <<endl<<str<<endl;
```

We now discuss *formatters*. The generic `find_format()` algorithm accepts a finder functor and a formatter functor. The finder functor determines what to find and how to find it. The formatter functor determines how the found sequence is replaced. Examples of predefined formatters are:

- Constant formatter (it always returns the specified string).
- Identity formatter (returns unmodified input string).
- Null or empty formatter (always returns an empty string).
- Regex formatter (format regex match using the specification in the format string).

The following code shows the use of formatters:

```
void TestGenericFindFormat()
{
    // The string to process.
    string str="The quick brown fox jumps over the lazy dog.";
    cout<<"Original string:"<<endl<<str<<endl;

    // Replace fox by cat.
    find_format(str, first_finder("fox"),
        const_formatter("cat"));
    cout<<"Fox replaced by cat:"<<endl<<str<<endl;

    // Remove lazy. The argument of empty_formatter is ignored
    // but is given so you don't have to specify a template argument.
    find_format(str, first_finder("lazy "), empty_formatter("xyz"));
    cout<<endl<<"Lazy removed:"<<endl<<str<<endl;

    // Replace all 'the' by 'a'.
    find_format_all(str,
        first_finder("the", is_iequal()), const_formatter("a"));
    cout<<endl<<"'the' replaced by 'a':"<<endl<<str<<endl;

    // Replace all spaces by a '-'.
    // The token_finder finds character that fulfills the predicate
    // (in this case if a character is a space or punctuation)
    find_format_all(str,
        token_finder(is_space() || is_punct()), const_formatter("-"));
    cout<<endl<<"Spaces & punctuation replaced by '-':"<<endl<<str<<endl;
}
```

We now present the output from this code so that we can check what is going on:

```
*** Generic find format ***

Original string:
The quick brown fox jumps over the lazy dog.
Fox replaced by cat:
The quick brown cat jumps over the lazy dog.

Lazy removed:
The quick brown cat jumps over the dog.

'the' replaced by 'a':
a quick brown cat jumps over a dog.

Spaces & punctuation replaced by '-':
a-quick-brown-cat-jumps-over-a-dog-
```

Finally, we show how the library supports the use of regular expressions to find a string. We discuss regular expressions in detail in chapter 12. For the moment, we can think of a *regular expression* as a pattern that describes legal or well-formed expressions in a certain language. For example, we can describe the format of a credit-card as follows:

```
regex_finder(regex("\\d{3,4}[- ](\\d{4})[- ](\\d{4})[- ](\\d{4})"))
```

Credit card numbers have 4 groups of digits separated by a space or '-'. Each group has 4 digits but the first group can have 3 digits. The `regex_finder` is needed when searching for substrings that match it. It is a pattern.

The next example creates a string and then formats it by replacing the numeric (sensitive) credit-card information by stars ('*'). The code processes the complete input string `str` and formats all occurrences of the regular expression using `regex_formatter()`:

```
void TestRegEx()
{// Search for credit cards numbers and replace the first 3 parts by *

    // The string to process.
    string str;
    str+="Name: John Smith\n";
    str+="Address: Schipluidenlaan 4\n";
    str+="Zipcode: NL-1062 HE\n";
    str+="City: Amsterdam\n";
    str+="Country: The Netherlands\n";
    str+="Phone: +31-20-6240055\n";
    str+="Mastercard: 1234-1234-1234-5678\n";
    str+="Amex: 234-1274-1534-8348\n";
    str+="Visa: 1242 1523 2834 2344";
    cout<<"Original string:"<<endl<<str<<endl;

    // Replace creditcard numbers using a regular expression search.
    // Credit card number have 4 groups of digits separated by a space or
    // '-'. Each group has 4 digits but the first group can have 3 digits.
    find_format_all(str, regex_finder(
    regex("\\d{3,4}[- ](\\d{4})[- ](\\d{4})[- ](\\d{4})")),
        regex_formatter(string("**** **** **** \\1")));
    cout<<endl<<"Creditcard numbers censored:"<<endl<<str<<endl;
}
```

You can check the code by examining the output:

```
*** Regular expression ***

Original string:
Name: John Smith
Address: Schipluidenlaan 4
Zipcode: NL-1062 HE
City: Amsterdam
Country: The Netherlands
Phone: +31-20-6240055
Mastercard: 1234-1234-1234-5678
Amex: 234-1274-1534-8348
Visa: 1242 1523 2834 2344

Creditcard numbers censored:
Name: John Smith
Address: Schipluidenlaan 4
Zipcode: NL-1062 HE
City: Amsterdam
Country: The Netherlands
Phone: +31-20-6240055
Mastercard: **** **** **** 1234
Amex: **** **** **** 1274
Visa: **** **** **** 1523
```

We remark that the above regular expression functionality in String Algo is an adapter for the corresponding functionality in Boost.Regex.

10.7 Iterators

The library has two iterator types:
- Find iterator (iterates through a matching substring in the input string).
- Split iterator (iterates through the gaps between matching substrings in the input string).

Associated with each of these iterators is a factory to create an instance that is then used to iterate over multiple occurrences of the found sequence of elements in the input string. We first discuss find_iterator. An example is:

```
void TestFindIterator()
{
    // The find_iterator used for the result of the finding algorithms.
    find_iterator<string::iterator> fi, fiEnd;

    // The string to process.
    string str="Mouse=10.49, Keyboard=7.99, Card reader=9.99";
    cout<<"Original string:"<<endl<<str<<endl;

    // Find all the = and replace it by =$
    for (fi=make_find_iterator(str, first_finder("=")); fi!=fiEnd; fi++)
    {
        // Replace = by =$. Be careful with changing the source string.
        // If characters are removed, the next iterator will go wrong.
        str.replace(fi->begin(), fi->end(), "=$");
    }
    cout<<endl<<"'=' replaced by '=$':"<<endl<<str<<endl;

    // Find all digits and replace by *
    for (fi=make_find_iterator(str, token_finder(is_digit()));
        fi!=fiEnd; fi++)
    {
        // Replace digits by *. Be carefull with changing the source string.
        // If characters are removed, the next iterator will go wrong.
        str.replace(fi->begin(), fi->end(), "*");
    }
    cout<<endl<<"Digits replaced by '*':"<<endl<<str<<endl;
}
```

The output from this code is:

```
*** Find iterator ***

Original string:
Mouse=10.49, Keyboard=7.99, Card reader=9.99

'=' replaced by '=$':
Mouse=$10.49, Keyboard=$7.99, Card reader=$9.99

Digits replaced by '*':
Mouse=$**.**, Keyboard=$*.**, Card reader=$*.**
```

We now discuss split_iterator (with factory make_split_iterator()). It iterates through the gaps and matching substrings in the input string. As an example, the following code processes a comma-separated string and it prints the strings 'between the gaps', in this case the comma separator:

```
void TestSplitIterator()
{
    // The split_iterator used for the result of the finding algorithms.
    split_iterator<string::iterator> si, siEnd;

    // The string to process.
    string str="Mouse, Keyboard, Card reader, Speakers";
    cout<<"Original string:"<<endl<<str<<endl;

    int counter = 0;
    cout << endl << "Components " << endl;

    // Find the ',' and print the parts outside the comma.
    for (si=make_split_iterator(str, first_finder(", ")); si!=siEnd; si++)
    {
        cout<< ++counter << " " << copy_range<string>(*si)<<endl;
    }
}
```

The output from this code is:

```
*** Split iterator ***

Original string:
Mouse, Keyboard, Card reader, Speakers

Components
1 Mouse
2 Keyboard
3 Card reader
4 Speakers
```

10.7.1 Creating Custom Formatters

In addition to the built-in formatters it is possible to create user-defined formatters that satisfy special needs. The `find_format()` function also accepts custom formatters. In this section we use a custom formatter that replaces numbers with text. Furthermore, we use a regular expression to find numbers (one or more digits that we model as the regular expression '\\d+' which signifies one or more digits). First, we create a simple custom formatter (a function object) that converts numbers to text:

```
struct NumberFormatter
{ // Custom formatter that replaces a number with text.

    // Version 2: we could use an STL map
    template <typename TFindResult>
    string operator () (const TFindResult& match) const
    {
        // Convert the range to a string
        string str(match.begin(), match.end());

        // Check the string and return the number as text.
        if (str=="0") return "zero";
        if (str=="1") return "one";
        if (str=="2") return "two";
        if (str=="3") return "three";
        else return "many";  // everything greater then '3' is 'many'
    }
};
```

The following code uses this custom formatter. In this case, we replace the digits in an input string by their corresponding string values using the simple dictionary NumberFormatter:

```
void TestCustomFormatter()
{
    // The string to process.
    string str;
    str+="There is 1 apple, 2 pears, 3 oranges and 12 grapes.";
    cout<<"Original string:"<<endl<<str<<endl;

    // Find number (one or more digits) and use custom formatter to
    // replace them by words.
    find_format_all(str, regex_finder(regex("\\d+")), NumberFormatter());
    cout<<endl<<"Numbers replace by words:"<<endl<<str<<endl;
}
```

The output from this code is:

```
*** Custom formatter ***

Original string:
There is 1 apple, 2 pears, 3 oranges and 12 grapes.

Numbers replace by words:
There is one apple, two pears, three oranges and many grapes.
```

10.8 Classification

This category contains unary predicates that test if a string fulfills a certain condition:
- Recognise spaces.
- Recognise alphanumeric characters.
- Recognise letters.
- Recognise upper-case/lower-case characters.
- Recognise characters from a set of characters (for example, '/', '*').
- Recognise decimal digits.
- Others.

These predicates can be combined using logical operators such as ! (NOT), || (OR) and &&
(AND). They can be used in conjunction with functions ending in all(), for example
replace_all(), find_all() and erase_all().
As final example, we test a string to determine if it consists of hexadecimal digits and if it
consists of alphanumeric characters. The result is true in all cases:

```
boolalpha(cout);
string sH("FFFFFFD6");
cout << "Is a hexadecimal? " << all(sH, is_xdigit()) << endl;
cout << "Is alphanumeric? " << all(sH, is_alnum()) << endl;

// Same test but now using boolean logic
cout << "Is hexadecimal and alphanumeric? "
     << all(sH, is_xdigit() && is_alnum() ) << endl;
```

The ability to combine predicates in this way adds to the applicability of this library.

10.9 Creating Name-Value Maps

The following example is concerned with semi-colon-delimited text and we have included it
to show the use of the functions in the library. The objective is to extract all the key-value
pairs from text and insert them into a map for further processing. We design the code as

follows: read in name-value pairs, create the vector of 'outer patterns' of the form 'K = V' and then extract the separate keys and values from this vector. The input string is:

```
string testString("10=3.14;11=hi;45=what?;80=1234");
```

We now wish to split the string into pieces:

```
// Outer machinery
vector<string> outerArray;
split(outerArray, testString, is_any_of(";"));
```

In other words, the variable `outerArray` will contain elements of the form 'a = b'. We now wish to extract the values *a* and *b* and we use the variable `innerArray`:

```
// Inner machinery
map<string, string> result;
vector<string> innerArray;
```

Finally, we create `innerArray` and from it, the desired map:

```
for (int j = 0; j < outerArray.size(); ++j)
{ // Prints all the vector elements

    cout << outerArray[j] << endl; // Print K-V pairs
    split(innerArray, outerArray[j], is_any_of("=")) ;

    result.insert( make_pair(innerArray[0], innerArray[1]) );
}
```

We chose this example to show the usefulness of string algorithms in a particular context. We shall see in later chapters how to achieve the same goal using less code.

10.10 The Range Library

Many generic applications are specified in terms of two or more iterators. For example, when computing the intersection of two set-like containers we can use the `set_intersection()` algorithm:

```
set<double> s1;
set<double> s2;

// Insert elements into s1 and s2 ...
...

// Determine intersection of s1 and s2
set<double> myIntersect;
set<double>::iterator i = myIntersect.begin();
insert_iterator<set<double> > insertIter(myIntersect, i);
set_intersection(s1.begin(), s1.end(), s2.begin(), s2.end(), insertIter);
```

We may wish to simplify this code and there are different ways of doing this, for example, wrapping this code in a utility function or a user-defined set class. It is obvious that part of the complexity is due to the fact that we need to use iterators. We resolve the problem by encapsulating a pair of iterators in a *range object*. The range is modelled as a composition of two iterators. In short, we create an *adapter object*. The advantages of this approach are:
• More compact and maintainable code.
• Simpler implementation and specification of generic range algorithms.

The Boost.Range library supports ranges of iterators by two classes:

- `iterator_range`: encapsulates two iterators in such a way that they fulfill the *ForwardRange* concept. We use this class when we wish to create general code.
- `sub_range`: a derived class of `iterator_range`. It is more user-friendly than `iterator_range` because its template argument is easier to specify.

The following files need to be included in your code:

```
#include <boost/range/iterator_range.hpp>
#include <boost/range/sub_range.hpp>
```

We first discuss *iterator_range*. Its public interface has the following functions:

- Constructors.
- Comparison operators: `==, !=, <, >, <=, >=`.
- Forward range functions such as `begin()` and `end()` (these return an iterator).
- External construction functions: functions to create `iterator_range` instances, primarily `make_iterator_range()` and `range_iterator()`.
- Stream output: `<<`.

The following code creates two `iterator_range` instances and we print them on the console:

```
void check_iterator_range()
{
    typedef string::iterator                iterator;
    typedef string::const_iterator          const_iterator;

    // Boost ranges
    typedef iterator_range<iterator>        irange;
    typedef iterator_range<const_iterator>  cirange; // const iterators

    string       str  = "hello world";
    const string cstr = "const world";

    irange r = make_iterator_range( str );
    r = make_iterator_range( str.begin(), str.end() );
    cout << r << endl;

    cirange r2 = make_iterator_range( cstr );
    r2 = make_iterator_range( cstr.begin(), cstr.end() );
    cout << r2 << endl;
}
```

The class `sub_range` inherits the functionality from `iterator_range`. Here is the same code as above using `sub_range`:

```
typedef sub_range<string>        srange;
typedef sub_range<const string>  csrange;

string       str  = "hello world";
const string cstr = "const world";

srange r = make_iterator_range( str );
r = make_iterator_range( str.begin(), str.end() )
cout << r << endl;

csrange r2 = make_iterator_range( cstr );
r2 = make_iterator_range( cstr.begin(), cstr.end() );
cout << r2 << endl;
```

Finally, we can compare `iterator_range` and `sub_range` to find the occurrence of a substring in a string; we see that the second option is easier to use because the instantiated template argument is simpler and it leads to somewhat more readable code:

```
// Comparing iterator_range and sub_range
string S1("Jesse James");
iterator_range<string::iterator> ir = find_first(S1, as_literal("se"));
sub_range<string> sr = find_first(S1, as_literal("se"));

cout << ir << endl;
cout << sr << endl
```

10.11 Summary and Conclusions

In this chapter we discussed the string manipulation functionality in the String Algorithm library. The library contains functions for string modification, searching in strings and regular expression pattern matching. You may find that the library contains enough functionality to suit a wide range of your text processing applications.
In chapter 12 we introduce the Boost.Regex library that is also concerned with string processing based on regular expressions.

The functionality in the current library is extensive and it may be hard to remember the precise syntax of its functions, especially if they are not used on a regular basis. Furthermore, we run the risk of copying code from previous projects and modifying it to suit new requirements. An alternative is to determine how to group related functionality into global functions or classes, The low-level details will then be hidden and the developer can use them at a higher level of abstraction rather than just using the functionality of the library '*as is*'. In general, we aggregate lower-level functions into modules that are easier to use. It is a form of *information hiding*.

11 Tokenizer

11.1 Introduction and Objectives

We discuss Boost.Tokenizer in this relatively short chapter. It is used when we wish to break a string or other sequence of characters into tokens. A *token* is a logically related group of characters. The term is found in compiler design (see Aho 1977) and examples of tokens are keywords, identifiers and punctuation symbols.

The main functionality is contained in three entities:
- The Tokenizer class (provides a container view of tokens).
- Token iterator (iterator view of the token in a parsed sequence).
- Tokenizer Function concept (parses a sequence until exactly one token has been found).

We use the following convenience files in our code:

```
#include <boost/tokenizer.hpp>
```

We use the following user-defined aliases:

```
typedef boost::tokenizer<boost::escaped_list_separator<char> > Tokenizer
typedef boost::tokenizer<boost::char_separator<char> > DefaultTokenizer
```

11.2 What is a Token?

In compiler theory a token is an atomic unit and it can be a keyword, identifier, operator symbol or punctuation. We consider a compiler as a program that produces a target (executable) program from a source program (see Figure 11.1). There are a number of phases, one of which is called *lexical analysis* and this is the phase that produces tokens. The lexical analyzer is the interface between the compiler and the source program. It reads the source program one character at a time. In order to find a token, the lexical analyzer examines successive characters in the source program. It starts from the first character not yet grouped into a token. It may need to search more characters beyond the next token in order to determine what the next token actually is. Then the syntax analyzer checks that the generated tokens are permitted by the specification in the source language. We impose a tree-like structure on the tokens for subsequent processing and we need to identify which parts should be grouped together in order to form a parse tree.

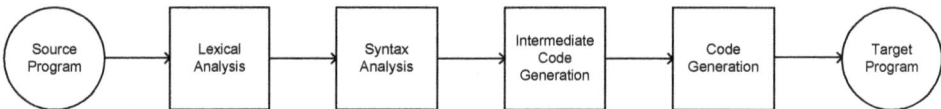

Figure 11.1 Phases of a compiler

For example, the FORTRAN code:

```
IF (5.EQ.MAX) GOTO 100
```

has tokens IF; (;5;.EQ;.MAX;); GOTO; 100. The lexical analyzer discovers these tokens.

In general, we first describe the possible tokens that can appear in an input stream. To this end, we use regular expression notation to describe all the tokens of the language that we are processing. We discuss regular expressions in more detail in chapter 12. Second, we need a mechanism which we can use to recognise these tokens in the input stream. Finally, we may also need to perform actions as the tokens are recognised, for example:

- Entering the value of the token in a table.
- Producing diagnostic messages.
- Generating output.

These are sometimes called *semantic actions* and we shall implement them in chapter 13. We now discuss how Tokenizer supports lexical analysis.

11.3 The Token Class, Token Iterator and Token Function

We give an introduction to the most important functionality in the library and we show how to use it by giving some examples.

11.3.1 Token Class

The class `tokenizer` allows us to break a string or a character sequence into a series of tokens. It is a template class with three parameters:

- A tokenizer functor that represents the delimiter between tokens.
- An iterator that determines how we navigate in the string.
- The token type; in most cases this is a string.

The declaration of the class is:

```
template <typename TokenizerFunc = char_delimiters_separator<char>,
    typename Iterator = std::string::const_iterator,
    typename Type = std::string>
class tokenizer { … };
```

We notice the presence of default parameters which means that you can avoid having to define specific parameters if your application uses strings and standard token separators. An example of use is:

```
// Default tokenizer
string str = "The quick, brown fox; jumps* over/ the lazy dog";
tokenizer<> tokA(str);
for (tokenizer<>::iterator iter = tokA.begin();
     iter != tokA.end(); ++iter)
{
    cout << *iter << "/";
}
```

The output from this code is: `The/quick/brown/fox/jumps/over/the/lazy/dog/`. In other words, we have broken the input string into its separate fields. We see that the delimiters are based on space and punctuation (for example, comma, exclamation marks, semi-colon and colon).

Finally, we can tokenize the FORTRAN code in section 11.2 as follows:

```
// Default tokenizer. FORTRAN source code
string strF = "IF (5.EQ.MAX) GOTO 100";
tokenizer<> tokF(strF);
for (tokenizer<>::iterator iter = tokF.begin();
     iter != tokF.end(); ++iter)
{
    cout << *iter << endl;
}
```

The output produces the tokens IF, 5, MAX, GOTO, 100.

11.3.2 TokenizerFunction Concept

The *TokenizerFunction* concept is a functor that parses a sequence until either exactly one token has been found or the end has been reached. It has three implementations:

- `char_delimiters_separator`: this can be used to break text up into tokens. It is the default *TokenizerFunction* for `tokenizer` and `token_iterator_generator`, as can be seen from the definition of class `tokenizer` in section 11.3.1.
- `offset_separator`: this can be used with `tokenizer` to break text into tokens. The `offset_separator` breaks a sequence of `char` into `strings` based on a sequence of offsets. For example, if we define the string '12252001' and offsets (2, 2, 4) it would break the string into 12 25 2001.
- `escaped_list_separator`: the `escaped_list_separator` parses a superset of the csv (comma separated value) format. Escape characters are interpreted differently from normal ASCII characters.

11.3.3 Token Iterator

The token iterator provides an iterator view of the tokens in parsed sequences:

```
template <
    typename TokenizerFunc = char_delimiters_separator<char>,
    typename Iterator = string::const_iterator,
    typename Type = string>
class token_iterator_generator { … };
```

We also need a function that creates token iterators:

```
template <typename Type, typename Iterator, typename TokenizerFunc>
typename token_iterator_generator<TokenizerFunc, Iterator, Type>::type
    make_token_iterator(Iterator begin, Iterator end,
                        const TokenizerFunc& fun);
```

We are now in a position to give some examples that integrate the `tokenizer` class, iterator and creational function.

11.3.4 Examples

Our first example uses `escaped_list_separator<char>` because the input string contains embedded escape characters;

```
string strB = string("Field 1,Field 2 with \"embedded quote\",") +
              string("Field 3 Field 1,Field 2 with \n new line,Field 3");
```

The code is:

```
tokenizer<escaped_list_separator<char> > tokB(strB);
for (tokenizer<escaped_list_separator<char> >::iterator iter =
    tokB.begin(); iter != tokB.end(); ++iter)
{
   cout << *iter << " ";
}
cout << endl;
```

The output is:

```
Field 1 Field 2 with embedded quote Field 3 Field 1 Field 2 with
new line Field 3
```

We now discuss the use of `offset_separator`. In this case we parse a string and we return its tokens based on a certain block size:

```
string s5("12252001001");
int offsets[] = {2, 2, 4, 3}; // Break up into blocks of size 2, 2, 4, 3
offset_separator fOff(offsets, offsets + 4);

typedef token_iterator_generator<offset_separator>::type Iter;

Iter beg = make_token_iterator<string>(s5.begin(), s5.end(), fOff);
Iter end = make_token_iterator<string>(s5.end(), s5.end(), fOff);

for (;beg != end; ++beg)
{
    cout << *beg << ",";     // prints 12,25,2001,001
}
```

11.4 Conversions and Casting Examples

In some applications we may wish to use Tokenizer to find tokens in an input string and then convert these tokens to some numeric format. A typical example is converting a comma-separated string to a `vector<double>` instance. To this end, we can use `lexical_cast` and we define the following utility function:

```
template <typename T> vector<T> extract(const string& Input)
{ // Extact a vector of type T from a string

    vector<T> result;

    DefaultTokenizer myToken(Input);

    for (Tokenizer2::iterator it = myToken.begin(); it != myToken.end(); ++it)
    {
        result.push_back(boost::lexical_cast<T>(*it));
    }

    return result;
}
```

We now take an example to show how this works; the lexical cast may fail and for this reason we define a `try/catch` block. First, we define two strings, one containing non-numeric data and the other containing numeric data. We use a `vector<double>` instance to hold the converted tokens:

```
string s(" aa bb");
string s2("11 23 89");
vector<double> vec;
```

In the first case the conversion will fail because we cannot convert `string` to `double`:

```
// Convert strings to doubles, exception
try
{
    vec = extract<double>(s);
}
catch(boost::bad_lexical_cast& error)
{
    std::cout << error.what() << endl;
}
```

In the second case the conversion will be successful:

```
// Now try with correct input string
try
{
    vec = extract<double>(s2);
}
catch(boost::bad_lexical_cast& error)
{
    std::cout << error.what() << endl;
}

BOOST_FOREACH(const double& x, vec)
{
    cout << x << " ";
}
```

The output is: 11, 23, 89.

As last example we consider the problem of converting a string in comma-separated form to a vector<double> instance:

```
string s4 = "1,2,3,4";
boost::char_separator<char> sep4(",");

DefaultTokenizer tokens4(s4, sep4);
vector<double> result;
for (DefaultTokenizer::iterator it = tokens4.begin();
     it != tokens4.end(); ++it)
{
    result.push_back(boost::lexical_cast<double>(*it));
}

cout << endl;

BOOST_FOREACH(const double& x, result)
{
    cout << x << ", ";
}
```

You can compare this solution with String Algorithm library's split functions as discussed in section 10.5.

11.5 Summary and Conclusions

In this chapter we introduced the Boost.Tokenizer library that implements a lexical analyser. Its main use is in breaking a string into a series of tokens. You can define how to distinguish tokens from each other by using tokeniser functions. The library is useful for applications involving lexical analysis.

In the interest of reusability a useful project would be to create a generic module based on the Tokenizer library that hides most of its low-level details from view. The module will be able to handle arbitrary data types and to recover gracefully in exceptional situations. The module could also use functionality from the String Algorithm library for preprocessing activities such as trimming, checking the data and conversions to upper case, for example.

12 Regex

12.1 Introduction and Objectives

In this chapter we discuss pattern matching in text-processing applications. In particular, we discuss how Boost supports regular expressions.
Some of the applications of Boost.Regex are:

- Input validation (for example, requiring that input be numeric).
- Pattern matching in text (determine if a regular expression matches a character sequence).
- Searching (find a substring that matches a regular expression).
- Text replacement (search for matches of a string and replace these matches by another string).
- Parsing text into more structured forms (for example, extracting data from a HTML page for storage in a database).

We use the following convenience file in our code:

```
#include <boost/regex.hpp>
```

Having read this chapter and studied the code examples you can consult the online Boost.Regex documentation for more advanced topics such as discussions on Perl and POSIX regular expression syntax, regex traits and interfacing with non-standard string types.

12.2 Alphabet, Words and Language

Let A be a non empty set of characters (or *symbols*). A *word* or string on A is a finite sequence of its characters. We sometimes call A the *alphabet*. Examples of words are:

$$u = abcbb, v = zzxaaa.$$

We can write these words in the equivalent forms $u = abcb^2, v = z^2xa^3$. Words that are empty are denoted by λ. This is called the *empty word*. We denote the set of all words on the alphabet A by A^*.
The length of a word u is denoted by $|u|$ or $l(u)$. For example, in the above cases, $l(u) = 5$ and $l(v) = 6$.

Let u and v be two words in an alphabet A. The *concatenation* of u and v is the word obtained by placing the letters of u followed by the letters of v; for example, if $u = abc, v = xyz$, then $uv = abcxyz$. A particular case is the concatenation of a word with itself, for example $u^2 = uu, u^3 = uu^2, u^n = uu^{n-1}, n \geq 4$.
Let $u = a_1a_2 \ldots a_n$ be a word on an alphabet A. A sequence $w = a_ja_{j+1} \ldots a_k$ $(1 \leq j, k \leq n)$is called a *subword* of u. A special case is when $j = 1$ and then w is called the *initial segment* of u.

A *language* L over an alphabet A is a collection of words on A. Thus, L is a subset of A^*, the set of all words on A. As an example, let A = {0, 1} be the binary alphabet. Then two important (programming) language alphabets are the ASCII and EBCDIC character sets. For example the ASCII code for 'A' is binary '100 0001' (decimal 65) while the ASCII code for 'z' is binary '111 1010' (decimal 122). Other examples of languages are:

$$M = \{a, ab, ab^2, \ldots\}$$
$$N = \{a^m b^n : m > 0, n > 0.\}$$

We see that M consists of words beginning with the letter a and ending with zero or more letter b's while N consists of words beginning with one or more a's and ending with one or more b's.

Let L and M be languages over the alphabet A. Then the concatenation of L and M is defined by:

$$LM = \{uv : u \in L, v \in M\}.$$

For example, if L = {a,b} and M = {c,d,e} then LM = {ac,ad,ae,bc,bd,be}. Powers of a language are defined recursively by:

$$L^0 = \{\lambda\}, L^1 = L, L^2 = LL, L^m = L^{m-1}L, \quad m > 1.$$

The *Kleene closure* (also known as the *Kleene star*) L^* of L is defined as the infinite union:

$$L^* = L^0 \cup L^1 \cup \ldots = \cup_{k=0}^{\infty} L^k.$$

12.3 An Introduction to Regular Expressions

A Kleene star is a unary operation on sets of strings or on sets of symbols . More precisely, if $\sum$ is an alphabet then the Kleene star is the set of all strings of finite length consisting of symbols in $\sum$, including the empty string λ.

A *regular expression* denotes a language and we can give rules for the construction of the denoted languages with the regular expression construction rules. In particular, each of the following is a regular expression over the alphabet A:

a)   The empty word λ and the empty expression (the pair '()') are regular expressions.

b)   Each letter a in A is a regular expression.

c)   If r is a regular expression then (r^*) is also a regular expression, where (r^*) is the set of all words from r.

d)   If $r1$ and $r2$ are regular expressions, then $r1r2$ is a regular expression.

e)   If $r1$ and $r2$ are regular expressions, then the concatenation $r1Vr2$ is also a regular expression where 'V' denotes the union of $r1$ and $r2$.

In general, we say that a language L over A is *regular if* there is a regular expression r over A such that L = L(r), that is r generates L.

We give some examples of regular expressions and languages. Let r = a*, that is zero or more occurrences of a. Then $L(r)$ consists of all powers of a, including the empty word. Now let r = aa*. Then $L(r)$ consists of all positive powers of a.

Finally, we take an example of a regular language:

$$L = \{b^m ab^n : m > 0, \quad n > 0\}$$

This language consists of all words that begin with one or more b's followed by a single a and then followed by one or more b's. A corresponding regular expression is r = bb* abb*.

We use different notation for regular expressions:

$a\{n\}$ matches a n times

$a\{n,\}$ matches a n or more times

$a\{,n\}$ matches a at most n times

$a\{n,m\}$ matches a repeated between n and m times inclusive

$a + \{n\}$ matches a one or more times

$a * \{n\}$ matches a zero or more times

$a|b$ match a or b.

We now begin our discussion of how Boost.Regex implements regular expressions.

12.4 Regex Functionality

Boost.Regex has functionality for regular expressions:
- Defining regular expressions as objects.
- Determine if a regular expression matches a character sequence.
- Search for a subsequence in a character sequence.
- Replace all matches of a regular expression in a character sequence.

Furthermore, Boost.Regex has an iterator and iterator adapter that enumerate all of the regular expression matches found in a sequence. The library supports exception handling by catching badly formed regular expressions at run-time.

12.5 The Class `basic_regex`

This template class encapsulates a regular expression. It is responsible for parsing and compilation of regular expressions. It has two template parameters:
- The character type which can be `char` or `wchar_t`.
- The traits that determine the behaviour of the character type.

The interface is:

```
namespace boost
{
    template <class charT, class traits = regex_traits<charT> >
    class basic_regex;

    typedef basic_regex<char>      regex;
    typedef basic_regex<wchar_t>   wregex;
}
```

In this chapter we work with standard types and for this reason we use the class `regex`. The main member functions are:
- Constructor (with a character array as input argument).
- Does a `regex` instance contain a valid regular expression?
- The number of marked subexpressions (a *marked subexpression* is a part of the regular expression that is enclosed within brackets).

In this section we concentrate on constructing regular expressions and to this end we take two initial examples:

```
regex myReg("[a-z]*");
regex myReg2("[a-z]+");
```

The first regular expression describes strings containing zero or more lower-case characters while the second regular expression describes strings containing one or more lower-case characters. There are many different ways to create regular expressions and we group them into categories or character classes. We discuss each category and we give some examples of use:

- Alphanumeric characters. We can define lower and upper-case strings and we can define strings that shall not contain alphanumeric characters:

```
// Alphanumeric characters
regex rC("(\\w)*");              // Alphanumeric (word) A-Za-z0-9
regex rC1("(\\W)*");             // Not a word
regex rC2("[A-Za-z0-9_]*");      // Alphanumeric (word) A-Za-z0-9
```

- Digits and non-digits: strings that consist of digits (0 to 9 inclusive). We can also define strings that shall not contain digits:

```
// Working with digits
regex rD("(\\d)*");              // Digits (0-9)
regex rD1("(\\D)*");             // Not a digit(s)
regex rD2("[2-6]*");             // Zero or more digits in range closed 2..6
```

- Escape characters: an escape character is a single character designated to invoke an alternative interpretation, for example form feed \f, newline \n, bell \a, tab \t and carriage return \r. Some examples are:

```
// Escape characters
cout << "Escape characers " << endl;
regex rE("\\a*");               // Bell output
regex rE1("\\n");               // Newline character
regex rE2("\\v");               // Output vertical tab
```

- Boolean logic: we can create regular expressions that define OR logic as well as regular expressions that disallow certain characters (NOT logic). Examples are:

```
regex rZ("(\\d|\\w)*");         // Strings containing digits or letters
regex rA1("[1-5]*");            // Zero or more of any digit in range [1..5]
regex rA2("[^1-5]*");           // NOT in range([1..5])
```

- Quantification: A *quantifier* that is placed after a token specifies how often that preceding element is allowed to occur. The main quantifiers are:
  - ? zero or one of the preceding element.
  - * zero or more of the preceding element.
  - + one or more of the preceding element.

We can quantify the above multiplicities by specifying lower and upper limits of the number of preceding elements:
  - {n} exactly n preceding elements.
  - {n, m} between n and m preceding elements (including the end values).
  - {n, } n or more preceding elements.
  - {,m} at most m preceding elements.

Some examples are:

```
regex myReg3("A*");             // zero or more A
regex myReg4("A+");             // one or more A
```

```
regex myReg5("(\\d {2})");      // two digits
regex myReg6("\\d {2, 4}");     // 2, 3 or 4 digits
regex myReg7("\\d {1,}");       // at least one digit
```

We are now in a position to test strings against regular expressions.

12.6 Regular Expression Matching

Having described how Boost.Regex supports regular expressions we now determine whether
a regular expression matches a string. This feature is useful when we validate input text in
applications, for example. To this end, we use the free function `regex_match()` which
accepts a regular expression, a character sequence to match against and an optional *flags
type* (for example, whether to take case sensitivity into account). The function returns *true* if
the match is successful, otherwise it returns *false*.

We give examples of use. First, we define default regular expressions and a regular
expression that is case-insensitive based on PERL syntax:

```
// Lower-case characters
regex myReg("[a-z]*");
regex myReg2("[a-z]+");

// Define RE using case insensitive and PERL syntax
regex myRegci("[a-z]+", boost::regex::icase|boost::regex::perl);
```

Next, we define character sequences to match against the regular expressions:

```
string s1("aza");
string s2("1");
string s3("b");
```

Finally, we match the sequence and we print the return value of each call to
`regex_match()`; you can check the return value in each case:

```
cout << s1 << ", " << regex_match(s1,myReg) << endl;    // true
cout << s2 << ", " << regex_match(s2,myReg) << endl;    // false
cout << s3 << ", " << regex_match(s3,myReg) << endl;    // true

cout << s3 << ", " << regex_match(s3,myReg2) << endl;   // true
to_upper(s3);                           // Now convert to upper case
cout << s3 << ", " << regex_match(s3,myReg2) << endl;   // false

// Now match with the case-insensitive flag and Perl syntax (default)
cout << s3 << ", " << regex_match(s3,myRegci) << endl;  // true
```

The next example shows how to define and match regular expressions using Boolean OR:

```
// Alternatives; a choice between 'new' and 'delete'
regex myAltReg("(new)|(delete)");
string s4("new");
string s5("delete");
string s6("malloc");

cout << s4 << ", " << regex_match(s4,myAltReg) << endl; // true
cout << s5 << ", " << regex_match(s5,myAltReg) << endl; // true
cout << s6 << ", " << regex_match(s6,myAltReg) << endl; // false
```

The following example uses quantifiers:

```
// Use of Kleene star syntax
regex myReg3("A*");              // zero or more A
regex myReg4("A+");              // one or more A
regex myReg5("(\\d{2})";         // two digits
regex myReg6("\\d{2, 4}");       // at least two and at most four digits
regex myReg7("\\d{1,}");         // at least one digit

string testA("1");
cout << "Kleene star examples\n";
cout << testA << ", " << regex_match(testA,myReg3) << endl;   // false
cout << testA << ", " << regex_match(testA,myReg4) << endl;   // false
cout << testA << ", " << regex_match(testA,myReg5) << endl;   // false
cout << testA << ", " << regex_match(testA,myReg6) << endl;   // false
cout << testA << ", " << regex_match(testA,myReg7) << endl;   // true
```

12.7 Searching

Boost.Regex has functionality for searching in a character sequence for a given pattern. In particular, we can find a subsequence of the input that matches a regular expression. The choices are:

a) using the free function `regex_search()`.

b) using `sregex_iterator`.

c) using `sregex_token_iterator`.

We discuss option b) in detail here because it is easy to apply and the functionality associated with options a) and c) can be more easily realised using StringAlgo in our experience.

The class `sregex_iterator` enumerates all the matches in a sequence in a regular expression. When it is dereferenced it will return a reference to an instance of `match_results` that acts as an indexed collection of sub-expression matches. In order to create a `sregex_iterator` we provide the iterators denoting the start and end of the input sequence and the regular expression.

We take an example that prints only the numeric values in a string:

```
// Match only numeric values
regex myReg12("[0-9]");
string S4A = "01234DD5679A";

sregex_iterator it4A(S4A.begin(), S4A.end(), myReg12);
sregex_iterator end4A;

while (it4A != end4A)
{
   cout << *it4A++ << ",";    // prints numerics only
}
```

We note that `sregex_iterator` is an alias:

```
typedef regex_iterator<string::const_iterator> sregex_iterator;
```

The next example processes all tokens that are not in a predefined list; in this case we print only the even numbers:

```
// Negated character classes, using metacharacter '^'
regex myReg11("[^13579]");
```

```
string S4 = "012345679";

sregex_iterator it4(S4.begin(), S4.end(), myReg11);
sregex_iterator end4;

while (it4 != end4)
{
    cout << *it4++ << ", ";    // prints 0,2,4,6
}
```

Finally, we process a comma-separated string containing numeric data (notice how we use an optional quantifier applied to commas, that is the optionality is zero or one). The output will contain an array of numeric data:

```
// Regex iterator
regex myReg9("(\\d+),?");
string S2 = "1,1,2,3,5,8,13,21";

sregex_iterator it(S2.begin(), S2.end(), myReg9);
sregex_iterator end;

while (it != end)
{
    cout << *it++ << " ";
}
```

Finally, we discuss `sregex_token_iterator` which is an iterator adapter and it represents a new view of an existing iterator sequence. In this case it enumerates all the occurrences of a regular expression within that sequence and then it presents one or more character sequences for each match found. In order to create a `sregex_iterator` we provide the iterators denoting the start and end of the input sequence, the regular expression and finally an extra parameter that determines how the regular expression should be processed.

We use `sregex_token_iterator` for the following regular expression:

```
regex myReg10("/");
string S3 = "2009/12/1";
```

The regular expression is a forward slash; in order to match it we use the form:

```
sregex_token_iterator itToken(S3.begin(), S3.end(), myReg10, 0);
```

while if we wish to extract the sequence (2009, 12, 1) we use the form:

```
sregex_token_iterator itToken(S3.begin(), S3.end(), myReg10, -1);
```

12.8 Text Replacement

The function `regex_replace` performs text substitution. The input to this function is a string to be parsed, a regular expression and a string that formats the matched string. As an example, consider the regular expression and candidate string:

```
// Replacing
regex myReg8("(Colo)(u)(r)", boost::regex::icase|boost::regex::perl);
string S = "Colour, colours, color, colourize";
```

We note that the regular expression has three subexpressions that we can address as $1=Colo, $2=u, $3=r. We replace the original string S by one that does not contain the contents of $2. In other words, we keep the contents of $1 and $3:

```
S = regex_replace(S, myReg8, "$1$3");
cout << "Replaced string: " << S << endl;
```

The string S is now in American English form.

12.9 Dynamic Regular Expressions and Exception Handling

A bad regular expression is one that does not conform to the rules on how to form regular expressions. In such cases the regular expression cannot be compiled by the regular expression engine. Then an exception of type regex_error will be thrown. We take a hard-wired example of a bad expression and we see that it throws an exception at creation time:

```
try
{
    regex myReg("\\d {2,3");   // BAD, BAD ==> {2,3}
}
catch(regex_error& exc)
{
    cout << "Bad expression " << exc.what() << endl;
}
```

We can also create regular expressions at run-time and match strings against them. Again, we define a try/catch block in case you type a non-conforming regular expression:

```
try
{
    // Define a regular expression
    cout << "Give a regular expression: ";
    string regString; getline(cin, regString);

    // Now define RE; throw an exception if badly formed
    regex myReg(regString);

    cout << "Enter a string to be matched: ";
    string inputString; getline(cin, inputString);

    if (regex_match(inputString, myReg) == true)
    {
        cout << "RE is good\n";
    }
    else
    {
        cout << "RE is NOT good\n";
        return 0;
    }
}
catch(regex_error& exc)
{
    cout << "Bad expression " << exc.what() << endl;
}
```

12.10 Regex and Callbacks

We conclude this chapter with a discussion of using callback functions in conjunction with Regex. What do we mean by this statement? In this case we wish to call a function object when we find a match of a subexpression in text.

The example we take is concerned with finding the sum of the values in a collection. The information is embedded in a string that needs to be matched against a regular expression:

```
// Regex iterator
regex myReg9("(\\d+),?");
string S2 = "1,1,2,3,5,8,13,21";

sregex_iterator it(S2.begin(), S2.end(), myReg9);
sregex_iterator end;
```

We can see immediately that the sum is 54. We automate this process and to this end we iterate in the string S2. We process a match in it as soon as it is found. Thus, we first create a callback functor:

```
class RegexCallback
{ // Function object

private:
    int sum;

public:
    RegexCallback() : sum(0) {}

    template <typename T> void operator () (const T& value)
    {
        sum += atoi(value[1].str().c_str());
    }

    int Sum() const
    {
        return sum;
    }
};
```

We now create an instance of RegexCallback and we deliver it as an argument to the function for_each():

```
RegexCallback callback;
int mySum = for_each(it, end, callback).Sum();
cout << "Sum: " << mySum << endl;   // Answer == 54
```

We shall see more examples of this kind of functionality when we discuss Boost.Xpressive in chapter 13.

12.11 Summary and Conclusions

We have introduced the Boost.Regex library that supports regular expressions in C++. It improves the robustness of the input validation process in applications. It can be used in combination with StringAlgo, in particular with the latter's string processing capabilities.

13 An Introduction to Expression Templates and Xpressive

13.1 Introduction and Objectives

In this chapter we introduce the Boost.Xpressive library. It supports lexical analysis (by creating tokens) and the creation of regular expression objects. It also supports matching, searching, splitting and tokenisation operations. Boost.Xpressive goes beyond lexical analysis. In particular, we can create both compile-time (as expression templates) and run-time (strings) regular expressions and these can be freely mixed in nested expressions. Furthermore, Boost.Xpressive has a number of features that are useful in more advanced text-processing applications:

- *Named captures*: you can assign a name (rather than a number) to a capture; this feature is useful when working with complex regular expressions.
- *Grammars*: this allows you to define a grammar for simple languages, represent sentences in the language and then interpret these sentences in much the same way as in compiler theory (Aho 1977) and design patterns (GOF 1995). In particular, a regex can refer to another regex, thus supporting composite regexes.
- *Semantic actions*: this feature allows us to do something when part of a regular expression matches. For example, when scanning an input string of the form 'a = 1, b = 99, c = 76', as soon as a '=' is matched then this would be the trigger to insert the name and value into a `map<string, string>`. In this case a regular expression has two parts, namely a *pattern* and an *action*.

We discuss these topics in later sections. If you need them in your applications then Boost.Xpressive is a good choice. On the other hand, if you need to define, match and search in static regular expressions then Boost.Regex (possibly in combination with the Boost.String Algorithm library) may be sufficient.

We include the following convenience file:

```
#include <boost/xpressive/xpressive.hpp>
```

When we wish to make a distinction between static and dynamic regular expressions we use separate header files as follows:

```
#include <boost/xpressive/xpressive_static.hpp>    // Static regex
#include <boost/xpressive/xpressive_dynamic.hpp>   // Dynamic regex
```

Furthermore, we use the following namespaces:

```
using namespace boost::xpressive;
using namespace std;
```

Regarding Xpressive, we concentrate on its support for matching, creating nested grammary and semantic actions. We now discuss a number of datastructures in Computer Science.

13.2 Binary Trees and Expression Trees

Before we discuss C++ expression templates and Boost.Xpressive we introduce a fundamental structure called a *binary tree*. We define what it is and we give some examples of binary trees. We then discuss expression trees.

By definition, a *binary tree* T is a set of elements (called *nodes*) such that
a) T is empty (the *empty tree*).
    or
b) T contains a special node (called the *root of* T) and the remaining nodes of T form an
    ordered pair of disjoint binary trees T1 and T2.

We see that this is a recursive definition; the trees T1 and T2 are called the left and right
subtrees of T of the root tree T, respectively. One or both subtrees may be empty and thus
we see that every node in a tree has 0, 1 or 2 *successors*. A node with no successors is called
a *terminal*.

We can represent a binary tree pictorially as in Figure 13.1, for example. This tree has 11
nodes with A playing the role of root node. Nodes D, F, G, L and K are terminals. Node B is
a *left successor* of node A and node C is a *right successor* of A. The *left subtree of* C
consists of node G while its *right subtree* consists of nodes H, J, L and K. Node H has two
successors J and K while node E has one successor. We say that nodes G and H are *children*
of node C or that node C is the *parent* of nodes G and H.

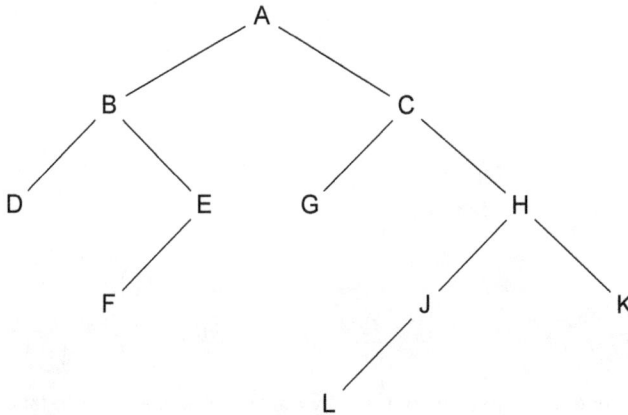

Figure 13.1 Binary Tree Example

We can represent *algebraic expressions* involving binary operations as a binary tree. For
example, let us consider the algebraic expression:

```
E = (a - b) / ((c * d) + e)
```
(13.1)

In this case we create 'internal' node structures in which the root node is an operator and left
and right subtrees correspond to the operands. For example, the operands of + are (c * d)
and e. We represent this algebraic expression as a binary tree in Figure 13.2. In this context
we call it an *expression tree*.

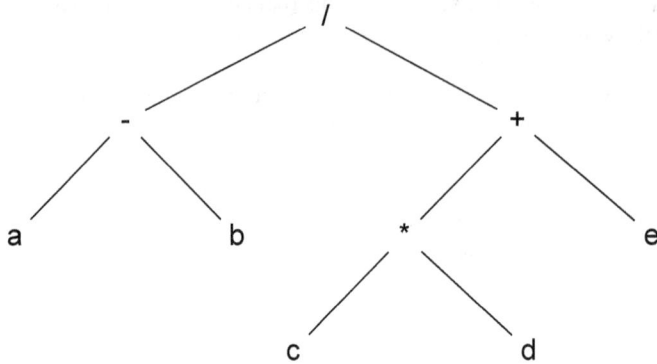

Figure 13.2 Expression Tree

13.2.1 Traversing Binary Trees

If we examine the binary tree in Figure 13.3 (a) having root node V, left successor L and right successor R we can then visit these nodes in six different ways, namely VLR, LVR, LRV, VRL, RVL, RLV.

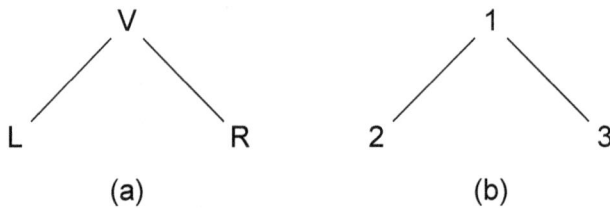

(a)   (b)

Figure 13.3 Basic structure

We reduce these six options to three options by constraining traversal to take place at node L before node R. The remaining options are:

VLR (or *preorder*)
1. Process the root V.
2. Traverse left subtree of V in preorder.
3. Traverse right subtree of V in preorder.

LVR (or *inorder*)
1. Process the left subtree of V in inorder.
2. Process the root V.
3. Traverse the right subtree of V in inorder.

LRV (or *postorder*)
1. Traverse the left subtree if V in postorder.
2. Traverse the right subtree of V in postorder.
3. Proces the root node V.

We now discuss each of these traversal options with reference to Figure 13.3 (b). With preorder, the traversal is 1,2, 3, with inorder it is 2,1,3 while with postorder it is 2,3,1. Taking the binary tree of Figure 13.1 again, the node ordering becomes:

- Preorder: A B D E F C G H J L K.
- Inorder: D B F E G C L J H K.
- Postorder: D F E B G L J K H C A.

13.2.2 Extended Binary Trees

An extended *binary tree* (or *2-tree*) is a binary tree in which each node has either 0 or 2 children. The nodes with two children are called *internal nodes* while the nodes with 0 children are called *external nodes*. We distinguish between internal and external nodes by using circles for the internal nodes and squares for the external nodes. We can convert an arbitrary binary tree to an extended binary tree by replacing each empty node by a new node as shown in Figure 13.4. A special case of a 2-tree is a tree T corresponding to an algebraic expression E that uses only binary operations. In general, the variables will appear as the external nodes and the operations in E will appear as the internal nodes. See the example in Figure 13.5 for the expression in equation 13.1.

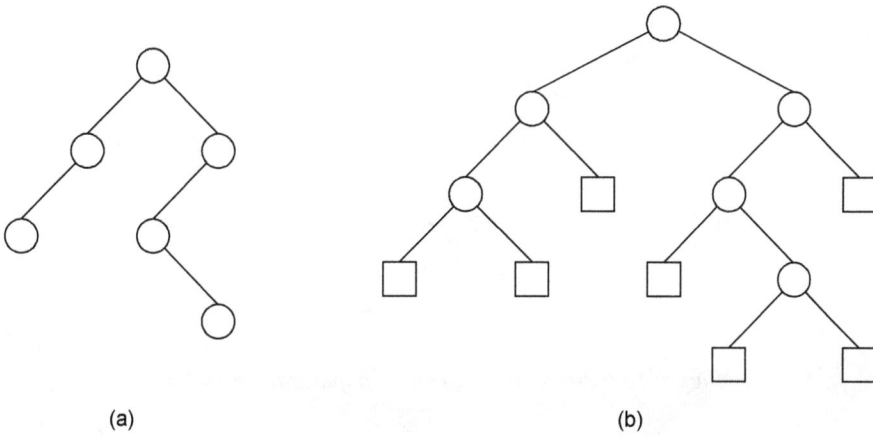

(a)   (b)

Figure 13.4 Binary Tree and Extended Binary Tree

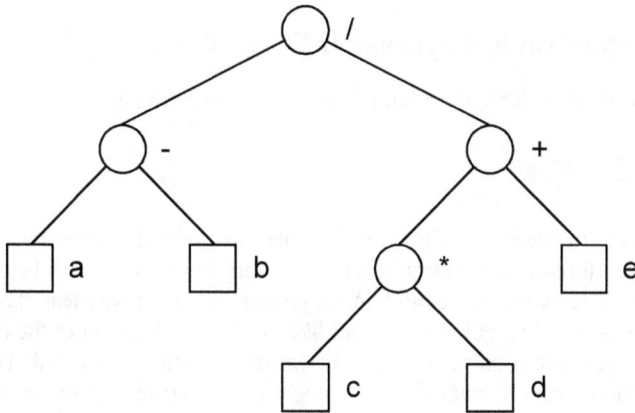

Figure 13.5 Algebraic expression as 2-tree

A final example is concerned with finding the roots of the quadratic equation:

$$ax^2 + bx + c = 0$$

$$x = \frac{-b \pm \sqrt{b^2 - 4ac}}{2a}.$$

The corresponding 2-tree for one of the roots of this quadratic equation is given in Figure 13.6.

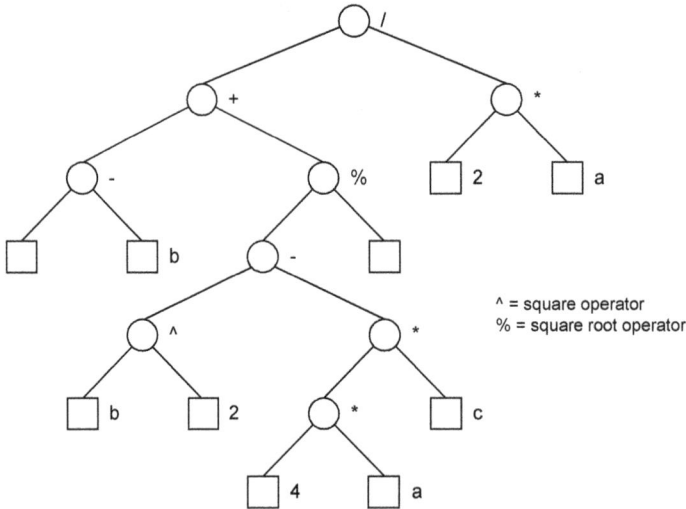

Figure 13.6 2-tree for one root of a quadratic equation

We conclude this section with the remark that the Boost.Intrusive library contains functionality for special containers based on tree structures. A discussion of this library is outside the scope of the current book.

13.3 An Introduction to Expression Templates

In order to motivate what expression templates are and why we need them, let us consider the expression:

```
A = B + (C + D)
```

where A, B, C and D are matrices. When implemented in C++ using operator overloading we will encounter a performance hit because temporary objects are created when executing the above expression. The expression evaluation is *greedy* by which we mean that computation begins as soon as is possible. What we would like is a lazy evaluation of the expression, in other words that the expression be parsed in its entirety and then evaluated. This issue is addressed by *domain-specific embedded languages* (DSEL) (see Abrahams 2005, Josuttis 2003) which can be created in Boost.Xpressive and Boost.Spirit, for example.

In general, the main uses of expression templates are:
- Creating DSELs in C++.
- Support lazy evaluation of C++ (mathematical) expressions.
- To pass an expression (and not the result of its evaluation) as a parameter to a function.

One of the advantages of domain-specific languages is that we can solve problems using a notation that is close to the problem domain in question. We take an example of matrix and vector operations in Numerical Analysis (see Golub 1996). We note that α, μ and β are scalars, x and y are vectors and A, B and C are matrices:
- Vector scale: $y = \alpha x$.
- Dot product: $\mu = x^T x$ (x^T is the transpose of x).
- Saxpy: $y = ax + y$.
- Matrix-vector multiplication: $y = \alpha Ax + \beta y$.
- Rank-1 update: $A = A + \alpha xy^T$.
- Matrix multiplication: $C = \alpha AB + \beta C$.
- Matrix-vector multiplication: $y = \alpha Ax + \beta y$.
- Rank-1 update: $A = \alpha x^T + A$.
- Rank-2 update: $A = \alpha xy^T + \alpha yx^T + A$.
- General product: $C = \alpha AB + \beta C$ (or $\alpha BA + \beta C$).

When implementing these features in C++ we would like the code to be expressive and close to mathematical notation and we would also like it to be efficient. These goals are achieved by using operator overloading and expression templates (see Josuttis 2003). We use templates to represent parts of an expression. In general, the template represents the particular kind of operation while the parameters represent the operands. The expression can then be passed to a function or evaluated at a later time.

Expression templates use the *Recursive Type Composition* pattern. In other words, we can define instances of templates that contain other instances of the same template as member data. The *Interpreter* pattern (GOF 1995) defines a representation for a given language and it provides an interpreter that uses the representation to parse sentences in the language. For example, we can define a grammar for regular expressions by representing each kind of expression as a class as shown in Figure 13.7. We define the grammar using the following Backus Naur Form (BNF) syntax:
- expression ::= constant | alternate | sequence | repeat | '(' expression ')'
- alternate ::= expression '|' expression
- sequence ::= expression '&' expression
- repeat ::= expression '*'
- literal ::= 'a' | 'b' | 'c' ... { 'a' | 'b' | ...}*

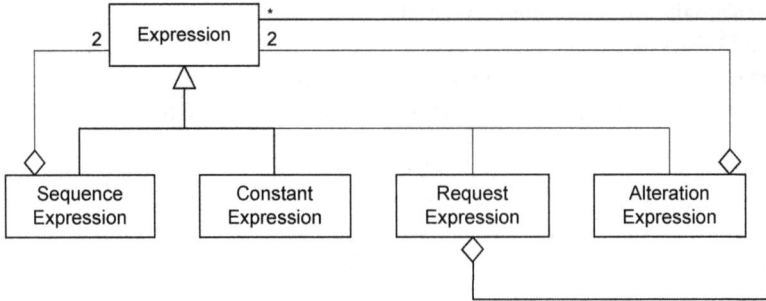

Figure 13.7 Expression Hierarchy

The symbol 'expression' is the start symbol and 'literal' is a terminal symbol that defines simple words.
It is possible to create an interpreter for the classes in Figure 13.7 by defining the `Interpret()` member function for each class.

We discuss a special version of the *Interpreter* pattern by defining the classes `Expression` and `BinaryExpression`. Use is made of the *Curiously Recurring Template Pattern* (CRTP) that we discuss in Appendix A. We say that CRTP uses *static polymorphism* rather than *dynamic polymorphism* because the 'base' class has a template parameter that will be instantiated for a particular kind of expression (for example, a binary expression):

```
template <typename E> struct Expression
{ // Base class that uses the CRTP pattern
  // (E will be a 'derived' class)

   E expr;

   Expression(E e) : expr (e) {}
   double operator () (double d) { return expr(d); }
};
```

We see that this class is a function object and when is invoked it will call the corresponding operator of its template parameter. The case of interest is when the template E is instantiated as a binary expression:

```
template <typename L, typename H, typename OP> struct BinaryExpression
{ // Binary operator: <operand> OP <operand>

   L l;
   H h;

   BinaryExpression(L l, H h) : l(l), h(h) {}
   double operator () (double d)
   {
      return OP::apply(l(d), h(d));
   }
};
```

We see that this class has three template parameters representing the left and right-hand generic operands `L` and `H` and a generic operator `OP`. In the current scope we consider variables and constants as operand classes:

```
struct Var
{ // Models variables in expressions
   double operator () (double v) { return v; }
```

```
};

struct Constant
{ // Models constants in expression

    double c;

    Constant(double d) : c (d) {}
    double operator () (double) { return c; }
};
```

Again, we see that these classes are function objects.

Returning to `BinaryExpression`, we note that it requires its instantiated `OP` classes to implement the `apply()` method. This is then our chance to define the kinds of operators that we are interested in, for example:

```
struct Add
{ // Add two numbers
    static double apply(double l, double h) { return l + h; }
};

struct Subtract
{ // Subtract two numbers
    static double apply(double l, double h) { return l - h; }
};

struct Multiply
{ // Multiply two numbers
    static double apply(double l, double h) { return l * h; }
};
```

The final step is to create a number of functions that evaluate expressions. The first functon evaluates a binary operation given two operands and an operator:

```
template <typename T, typename Func> double Evaluate(T t1, T t2, Func f)
{ // Evaluate a single expression

    return f.apply(t1, t2);
}
```

Some examples of use are:

```
// Evaluate a binary operator
Add myAddOperator;
Multiply myMultOperator;
Subtract mySubOperator;

double d1 = Evaluate(1.0, 2.0, myAddOperator);      // 3
double d2 = Evaluate(1.0, 2.0, myMultOperator);     // 2
double d3 = Evaluate(1.0, 2.0, mySubOperator);      // -1
cout << d1 << ", " << d2 << ", " << d3 << endl;
```

We now wish to add some more expressiveness to this simple system; let us say that we wish to define mathematical operators such as '*' and '+'. To this end, we define global operators:

```
template <typename A, typename B>
Expression<BinaryExpression<Expression<A>, Expression<B>, Add> >
    operator + (Expression<A> a, Expression<B> b)
{
    typedef BinaryExpression<Expression<A>, Expression<B>, Add> ExprT;
```

```
    return Expression<ExprT>(ExprT(a,b));
}

template <typename A, typename B>
Expression<BinaryExpression<Expression<A>, Expression<B>, Multiply> >
  operator * (Expression<A> a, Expression<B> b)
{
    typedef BinaryExpression<Expression<A>, Expression<B>, Multiply> ExprT;
    return Expression<ExprT>(ExprT(a,b));
}
```

We now give an example on how to use these functions. First, we define:

```
// Define some shorthand notation
typedef Expression<Var> Variable;
typedef Expression<Constant> Literal;
typedef BinaryExpression<Variable, Literal, Add> VarLitAdder;
typedef BinaryExpression<Variable, Variable, Add> VarVarAdder;
typedef Expression<VarLitAdder> Adder;
typedef Expression<VarVarAdder> Adder2;
```

and we create the instances:

```
Variable x( (Var()) );
Variable y( (Var()) );
Literal myLiteral(Constant(50.00));
VarLitAdder vladder(x, myLiteral);
Adder expr(vladder);
```

Next, we define a function to evaluate the expression:

```
// Evaluate the expression function
template <typename Itr, typename Func >
void evaluate(Itr begin, Itr end, Func func)
{ // Evaluate a range of xpressions

    for (Itr i = begin; i != end; ++i) cout << func (*i) << endl;
}
```

We now create a vector whose elements we will use in the evaluator:

```
vector<double> vec;
vec.push_back(10);
vec.push_back(20);
```

Finally, we evaluate a composite expression:

```
evaluate(vec.begin(), vec.end(), x*(x + myLiteral + x));
```

You can check that the output is 700, 1800. In general, we would not create our own interpreters but we would use the libraries in Boost.

13.4 An Introduction to Xpressive

Boost.Xpressive is an object-oriented regular expression template library for C++.
The regular expressions that Boost.Xpressive supports can be written as strings and parsed at run-time and we can also define them as expression templates that are parsed at compile-time. The advantages of compile-time parsing are:
• The syntax of regular expressions and parameter types is checked at compile time, thus allowing the early identification of errors.

- Possibility of compiler optimisation support; this improves the performance of matching and searching algorithms.
- The ability to create complex grammars.
- Clarity of code and less opportunity for making errors.

We use Boost.Xpressive when we need to parse complex input. The advantages of having a parse generator in Boost.Xpressive are:
- We can define, match and search regular expressions at run-time.
- Support for backtracking, allowing developers to exhaustively attempt to match each possibility in a pattern.

An application area for Boost.Xpressive is the parsing of input data. For example, in applications we may process real-time market data feeds or market quote information. The formats corresponding to this kind of information may be complex and may change. A library such as Boost.Xpressive allows us to create C++ code that can adapt to changing requirements. A second area constitutes those applications that use a combination of compile-time and run-time regular expressions. A typical application is user-driven data filtering.

We discuss the syntax of Boost.Xpressive and its functionality in the following sections.

13.5 First Encounters with Xpressive

There are a number of template classes and functions in Boost.Xpressive. We first describe them in general terms and then we proceed to discuss each one in detail:

- basic regex class `basic_regex<>`: the most important class and it contains a compiled regular expression. In applications you need to create an object of type `basic_regex<>`.
- `regex_match()`: checks if a string matches a regex. In order to succeed, the whole string – from beginning to end – must match the regex.
- `regex_search()`: searches a string to find a substring that matches a regex. It tries to find a match at every position in the string, starting from the beginning and stopping when it finds a match or when the string is exhausted.
- `match_results`: the output from `regex_match()` and `regex_search()`. It is similar to a vector of `sub_match<>` objects. The latter class is a pair of iterators representing the beginning and end of the marked sub-expression, respectively.
- `regex_replace()`: given an input string, a regex object and a substitute string, this function builds a new string by replacing those parts of the input string that match the regex with the substitution string.
- `regex_iterator<>`: STL-compatible iterator to find all the places in a string that match a regex. We can find the next match by incrementing the iterator. Dereferencing this iterator results in a `match_results` object.
- `regex_token_iterator<>`: this has the same functionality as `regex_iterator<>` except that we get a string when we dereference it. By default, it returns the whole substring that was matched by the regex.
- `regex_compiler<>`: this is a *factory* for `basic_regex` objects. It compiles a string into a regular expression. In general, you do not have to use this class directly because `basic_regex` has a static factory method called `compile()` that uses it.

The basic regex classes are defined in terms of the aliases:

```
typedef basic_regex<string::const_iterator> sregex;
typedef basic_regex<char const*> cregex;
```

while the match results classes are defined as:

```
typedef match_results<string::const_iterator> smatch;
typedef match_results<char const*> cmatch;
```

Thus, we can define regular expressions based on either strings or character pointers. We use strings in this book. In the same way, xpressive has defined the typedefs `sregex_iterator`, `sregex_token_iterator` and `sregex_compiler`.

We now discuss a number of the above features in more detail. In particular, we concentrate on matching. We provide code examples for the other functions in the code distribution.

13.6 Regex Object and Matches

Our first example introduces some code. In this case we create a dynamic regex object based on a string representing a regular expression. We then match it against an input string. We print the submatches in the `smatch` vector, first hard-coded and then using a more flexible mechanism:

```
#include <iostream>
#include <boost/xpressive/xpressive_dynamic.hpp>  // Dynamic regex

using namespace boost::xpressive;

string str("Hello World Again!");

// Create a dynamic regex; three words followed by a '!'
sregex rex = sregex::compile( "(\\w+) (\\w+) (\\w+)!" );
smatch what;

// Check if matched
if (regex_match(str, what, rex))
{ // All the (sub)matches in a match_results objects

    cout << "Number of submatches: " << what.size();
    cout << what[0] << endl;       // Full match
    cout << what[1] << endl;       // First capture 'Hello'
    cout << what[2] << endl;       // Second capture 'World'
    cout << what[3] << endl;       // Third capture 'Again'
}
else
{
    cout << "No match found\n";
}

// Now loop over all matches
for (int n = 0; n < what.size(); ++n)
{
    cout << n << ": " << what[n] << endl;
}
```

The next example defines regular expressions for key-value assignments in comma-separated format:

```
rexA = sregex::compile( "(\\w+=\\w+,)*" );
```

```
// Simple comma-separated string
string strA( "a=1,b=2," );
smatch whatA;

if (regex_match(strA, whatA, rexA))
{ // All the matches in a match_results objects

    cout << "Number of submatches CSV: " << whatA.size() << endl; // 2

    for (int n = 0; n < whatA.size(); ++n)
    {
        std::cout << n << ": " << whatA[n] << std::endl;
    }
}
else
{
    cout << "No match found, # submatches: " << whatA.size() << endl;
}
```

Our final example in this section is to define regular expressions that recognise dates:

```
// Date format matching
sregex rexB = sregex::compile( "\\d{1,2}[/]\\d{1,2}[/|-]\\d{4}" );
string strB( "14/12/2007" );
smatch whatB;

if (regex_match(strB, whatB, rexB))
{ // All the matches in a match_results object

    cout << "Number of submatches for dates: "
        << whatB.size() << endl;   // 1 date matched

    for (int n = 0; n < whatB.size(); ++n)
    {
        cout << n << ": " << whatB[n] << endl;
    }
}
else
{
    cout << "Number of submatches dates: " << whatB.size() << endl;
    cout << "No match found\n";
}
```

We see that is not difficult to create regular expressions in Boost.Xpressive.

13.7 Nested Regex and simple Grammar

We now discuss how to define regular expressions that consist of other regular expressions. We consider defining regular expressions for two-dimensional shapes such as points, line segments, circles and polylines:

```
// 2d Shape expressions
sregex PointExpr = ("(" >> (s1 = +_d) >> "," >> (s2 = +_d) >> ")");
sregex LineSegmentExpr = PointExpr >> ';' >> PointExpr;
sregex CircleExpr = PointExpr >> ';' >> "\\d{1}";
sregex PolylineExpr = PointExpr >> *(';' >> *(PointExpr));
```

Note the presence of the placeholders s1 and s2 that we discuss later in section 9.

In the above examples we use the operator '>>' to build up a regular expression from a combination of other regular expressions and literals; for example, the expression:

```
sregex CircleExpr = PointExpr >> ';' >> "\\d{1}";
```

defines a circle that consists of a point, a semicolon and one digit. Then a string that conforms to this expression would be:

```
string strCircle("(0,0);10.0");
```

This way of defining regular expressions certainly improves readability.

Other examples of shapes are:

```
string strPolyline("(0,0);(1,1);(2,3)");
string strPoint("(0,0)");
string strLineSegment("(0,0);(1,1)");
```

Having defined the regular expressions and strings we now wish to see if they match. We use the regex_match and match_results (smatch) classes that we discussed in sections 5 and 6:

```
smatch what;
if (regex_match(strPolyline, what, PolylineExpr))
{
    cout << "Polyline match found\n";
    for (int n = 0; n < what.size(); ++n)
    {
        cout << n << ": " << what[n] << endl;
    }
}
else
{
    cout << "no match\n";
}

if (regex_match(strLineSegment, what, LineSegmentExpr))
{
    cout << "Line Segment match found\n";
    for (int n = 0; n < what.size(); ++n)
    {
        cout << n << ": " << what[n] << endl;
    }
}
else
{
    cout << "no match\n";
}

if (regex_match(strPoint, what, PointExpr))
{
    cout << "Point match found\n";
    for (int n = 0; n < what.size(); ++n)
    {
        cout << n << ": " << what[n] << endl;
    }
}
else
{
    cout << "no match\n";
}
```

We conclude this section with a discussion on how to define *self-referencing regular expressions*. This allows us to define expressions in a cyclic manner, for example expression *A* defined in terms of expression *B* which is defined in terms of expression *C* which in its turn is defined in terms of *A*. In other words, we can *forward-declare* regex objects in a *cyclic grammar* (a grammar is a set of rules that defines a language). We define regex objects in this grammar by reference if they have not yet been initialised and by value if they have been initialised and whose values do no change. We use the `by_ref()` function template to allow us to embed a `regex` object in another one by reference.

We take an example of a simple grammar that matches mathematical expressions. It is meant to show how to define self-referencing expressions. The hierarchy of `regex` objects is defined by:

```
// Defining simple grammars
sregex group, factor, term, expression;

group       = '(' >> by_ref(expression) >> ')';
factor      = +_d | group;
term        = factor >> *(('*' >> factor) | ('/' >> factor));
expression  = term >> *(('+' >> term) | ('-' >> term));
```

We can now define sentences in the language defined by this grammar:

```
std::string mathsExpr("349*(2+3)");

smatch whatM;

if (regex_match(mathsExpr, whatM, expression))
{ // All the matches in a match_results object

    cout << "Number of submatches for maths expression: "
         << whatM.size() << endl;

    for (int n = 0; n < whatM.size(); ++n)
    {
        cout << n << ": " << whatM[n] << endl;
    }
}
else
{
    cout << "Number of submatches dates: " << whatM.size() << endl;
    cout << "No match found\n";
}
```

13.8 Semantic Actions

Semantic actions are C++ functions or function objects that are called whenever the parser successfully recognises a portion of the input. We can attach a semantic action to any point in the grammar specification. In general, if we have a parser *P* and a C++ function *F* we then wish to make the parser invoke *F* whenever it matches an input; the notation would read *P[F]*. In general, the function or function object signature depends on the type of the parser to which it is attached.

Some of the uses of semantic actions are:
- Parsing an input string that matches a certain regular expression and creating or updating an STL container from the data in the string.
- Executing commands.

- Implementing semantic actions using function pointers, function objects, free functions and member functions using Boost.Bind.

In this section we focus on the first feature. There are a few steps that need to be taken and while they are not difficult to implement in C++ each step must be correct. We take an example of processing two-dimensional point data in a semi-colon-separated format describing polylines (ordered points) and producing an STL map whose first elements are integers representing the index of a point in the polyline and whose second element is the point corresponding to the index. To this end, we introduce a number of topics:

- Using expression templates in combination with regular expressions, in particular action encoding and execution.
- Using sub-match placeholder names.
- Semantic actions with variables and operators.
- Lazy functions: attach a user-defined function to a regular expression.

We take an example that processes a string containing two-dimensional point coordinates. The string represents a polyline that is an aggregation of points. A typical input string is:

```
std::string strPolyline("(0,0);(1,1);(2,3);(9,7);(8,99);(7,929)");
```

We create an STL map whose keys are integers and whose values are the points constructed from the input string. First, we define the Point class:

```
struct Point
{
    int x,y;

    Point() { x = y = 0; }
    Point(int X, int Y) { x = X; y = Y; }
    friend ostream& operator << (ostream& os, const Point& pt)
    {
        os << "(" << pt.x << "," << pt.y << ")";
        return os;
    }
};
```

The goal now is to define a regular expression to model points; the semantic action ensures that the coordinates are extracted and used to create an instance of Point which is then inserted into the map. We then just need to do one more thing; since directly using points is not a semantic action we need to modify Point. To this end, we use our code with a xpressive::function and we define a wrapper class for Point:

```
struct point
{ // Wrapper for the class in semantic action

    typedef Point result_type;
    Point operator () (int x, int y) const
    {
        return Point(x,y);
    }
};

function<point>::type const point_ = {};
```

We are now in a position to define the regular expression and the corresponding semantic action (the latter is defined between the brackets '[' and ']'):

```
std::map<int, Point> result;
```

```
// 2d Shape expressions
int i = 0;
sregex PointExpr = ("(" >> (s1 = +_d) >> "," >> (s2 = +_d) >> ")")
    [ ref(result)[++ref(i)] = point_(as<int>(s1), as<int>(s2)) ];
```

We note the presence of the placeholders s1 and s2 that contain the x and y coordinates of a point, respectively. We need to convert these sub-match variables to integers using Boost.Lexical cast. The effect is to add a point to the polyline. Finally, please note that we use xpressive references in the above code; such a reference returns a lazy reference that we can use in expressions that are executed lazily. This is in contrast to boost::ref() that returns a plain reference wrapper to an object.

Continuing, we define the regular expression for polylines:

```
sregex PolylineExpr = PointExpr >> *(';' >> *(PointExpr));
```

Finally, we match the input string strPolyline against the regular expression:

```
smatch what; // match_results
if (regex_match(strPolyline, what, PolylineExpr))
{
    cout << "Polyline match found\n";
    for (int n = 0; n < what.size(); ++n)
    {
        cout << n << ": " << what[n] << endl;
    }
}
else cout << "no match\n";
```

The output is:

```
Polyline match found
0: (0,0);(1,1);(2,3);(9,7);(8,99);(7,929)
[1: (0,0)]
[2: (1,1)]
[3: (2,3)]
[4: (9,7)]
[5: (8,99)]
[6: (7,929)]
```

We have now completed the discussion of the example.

13.9 More Semantic Actions

We give some more examples. The first example is simpler than the example in section 13.8 because we do not have to define a wrapper class to support lazy function evaluation. This is because xpressive converts the relevant code automatically into a semantic action since we are using call by value. We define a regular expression and corresponding semantic action to parse strings of the form:

```
string str("8=FIX.4.2;9=204;35=D;49=xxx;56=xxx;");
```

The data structure, regular expression and related semantic action are defined by:

```
map<int, string> result;
sregex pair = ( (s1= +_d) >> "=" >> (s2= +(_w|'.')))
    [ ref(result)[as<int>(s1)] = s2];
sregex rx = pair >> *(';' >> *(pair));
```

Finally, the code to match the string is:

```
if (regex_match(str, rx))
{

    map<int, string>::const_iterator it;
    for (it = result.begin(); it != result.end(); ++it)
    {
        cout << it->first << "," << it->second << endl;
    }
}
else
{
    cout << "no match\n";
}
```

The second example uses some new notation to help us create more complex regular expressions. Instead of using names such as s1 and s2 for placeholders we can use *custom mark tags*; in this case we create four tags, each one having its own integer identifier:

```
string str("Birthday is 8/29/1952");

mark_tag day(1), month(2), year(3), delim(4);

// This regex finds a date
sregex date = (month= repeat<1,2>(_d))               // find the month
    >> (delim= (boost::xpressive::set= '/','-')) // followed by a delimiter
    >> (day=   repeat<1,2>(_d)) >> delim          // and a day + delim
    >> (year=  repeat<1,2>(_d >> _d));            // and the year.

smatch what;

if (regex_search(str, what, date))
{
    cout << what[0]     << '\n';                   // whole match
    cout << what[day]   << '\n';                   // the day
    cout << what[month] << '\n';                   // the month
    cout << what[year]  << '\n';                   // the year
}
```

13.10 Conclusions and Summary

This chapter discussed advanced text and string processing using Boost.Xpressive. Whereas Boost.Tokenizer and Boost.Regex deal mainly with lexical analysis and text processing functionality, Boost.Xpressive supports expression templates, compile-time and run-time expressions that we can use in data-driven applications. Of particular usefulness is the support for semantic actions that can be associated with functionality when certain patterns in input strings are matched.

The library is a good candidate in our opinion when we wish to parse strings that reflect the structure of hierarchically organised objects as discussed in section 13.7 where we discussed two-dimensional shapes and which we discuss in the context of the CADObject library in chapter 17. Furthermore, the support for semantic actions and user-defined assertions means that we can integrate dynamic regular expression parsing with application code. For example, a useful initial exercise is to create a factory class that creates two-dimensional shapes from the command line.

14 MultiArray and Array

14.1 Introduction and Objectives

In this chapter we introduce the Boost Multi-dimensional Array Library that allows developers to define multi-dimensional arrays in C++. We are already familiar with special cases of such arrays; for example, a one-dimensional array is called a *vector*, a two-dimensional array is called a *matrix* and a three-dimensional array is sometimes called a *tensor*. It is possible to create these data structures using nested STL vectors, as the following code snippet shows:

```
int NR = 4;      // Number of rows
int NC = 3;      // Number of columns

// Create a nested vector ~ dense NRxNC matrix
vector<vector<double> > matrix(NR);     // Outer vector

for (int j = 0; j < NR; ++j)
{ // Create inner vectors, all of same size NC

    matrix[j] = vector<double>(NC, double(j));
}
```

In this case we simulate the structure of a dense square matrix with NR rows and NC columns by defining and initialising a nested vector. First, we create the outer vector of size NR and then we initialise each indexed value to be a vector<double> of size NC. Having initialised the matrix we can then, for example print its values:

```
// Print the values of the matrix
for (int i = 0; i < NR; ++i)
{
    cout << endl;
    for (int j = 0; j < NC; ++j)
    {
        cout << matrix[i][j] << ", ";
    }
}
```

This code works but there are also some problems and shortcomings associated with it, especially when we wish to add new functionality, improve run-time performance or maintain the software after changes have been made to the code. In general, a better approach would be to create a class called Matrix whose member data is a nested vector and that has appropriate functionality:

```
class Matrix
{
private:
    vector<vector<double> > mat;

public:
    // Your functionality here
};
```

This solution has a number of drawbacks:
a) We access the elements of the matrix using the concatenated operators [] []. It is not clear if this approach is efficient especially if we access the elements on a column-wise basis even though C uses a *row-major* regime. For example, the 2 x 3 matrix whose rows are {1,2,3} and {4,5,6} is laid out in memory as {1,2,3,4,5,6}. Accessing the elements in

row-major order is efficient whereas *column-major order* reads the data from memory in the order {1,4,2,5,3,6} which is not efficient.

b) It is difficult to create *views* of the matrix, for example selecting sub-matrices and ranges of columns and rows. We could create member functions to realise this functionality but this would be time-consuming and sub-optimal.

c) *Array base*: the start index in STL `vector<T>` is zero and this may not be the most appropriate choice in some applications. For example, developers with a Fortran background prefer to use arrays where the start index is one.

d) *Reshaping* a matrix: in this case we would like to change the shape of a matrix (for example, change a 2 x 3 matrix to a 3 x 2 matrix).

14.2 A Quick '101' Tour of MultiArray

We immediatly give an example of a three-dimensional array. We include the following header file in our code:

```
#include <boost/multi_array.hpp>
```

The class that allows us to create multi-dimensional data structures is called `multi_array`. We have a number of options when creating an instance of this class; the difference lies in when the array's *extents* (the number of elements in each dimension of the `multi_array`) is defined. In the first case we create the array object and afterwards we can define its extents by resizing it:

```
// Define structure of tensor
const int dim = 3; // 3d matrix
typedef boost::multi_array<double, dim> Tensor;
Tensor tensor;

// Define the extents of each separate dimension
const int NT = 3;
const int NSIM = 4;
const int NDIM = 3;
tensor.resize(extents[NT][NSIM][NDIM]);
```

The second option is to define the extents directly in the constructor:

```
// Useful shorthand
Tensor tensor2(extents[NT][NSIM][NDIM]);
```

Finally, we can create an array by defining its extents in a collection:

```
// Create a tensor using a Collections
array<Tensor::index, dim> extentsList = { NT, NSIM, NDIM };
Tensor tensor3(extentsList);
```

Having created an array we then access its data using indexing operators. We can choose between concatenated square brackets `[]` that accept integers as index and round brackets `()` that accept a collection as input. We first define an alias that allows us to access the indices relating to an array:

```
// Define a 3d loop to initialise the data
typedef Tensor::index Index;
```

The following code shows how to initialise an array using square bracket notation:

```
// Accessing elements using []
for (Index i = 0; i != NT; ++i)
```

```
{
    for (Index j = 0; j != NSIM; ++j)
    {
        for (Index k = 0; k != NDIM; ++k)
        {
            tensor[i][j][k] = i + j + k;
        }
    }
}
```

We can also define an index collection and use round brackets to access the array elements (this option tends to be more efficient than using square brackets):

```
// Accessing elements using () with a collection of indices
typedef boost::array<Tensor::index, dim> Indices;

Indices indices;
for (indices[2]=0; indices[2] < NDIM; indices[2]++)
{
    for (indices[0]=0; indices[0] < NT; indices[0]++)
    {
        for (indices[1]=0; indices[1] < NSIM; indices[1]++)
        {
            tensor(indices) = 0.0;
        }
    }
}
```

We now discuss Boost.MultiArray in detail.

14.3 Overview of MultiArray Functionality

The MultiArray concept defines an interface to hierarchically nested containers. In particular, we can define n-dimensional data structures using the template class provided by the library. The library provides operations for creating multi-arrays, accessing their elements, navigating in multi-arrays as well as creating views of multi-arrays. The underlying memory model supports a number of layouts, thus making the library suitable for a wide range of applications.

We discuss the following concepts:
- Memory layout.
- Creating multi-arrays.
- Traversing a multi-array.
- Creating specialised views of a multi-array.

14.4 Specifying Array Dimensions

When constructing a multi-array we first need to specify the number of dimensions N (N = 3 for a three-dimensional array) and the extent of each dimension. The extent is the number of indexable values in each dimension. We first define the multi-array class and the class to hold its indices:

```
// Creating 3d arrays
const int N = 3;
typedef boost::multi_array<int, N> IntegerCube;
typedef boost::array<IntegerCube::index, N> IntegerCubeIndices;
```

We now create instances of `IntegerCube`. There are two approaches; the first method consists of passing a collection (for example, a `boost::array` that we discuss in section 14.8) of extents to a constructor:

```
// Option 1: Specify the size and a collection of extents
IntegerCube::index rows = 3;
IntegerCube::index columns = 4;
IntegerCube::index layers = 2;
IntegerCubeIndices shape = {rows, columns, layers};

IntegerCube myCube(shape);
```

We remark that `index` is a signed integral type that is used for indexing into a multi-array. It has other uses such as representing strides and index bases.

The second method involves passing an `extents_gen` object to the constructor:

```
// Option 2: Specify an extents object
IntegerCube myCube2(boost::extents[rows][columns][layers]);
```

14.5 Accessing the Elements of a Multi-Array

Having created a multi-array we can now consider how to access its elements. The first method is reminiscent of C and it uses the operator `[]`. In the case of a three-dimensional structure we use concatenated operators:

```
// Accessing the elements of a multi-array
myCube[2][3][1] = 2;                   // upper limits in each direction
assert(myCube[2][3][1] == 2);
```

The second method allows us to access the elements of a multi-array by passing a collection of indices to the operator `()`. In this case three indices will be used, one for each dimension of the container:

```
// Using a collection of indices
IntegerCubeIndices idx = {2, 3, 1};
myCube(idx) = 3;
assert(myCube(idx) == 3);
```

In general, the second method is useful when we wish to write dimension-independent code (we define the index collection once and then we use it in subsequent code without having to refer to its elements).

We can print the elements of a multi-array using the index type:

```
// Print the elements of the multi-array
for (IntegerCube::index layer=0; layer<layers; layer++)
{
    for (IntegerCube::index row=0; row<rows; row++)
    {
        for (IntegerCube::index column=0; column<columns; column++)
        {
            cout<<myCube[row][column][layer]<<", ";
        }
        cout<<endl;
    }
    cout<<"-------"<<endl;
}
```

We could also use round brackets to access the elements as we saw in section 14.2.

14.6 Setting the Array Base

By default, all arrays have start index equal to zero. In some cases we may wish to change this default value to 1, for example. We can then create a multi-array and define its array base by the following methods:

- Use the `reindex` member function to set all bases to the same index value.
- Use the `reindex` member function and pass a collection of index bases.
- Specify a pair of range values with the `extent_range` type.

The first option sets the base index of all dimensions to 1:

```
// All bases == 1
IntegerCube::extent_gen extents;
IntegerCube myCubeA(extents[rows][columns][layers]);
myCubeA.reindex(1);       // All start indices == 1
myCubeA[1][1][1] = 2;
assert(myCubeA[1][1][1] == 2);
```

If we wish to set the base index for each separate dimension we use the `reindex` member function with a collection:

```
// Set each dimension base to a value
IntegerCubeIndices bases = {-1, 2, -1};
myCubeA.reindex(bases);
myCubeA[-1][2][-1] = 42;
assert(myCubeA[-1][2][-1] == 42);
```

Finally, we can use `extent_range` to define both the start index and the upper limit of the extent:

```
// Using extent_range
IntegerCube myCubeB(extents[IntegerCube::extent_range(-2,6)]
                           [IntegerCube::extent_range(1,6)]
                           [IntegerCube::extent_range(-3,6)]);

// Set the value at lower indices
myCubeB[-2][1][-3] = 99;
assert(myCubeB[-2][1][-3] == 99);
```

We note that the generated range is a closed/open range; hence the following code will result in a run-time error:

```
// myCubeB[6][6][6] = 919;
// assert(myCubeB[6][6][6] == 919);
```

However, the following code is correct:

```
// Set the value at upper indices
myCubeB[5][5][5] = 919;
assert(myCubeB[5][5][5] == 919);
```

For most applications, you probably will not need to modify the array base. However, in some applications (for example, numerical linear algebra) mathematicians may prefer to use multi-arrays whose base index is 1.

14.7 Storage Ordering

In some cases we wish to store the data in such a way that it can be used by Fortran routines or we may even wish to customise the order in which data is stored. To this end, each array class has constructors that accept a *storage ordering parameter*.

This option is used when interfacing with legacy code in languages such as Fortran, for example. The three kinds of storage are:

- `c_storage_order`: this is the default and it stores elements in memory with dimensions stored from last to first. This is the way elements are stored in C (*row-major order*).
- `fortran_storage_order`: stores elements in the same order as Fortran, that is from the first dimension to the last (*column-major order*).
- `general_storage_order`: this option allows us to customise the order in which dimensions are stored in memory and whether dimensions are stored in ascending or descending order.

Creating a multi-array with the Fortran storage is easy:

```
// Fortran storage order
IntegerCube myFortranCube(extents[rows][columns][layers],
                    boost::fortran_storage_order());
```

Finally, let us create a three-dimensional array and store it in the order of last dimension, then first dimension, then second dimension. The corresponding code is:

```
// User-defined storage order
const int N = 3;
typedef boost::general_storage_order<N> GeneralStorage;

// Last, then first, then second dimension
array_type::size_type ordering[] = {2, 0, 1};

bool ascendingYN = {false, true, true};

IntegerCube myStoredCube(extents[rows][columns][layers],
                    GeneralStorage(ordering, ascendingYN));
```

We conclude this section with a discussion of memory layout specifiers for two-dimensional arrays. First, let us consider the following rectangular matrix having 3 rows and 4 columns:

$$
\begin{pmatrix}
0 & 1 & 2 & 3 \\
4 & 5 & 6 & 7 \\
8 & 9 & 10 & 11
\end{pmatrix}
$$

In C++ we specify this matrix in row-major order as:

```
int mat[3][4] = {0, 1, 2, 3, 4, 5, 6, 7, 8, 9, 10, 11};
```

We take an example to show how to represent data in memory and how to specify memory layout in C and Fortran. The code is for illustrative purposes only and to give some insights. The objective is to show how to represent the above matrix using row-major and column-major storage. In the first case we define the one-dimensional data and *stride* arrays:

```
int arrayA[] = {0, 1, 2, 3, 4, 5, 6, 7, 8, 9, 10, 11};
int strideA[] = {4, 1};
```

We can then print the elements of the array as a matrix:

```
for (int i = 0; i < 3; ++i)
{
    cout << endl;
    for (int j = 0; j < 4; ++j)
    {
        cout << *(arrayA + i*strideA[0] + j*strideA[1]);
    }
}
cout << endl;
```

Similarly, we can lay out the same matrix by column as follows:

```
// Fortran storage (by column)
int arrayB[] = {0, 4, 8, 1, 5, 9, 2, 6, 10, 3, 7, 11};
int strideB[] = {1, 3};
for (int i = 0; i < 3; ++i)
{
    cout << endl;
    for (int j = 0; j < 4; ++j)
    {
        cout << *(arrayB + i*strideB[0] + j*strideB[1]);
    }
}
cout << endl;
```

Summarising, storage ordering is useful when you interface Boost.MultiArray with external packages whose internal data storage regime differs from the C storage regime. This is taken care of by MultiArray.

14.8 Array

The STL vector<T> container provides the semantics of dynamic arrays. The number of elements in this class is variable and it is possible to append elements to it at run-time. In some applications we may wish to work with arrays whose size is known at compile-time. To this end, the Boost.Array library is one solution. It consists of a single template class array<V, N> having two template parameters, one parameter N for the size of the array and the other parameter V for the underlying data type. The interface has the following functionality:

- Array assignment.
- Accessing the elements of an array using the operator [] and the at() member function.
- Iterators.
- Member functions to retrieve the first and last elements of an array.
- We can compare arrays using the binary operators ==, !=, <, >, <=, >=.
- We can exchange elements of two arrays using the swap() member function.

We take some simple examples. First, we create an array of `long` and we initialise its elements:

```
const int N = 4;
boost::array<long, N> myArr = {1, 2, 3, 4};
```

We can now print the elements of the array using an iterator and by using the indexing operator:

```
// Using iterators
boost::array<long, N>::const_iterator it;
for (it = myArr.begin(); it != myArr.end(); ++it)
{
    cout << *it << endl;
}

// Indexing operator
for (long i = 0; i < myArr.size(); ++i)
{
    cout << myArr[i] << endl;
}
```

It is also possible to initialise an array as follows:

```
const int M = 2;
boost::array<string, M> myStringArr;
myStringArr[0] = "Hello";
myStringArr[1] = "World";
```

We now take an array that models a simple fixed-sized polyline consisting of points. The elements of the array consist of instances of class `Point` whose interface is:

```
class Point
{
private:
    double x;                           // X coordinate
    double y;                           // Y coordinate

public:
    // Constructors
    Point();                            // Default constructor
    Point(double xval, double yval);    // Initialise with x and y value
    Point();

    // Accessing functions
    double X() const;                   // The x-coordinate
    double Y() const;                   // The y-coordinate

    // Modifiers
    void X(double newX);
    void Y(double newY);

    Point operator + (const Point& p2) const;
    double distance (const Point& p2) const; // Distance between 2 points

    Point& operator = (const Point& pt);
};
```

We now create an array of points:

```
const int N = 4;
boost::array<Point, N> myPointArr;
myPointArr[0] = Point(1.0, 2.0);
```

```
myPointArr[1] = Point();
myPointArr[2] = Point(-1.0, 9.8);
myPointArr[3] = Point(3.4, 6.32);
```

There are two ways to access the elements of this array but they differ in the way they handle exceptional situations, in particular *out-of-bounds indexing*. First, an assert is executed in the case of operator overloading:

```
// What happens when the index is out-of-range?
// myPointArr[N] = Point();       // Assertion 'index < N'
// myPointArr[N].X(1.0);          // Assertion 'index < N'
```

The program stops executing in this case. Second, the `at()` member function throws an exception when an index is out-of-bounds and we catch the exception in the usual way:

```
try
{
    cout << "Give an index: "; int index; cin >> index;
    Point pt = myPointArr.at(index);
    cout << "(" << pt.X() << "," << pt.Y() << ")" << endl;
}
catch(const exception& e)
{
    cout << e.what() << endl;
}
```

Our final remark is that we cannot use arrays of different sizes together. This increases the robustness of applications that use them. We take an example of two arrays:

```
// Assignment of arrays with incompatible dimensions
const int N1 = 3;
const int N2 = 4;

boost::array<double, N1> arr1;
boost::array<double, N2> arr2;
```

Then the following code will not compile:

```
arr1 = arr2; // Gives compiler error
```

14.9 Applications of Boost.Array

There are many applications of Boost.Array. Some examples are:

- N-dimensional geometry: we can create a template class that represents points and other objects in n dimensions. In this case we implement the class NPoint by using an embedded `boost::array` instance:

```
template <typename Type, int n> class NPoint
{
private:

    // Originally: Type arr[n]
    boost::array<Type, n> arr;

public:

    // member functions here..
};
```

We compute the distance between two points as follows:

```
const int N = 3;
NPoint<double, N> p1(0.0);
NPoint<double, N> p2(1.0);

cout << "Distance: " << p1.distance(p2) << endl;
```

- Creating multi-dimensional, compile-time data structures: a good example is a template matrix with N rows and M columns:

```
template <typename T, std::size_t NRows, std::size_t NColumns>
class Matrix
{ // Basic class, can be extended

private:
    boost::array<boost::array<T, NColumns>, NRows> mat;

public:
    Matrix();
    std::size_t Rows() const;
    std::size_t Columns() const;

    T& operator () (std::size_t r, std::size_t c);
    const T& operator () (std::size_t r, std::size_t c) const;
};
```

An example of use is:

```
const int NROWS = 3; const int NCOLUMNS = 3;
Matrix<double, NROWS, NCOLUMNS> myMatrix;
```

- Using Boost.Array with Boost.MultiArray: Part of the code for initialising a multi-array involves defining its extents. The following code shows how to define these extents using boost::array:

```
int main()
{
    const int N = 3;
    typedef boost::multi_array<int, N> Array;

    // Define the extents using boost::array
    boost::array<Array::size_type, N> arrayDims;
    arrayDims[0] = 2;
    arrayDims[1] = 3;
    arrayDims[2] = 4;

    Array myArray(arrayDims);

    int num = 0;
    for (Array::index i=0; i!=arrayDims[0]; ++i)
        for (Array::index j=0; j!= arrayDims[1]; ++j)
            for (Array::index k=0; k!=arrayDims[2]; ++k)
                myArray[i][j][k] = num++;

    return 0;
}
```

We discuss some other application areas in section 14.14.

14.10 Four-dimensional Arrays

In some applications we would like to distinguish between the separate dimensions in a multi-array. For example, in a four-dimensional multi-array one dimension could represent time while the other dimensions represent three-dimensional coordinates. We give an example of how to define such a multi-array and we assign values to its elements:

```
// Typedef to make working with quads easier
typedef boost::multi_array<double, 4> Quad;

// The dimensions
Quad::index dim1=3;                    //Time dimension
Quad::index dim2=4;
Quad::index dim3=2;
Quad::index dim4=2;

// Create a "quad" multi-array
Quad quad(boost::extents[dim1][dim2][dim3][dim4]);

// Fill cube using the operator [index][index][index][index] syntax
for (Quad::index d1=0; d1<dim1; d1++)
{
   for (Quad::index d2=0; d2<dim2; d2++)
   {
      for (Quad::index d3=0; d3<dim3; d3++)
      {
         for (Quad::index d4=0; d4<dim4; d4++)
         {
            quad[d1][d2][d3][d4]= d1*d2*d3*d4;
         }
      }
   }
}
```

14.11 Views and Slices

A feature of Boost.MultiArray is the ability to create a subview of a multi-array. For example, it is possible to:

- Create a *subview* that retains the same number of dimensions as the original array.
- Create a *subview* that has one dimension less than that of the original array (*slicing*).

A view is represented by the `array_view` class. A view on a multi-array does not copy the data of the multi-array but references the original data.

We take two examples to show how to create views.

14.11.1 Subviews and Zooming

This feature is concerned with the selection of a subset of the data in a multi-array. What kinds of views would we like to create? The answer depends on the kind of problem we are trying to solve but in general many applications in science, engineering and finance use matrices to store data and need the following kinds of functionality:

- Partitioning a matrix into blocks (Golub 1996); this feature is useful in parallel matrix multiplication using the *Geometric Decomposition pattern* (see Mattson 2005).
- Creating views by taking even (or odd) indices, for example; this feature is useful when solving partial differential equations (PDE) using the finite difference method (FDM), see Mitchell 1980, Duffy 2006.

- More complicated matrix patterns, such as decomposing a matrix into its upper and lower triangular sub-matrices.

We show how to create a sub view from a three-dimensional multi-array. We create the view using the operator [] on the multi_array instance giving it an index_gen object. The example creates a sub view of a 5x4x3 structure. The sub view contains the closed-open ranges [1,3)[1,3)[0,2) thus resulting in a 2x2x2 view:

```
typedef boost::multi_array<double, 3> Cube;

int main()
{
    // Create multi-array
    Cube cube(boost::extents[5][4][3]);

    // Fill the cube with values (code omitted)
    ...

    // Print the cube
    Print(cube);

    // Get a sub view with same number of dimensions
    Cube::index_range r1(1,3);
    Cube::index_range r2(1,3);
    Cube::index_range r3(0,2);
    Cube::array_view<3>::type view=cube[ boost::indices[r1][r2][r3] ];

    cout<<"Sub view [1,3)[1,3)[0,2):"<<endl;
    Print(view);
}
```

Now we discuss the problem of selecting the elements of a matrix from the start index to the end index and where the elements selected are determined by a number *n* that we call the *stride*. For example, for an array filled with 11 numbers 0 to 10, we get the following views when $n = 1, 2$ and 3:

```
n=1: All values are in the view: 0, 1, 2, 3, 4, 5, 6, 7, 8, 9, 10
n=2: Only 1 out of 2 values are in the view: 0, 2, 4, 6, 8, 10
n=3: Only 1 out of 3 values are in the view: 0, 3, 5, 9
```

How do we code this functionality for matrices (the stride in both directions)? We create a global function Zoom that accepts a multi-array and stride as input and that produces a view as output:

```
const int N = 2;
typedef boost::multi_array<double, N> Matrix;

Matrix::array_view<N>::type Zoom(Matrix& matrix, int zoom)
{
    // Create ranges with original start- and end-values
    // and custom stride.
    Matrix::index_range r1=Matrix::index_range().stride(zoom);
    Matrix::index_range r2=Matrix::index_range().stride(zoom);

    // Return view with custom stride.
    return matrix[boost::indices[r1][r2]];
}
```

We thus create a matrix view with a given stride or zoom factor. A test program shows how to use this function:

```
int main()
{
    // The dimensions
    Matrix::index dim1=10;
    Matrix::index dim2=10;

    // Create a multi-array
    Matrix matrix(boost::extents[dim1][dim2]);

    // Fill the matrix using the operator [int][int] syntax
    for (Matrix::index d1=0; d1<dim1; d1++)
    {
        for (Matrix::index d2=0; d2<dim2; d2++)
        {
            matrix[d1][d2]=d1 + d2*dim1;
        }
    }

    // Print the matrix.
    Print(matrix);

    // Zoom out
    for (int i=2; i<4; i++)
    {
        cout<<"\n\nZoom out "<<i<<":"<<endl;
        Print(Zoom(matrix, i));
    }
}
```

The output contains a display of the original matrix and two views corresponding to stride values of 2 and 3. The following is a subset of the output:

```
Number of dimensions: 2
Number of elements: 100
size_of(array): 64 bytes
Data size: 100*8=800 bytes
Dim 0 [0, 10) (size: 10) (stride: 10)
Dim 1 [0, 10) (size: 10) (stride: 1)
0, 1, 2, 3, 4, 5, 6, 7, 8, 9,
10, 11, 12, 13, 14, 15, 16, 17, 18, 19,
20, 21, 22, 23, 24, 25, 26, 27, 28, 29,
30, 31, 32, 33, 34, 35, 36, 37, 38, 39,
40, 41, 42, 43, 44, 45, 46, 47, 48, 49,
50, 51, 52, 53, 54, 55, 56, 57, 58, 59,
60, 61, 62, 63, 64, 65, 66, 67, 68, 69,
70, 71, 72, 73, 74, 75, 76, 77, 78, 79,
80, 81, 82, 83, 84, 85, 86, 87, 88, 89,
90, 91, 92, 93, 94, 95, 96, 97, 98, 99,

Zoom out 2:
Number of dimensions: 2
Number of elements: 25
size_of(array): 36 bytes
Data size: 25*8=200 bytes
Dim 0 [0, 5) (size: 5) (stride: 20)
Dim 1 [0, 5) (size: 5) (stride: 2)
0, 2, 4, 6, 8,
20, 22, 24, 26, 28,
40, 42, 44, 46, 48,
60, 62, 64, 66, 68,
80, 82, 84, 86, 88,
```

```
Zoom out 3:
Number of dimensions: 2
Number of elements: 16
size_of(array): 36 bytes
Data size: 16*8=128 bytes
Dim 0 [0, 4) (size: 4) (stride: 30)
Dim 1 [0, 4) (size: 4) (stride: 3)
0, 3, 6, 9,
30, 33, 36, 39,
60, 63, 66, 69,
90, 93, 96, 99,
```

It is a good idea to compile and run the code for this problem; please note that the function `Print()` is discussed in section 14.13.

14.11.2 Slicing

Another kind of view is possible when we examine a subset of an n-dimensional data structure as a data structure of dimension n-1. In particular, we would like to iterate in the n-dimensional structure and use the data in the (n-1)-dimensional data structure at each time level.

We define the three-dimensional multi-array class and the list class that contains its two-dimensional views:

```
const int N = 3;
typedef boost::multi_array<double, N> Cube;
typedef list<Cube::array_view<N-1>::type> List;
```

We now introduce the function that creates a two-dimensional slice. We show the code for the first dimension only (the code for the other cases is similar):

```
List Slice(Cube& cube, int dim)
{
    // Get the size of the slicing dimension.
    Cube::index size=cube.shape()[dim];

    // Create the list.
    // If we use a vector, we can't use the constructor with
    // size because the view does not have a default constructor.
    List l;

    // Code depends on which dimension we want to slice.
    // The dimension for the slice is another datatype than the
    // range of the other dimensions.
    switch (dim)
    {
    case 0:
        // Iterate all the indexes of the slicing dimension, create
        // a new view (slice) and add it to the list.
        // The index range created with the default constructor
        // specificies the complete range.
        for (Cube::index i=0; i<size; i++)
        {
            Cube::index r1(i);
            Cube::index_range r2;
            Cube::index_range r3;
            l.push_back(cube[boost::indices[r1][r2][r3]]);
        }
        break;
```

```
    case 1:
        // Similar code

    case 2:
        // Similar code
    }

    // Return the created list.
    return l;
}
```

We now define the three-dimensional data structure:

```
// The dimensions (a 3-list of 2X2 matrices)
Cube::index dim1=3;
Cube::index dim2=2;
Cube::index dim3=2;

// Create a multi-array
Cube cube(boost::extents[dim1][dim2][dim3]);

// Fill the cube using the operator [int][int][int] syntax
for (Cube::index d1=0; d1<dim1; d1++)
{
    for (Cube::index d2=0; d2<dim2; d2++)
    {
        for (Cube::index d3=0; d3<dim3; d3++)
        {
            cube[d1][d2][d3]=d1 + d2*dim1 + d3*dim1*dim2;
        }
    }
}
```

Finally, the test program is (note that the for-loop is executed once):

```
// List for slicing.
list<Cube::array_view<2>::type> l;

// Slice it on all dimensions.
for (int i=0; i<1; i++) // NB Just 1 iteration
{
    cout<<"\n\nSlicing on dimension "<<i<<":\n\n";
    l=Slice(cube, i);
    int j=0;
    for (List::iterator it=l.begin(); it!=l.end(); it++)
    {
        cout<<"Dimension: "<<i<<", Slice: "<<j++<<":"<<endl;
        Print(*it);
    }
}
```

The output from this program is:

```
Number of dimensions: 3
Number of elements: 12
size_of(array): 80 bytes
Data size: 12*8=96 bytes
Dim 0 [0, 3) (size: 3) (stride: 4)
Dim 1 [0, 2) (size: 2) (stride: 2)
Dim 2 [0, 2) (size: 2) (stride: 1)
0, 1, 2,
3, 4, 5,
6, 7, 8,
9, 10, 11,
```

```
Slicing on dimension 0:

Dimension: 0, Slice: 0:
Number of dimensions: 2
Number of elements: 4
size_of(array): 36 bytes
Data size: 4*8=32 bytes
Dim 0 [0, 2) (size: 2) (stride: 2)
Dim 1 [0, 2) (size: 2) (stride: 1)
0, 3,
6, 9,

Dimension: 0, Slice: 1:
Number of dimensions: 2
Number of elements: 4
size_of(array): 36 bytes
Data size: 4*8=32 bytes
Dim 0 [0, 2) (size: 2) (stride: 2)
Dim 1 [0, 2) (size: 2) (stride: 1)
1, 4,
7, 10,

Dimension: 0, Slice: 2:
Number of dimensions: 2
Number of elements: 4
size_of(array): 36 bytes
Data size: 4*8=32 bytes
Dim 0 [0, 2) (size: 2) (stride: 2)
Dim 1 [0, 2) (size: 2) (stride: 1)
2, 5,
8, 11,
```

14.12 MultiArray Adapters

Boost.MultiArray contains two adapters for `multi_array`:

- `multi_array_ref`; this class adapts an existing array to provide the `multi_array` interface. It does not own the data passed to it.
- `const_multi_array_ref`; this is similar to `multi_array_ref` but in this case the contents of the array are immutable.

We take an example that wraps a C array into a `multi_array`. The test data has 24 elements:

```
// Create a native array
double myData[]={0, 1, 2, 3, 4, 5, 6, 7, 8, 9, 10, 11, 12,
                13, 14, 25, 16, 17, 18, 19, 20, 21, 22, 23};
```

We now wish to arrange this data in a three-dimensional multi-array with the following structure:

```
typedef boost::multi_array<double, 3> Cube;
typedef boost::multi_array_ref<double, 3> CubeRef;

// The dimensions
CubeRef::index dim1=3;
CubeRef::index dim2=4;
CubeRef::index dim3=2;

// Create a multi-array ref
CubeRef cube(myData, boost::extents[dim1][dim2][dim3]);
```

The instance cube is a wrapper for the original data `myData`; if we change the value of one of its elements then the data in the cube will also change:

```
// Change some elements of the C array. The cube also changes
mydata[0]=99;
```

You can convince yourself of this fact by printing the data in the cube.

14.13 Utility Print Functions

We have created a number of functions to print multi-arrays of arbitrary dimension. For arrays in one and two dimensions it is not difficult to write some simple functions to display their data on the console but in higher dimensions the situation is more complex because we then need to use recursion.

There are two functions; first, the function `Print()` that accepts a multi-array as input argument. It displays high-level information pertaining to the multi-array and then it calls the recursive function `PrintRecursive()` function to print the data in the lower-order sub-arrays of the multi-array.

The code for these two functions is given by:

```
template <typename T> void PrintRecursive(const T& ma,
    vector<typename T::index> indices, typename T::size_type dim)
{
    // Determine the size of the current dimension
    T::size_type size=ma.shape()[dim];

    // Determine the start- and end-index of the current dimension
    T::index start=ma.index_bases()[dim];
    T::index end=start+size;

    // Iterate all elements of the current dimension
    for (indices[dim]=start; indices[dim]<end; indices[dim]++)
    {
        // If dimension 0 print value, else recursively print dimension
        if (dim==0) cout<<ma(indices)<<", ";
        else PrintRecursive(ma, indices, dim-1);
    }

    // End of dimension
    cout<<endl;
}


template <typename T>
void Print(const T& ma)
{
    // Create the counters for each dimensions
    T::size_type dims=ma.num_dimensions();
    vector<T::index> indices(dims);

    // Print the dimension information & size
    cout<<"Number of dimensions: "<<dims<<endl;
    cout<<"Number of elements: "<<ma.num_elements()<<endl;
    cout<<"size_of(array): "<<sizeof(ma)<<" bytes"<<endl;
    cout<<"Data size: "<<ma.num_elements()<<"*"<<sizeof(T::element)
        <<"="<<sizeof(T::element)*ma.num_elements()<<" bytes"<<endl;
    for (T::size_type i=0; i<dims; i++)
    {
        cout<<"Dim "<<i<<" ["<<ma.index_bases()[i]<<",
        "<<ma.index_bases()[i]+ma.shape()[i]<<")";
```

```
         cout<<" (size: "<<ma.shape()[i]<<")";
         cout<<" (stride: "<<ma.strides()[i]<<")";
         cout<<endl;
    }

    // Print the multi-array passing the highest dimension number
    PrintRecursive(ma, indices, dims-1);
}
```

Finally, we note that multi-arrays can be serialised but a discussion of this topic is outside the scope of the current book.

14.14 MultiArrays in Combination with other Data Structures

The examples in this chapter were essentially multi-arrays of scalar data (in this case, `double`). However, many applications in statistics, finance and engineering involve more complex data structures. In general, we need to manipulate M-dimensional data in an N-dimensional space. Some specific examples are:

- Three-dimensional partial differential equation (PDE) on a discrete grid (N = 3, M = 6): in this case we define cube cell data; each data point is an array of size 6 and contains information relating to some physical process, for example fluid velocity, pressure, density and temperature at a point in three-dimensional space.
- Sampling experiments (N = 4, M = 7); for example, an automobile manufacturer wishes to determine the safety of its automobiles based on four control parameters (for example, the angle of the steering wheel and the amount of leg space). Each control parameter has 7 possible values.
- Latin Hypercube Sampling (general N and M): this is a statistical process that samples a function of N variables; the range of each variable is divided into M equally probable intervals.

The above examples are for motivational purposes. We choose N = M = 2 for convenience. We model the data structure as a multi-array of 2-tuples. First, we define some aliases for readability reasons:

```
// Some shorthand notation for easy reading
const int dim = 2;    // 2d matrix
typedef multi_array<tuple<double, double>, dim> TupleMatrix;
typedef boost::multi_array<TupleMatrix, dim>::index Index;
```

We now develop the code to create an instance of `TupleMatrix`:

```
int main()
{
    // Define structure of a matrix
    TupleMatrix matrix;

    // Define the extents of each separate dimension
    const int NX = 4;
    const int NY = 3;
    matrix.resize(extents[NX][NY]);

    // Define a 2d loop to initialise the data
    for (Index i = 0; i != NX; ++i)
    {
        for (Index j = 0; j != NY; ++j)
        {
            matrix[i][j] = make_tuple(2.17, 3.14);
        }
```

```
    }
    print(matrix, NX, NY, "tuple matrix");

    return 0;
}
```

We show the body of the print function for this special matrix:

```
void print(const TupleMatrix& matrix, int NX, int NY,
           const std::string& annotation)
{
    cout << endl << "Start of matrix, " << annotation << endl;
    cout << "\nSize: " << matrix.size() << ", elements: "
         << matrix.num_elements() << ", dimensions: "
         << matrix.num_dimensions() << endl;

    // Start indices of matrix in each dimension
    const Index idx0 = matrix.index_bases()[0];
    const Index idx1 = matrix.index_bases()[1];

    for (Index i = idx0; i != NX; ++i)
    {
        cout << endl;
        for (Index j = idx1; j != NY; ++j)
        {
            cout << "*[" << matrix[i][j].get<0>() << ","
                 << matrix[i][j].get<1>() << "]*";
        }
    }

    cout << endl << "End of matrix" << endl;
}
```

This example is representative in the sense that it can be generalised to other complex datastructures. Please see exercise 8 in Appendix C.

14.15 Summary and Conclusions

We have given an introduction to Boost.MultiArray that offers a class template for multi-dimensional arrays. In the past these structures were created using nested containers from the C++ Standard Library (for example) but this approach can lead to code that is difficult to maintain. We now have a library at our disposal that we can use in many applications in engineering, finance and science.
The data in a multi-array can be numeric or non-numeric, simple or composite. A multi-array is a data container for dense multi-dimensional arrays and it does not provide functionality for array manipulation. This is in contrast to the Boost.uBLAS library that can be used in Numerical Linear Algebra applications. We use MultiArray to solve n-factor partial differential equations using the Finite Difference Method.

When creating applications using MultiArray we see that its functionality may need to be extended. We may wish to support a range of data types (for example, tuples and variants) and we may also wish to add new functionality to classes that use the library. We can achieve this end by a combination of member functions, global functions and by using the *Visitor* pattern or using the functionality that is already in Boost as we saw in section 8.5 when we discussed typesafe visitation of variants. In Volume II we use MultiArray in a number of applications.

15 Random Number Generation

15.1 Introduction and Objectives

In this chapter we introduce the Boost.Random library that contains functionality in the form of generators to produce random numbers and random number distributions. Truly random numbers do not exist in software and we then must use *pseudo-random number generators* that produce numbers that look random. These generators are in general linear or nonlinear one-step iterative methods that produce numbers based on a given initial value, or *seed*. The challenge lies in choosing a generator with a long period, which is the number of iterations before the generated numbers start repeating themselves.

We use the following headerfile:

```
#include <boost/random.hpp> // Convenience header file
```

The focus in this chapter is to discuss which random number generators are available in the library and how to use them. We give some examples. A discussion of applications where random number generators are used is outside the scope of this book.
We assume that the reader has some knowledge of random number generation. Applications to computational finance are discussed in Duffy 2009.

15.2 Overview of Random Number Generation

In this section we give some background information on random number generation. We distinguish between two categories of random numbers; first, *pseudo-random number* are those numbers that are produced by software algorithms, usually some kind of linear or nonlinear one-step or multi-step iterative scheme. These are sometimes called deterministic random number generators. The second category is the set of *non-deterministic random number generators* and the corresponding numbers are generated by some truly random generator such as a Zener diode, nuclear decay process or inter-arrival times of computer network packages, for example. We focus in this chapter on pseudo-random number generators (RNGs).

We first examine RNGs that are implemented by specialisations of the *linear congruential generator* (LCG):

$$X_{n+1} = (aX_n + c) \bmod m, \quad n \geq 0$$

m : modulus, $m > 0$

a : multiplier, $0 \leq a < m$

c : increment, $0 \leq c < m$

X_0 : seed, $0 \leq X_0 \leq m$.

We see that this algorithm generates numbers based on a one-step iterative method having an initial seed value. It uses modulo arithmetic (we recall from Chapter 9, section 5 that $a = b \pmod{m}$ if and only if $a - b$ is a multiple of m). The generated numbers start repeating themselves after a certain number of cycles (called the *period*). Boost has support for LCGs in the form of the following low-level class:

```
template <class IntType, IntType m>
class const_mod
{
public:
    static IntType add(IntType x, IntType c);
    static IntType mult(IntType a, IntType x);
    static IntType mult_add(IntType a, IntType x, IntType c);
    static IntType invert(IntType x);

    // etc.
};
```

In other words, this class allows us to use LCGs in code. This level of detail is probably not needed in general. Continuing, we give a short overview of common generators:

- Mersenne Twister.
- Linear congruential (LCG).
- Lagged Fibonacci.
- Inverse congruential.
- Additive combine.
- Shuffle output.

The Mersenne Twister (MT) algorithm is a pseudorandom generator based on a matrix linear recurrence relation. Its period is a so-called Mersenne prime ($M_p = 2^p - 1$, p prime) and this is a long period. MT is popular and it passes tests for statistical randomness.
We have already discussed LCG and in this case the period is at most m. A special example is the C language `rand()` function. A relatively new class of generators that improve LCGs are based on generalised Fibonacci sequences:

$$X_n = X_{n-p} + X_{n-q} \pmod{m} \ (p > q > 0)$$

$$m = 2^k, \text{ some } k > 0.$$

The main advantages in this case are that the period is very long and that the algorithm is efficient. A disadvantage is that it is sensitive to the choice of the initial seeds (we need p seeds).
The Inverse Congruential generator is nonlinear and it uses the inverse of the previous value to calculate the next value:

$$X_{n+1} = aX_n^{-1} + c \pmod{m}, \quad 0 < X_n < m.$$

A special case of such a generator in Boost is the class `hellekalek1995`. The Additive Combine generator is a combination of two LCGs. An example is the class `ecuyier1988`. Finally, the Shuffle Output generator mixes the output of some linear congruential uniform generator to produce better statistical properties. An example in Boost is the class `kreutzer1986`.

15.3 Random Number Generators in Boost

There are six main C++ template classes that implement random number generators. Each class has several template parameters that the user can instantiate; for example, in the case of the linear congruential generator (LCG) these parameters are defined as follows:

```
template <class IntType, IntType a, IntType c, IntType m, IntType val>
class linear_congruential
```

```
{
    // ...
};
```

In practice, the user does not have to worry about the initialisation of these parameters as they have been determined and optimised. For example, two common specialisations of LCG are:

```
typedef random::linear_congruential<int32_t, 16807, 0, 2147483647,
                              1043618065> minstd_rand0;
typedef random::linear_congruential<int32_t, 48271, 0, 2147483647,
                              399268537> minstd_rand;
```

Similarly, the Mersenne Twister and Lagged Fibonacci generators have declarations and synonyms:

```
template <class UIntType, int w, int n, int m, int r, UIntType a, int u,
    int s, UIntType b, int t, UIntType c, int l, UIntType val>
class mersenne_twister
{
    // ...
};

typedef random::mersenne_twister<uint32_t, 32, 351, 175, 19, 0xccab8ee7,
    11, 7, 0x31b6ab00, 15, 0xffe50000, 17, 0xa37d3c92> mt11213b;

typedef random::mersenne_twister<uint32_t, 32, 624, 397, 31, 0x9908b0df,
    11, 7, 0x9d2c5680, 15, 0xefc60000, 18, 3346425566U> mt19937;


template <class UIntType, int w, unsigned int p, unsigned int q,
          UIntType val = 0>
class lagged_fibonacci
{
    // ...
};

typedef random::lagged_fibonacci_01<double, 48, 607, 273>
    lagged_fibonacci607;
typedef random::lagged_fibonacci_01<double, 48, 1279, 418>
    lagged_fibonacci1279;
// ...
typedef random::lagged_fibonacci_01<double, 48, 44497, 21034>
    lagged_fibonacci44497;
```

In general, it is probably best to use these specialised classes in applications unless you have reasons for not doing so, for example when you have special requirements concerning the efficiency or reliability of your generator. It is your responsability to check that the generators satisfy your requirements. Other classes are:

```
template <class MLCG1, class MLCG2,typename MLCG1::result_type val>
class additive_combine
{
    // ...
};

typedef random::additive_combine<
    random::linear_congruential<int32_t, 40014, 0, 2147483563, 0>,
    random::linear_congruential<int32_t, 40692, 0, 2147483399, 0>,
    2060321752> ecuyer1988;
```

```
template <class IntType, IntType a, IntType b, IntType p, IntType val>
class inversive_congruential
{
    // ...
};

typedef random::inversive_congruential<int32_t, 9102, 2147483647-36884165,
    2147483647, 0> hellekalek1995;


template <class UniformRandomNumberGenerator, int k,
    typename UniformRandomNumberGenerator::result_type val = 0>
class shuffle_output
{
    // ...
};

typedef random::shuffle_output<
    random::linear_congruential<uint32_t, 1366, 150889, 714025, 0>,
    97, 139726> kreutzer1986;
```

Some examples of using these classes follow in which we define default objects:

```
boost::mt19937 rng;
boost::lagged_fibonacci607 rngB;
boost::minstd_rand0 rngC;
boost::rand48 rngD;
boost::ecuyer1988 rngE;
boost::kreutzer1986 rngF;
boost::hellekalek1995 rngG;
```

We now discuss how to initialise the seed. We can achieve this goal, either by a constructor taking a seed value as argument or by calling a modifier function to set the seed after the object has been default constructed, for example:

```
// Using seeds with random number generators
boost::mt19937 rng1;
rng1.seed(static_cast<boost::uint32_t>(std::time(0)));

boost::mt19937 rng2;
rng2.seed();

boost::mt19937 rng3(static_cast<boost::uint32_t>(std::time(0)));
```

The last issue to discuss is the actual generation of random numbers. Each random number class is a function object and thus it overloads the function call operator (). A random number will be generated as follows:

```
cout << rng3() << endl;
```

We can generate a sequence of random numbers by consecutive operator calls:

```
for (int n = 1; n <= 10; ++n)
{
    cout << rng2() << ", ";
}
```

We have now completed the discussion of random number generators in Boost. We compare their relative qualities (for example, efficiency and accuracy) in section 5.

15.4 variate_generator

This template class joins a random number generator with a random number distribution.
Now we wish to generate variates from the following distributions:
- Uniform (integer and double versions).
- Triangle.
- Bernoulli.
- Cauchy.
- Exponential.
- Geometric.
- Normal (Gaussian).
- Uniform distribution on a sphere.

This is useful functionality to have in a library because many applications need to generate
random variates from the above distributions. In particular, generating normal and
exponential variates have applications in computational finance, queuing theory and
network systems, to name just a few.
The class interface for variate_generator is given by:

```
template <class Engine, class Distribution>
class variate_generator
{
private:
    // ...

public:
    typedef typename decorated_engine::base_type engine_value_type;
    typedef Engine engine_type;
    typedef Distribution distribution_type;
    typedef typename Distribution::result_type result_type;

    // Constructor with RN class and desired distribution
    variate_generator(Engine e, Distribution d);

    result_type operator () ();

    template <class T> result_type operator () (T value);

    // Set and get functions for RN engine and distribution
    engine_value_type& engine();
    const engine_value_type& engine() const;

    distribution_type& distribution();
    const distribution_type& distribution() const;

    // ...
};
```

We see that the constructor accepts a random number generator e and distribution d. The
class variate_generator is a function object and calling the operator () will produce a
variate from the given distribution. Thus, in order to use this class we first need to create
instances of the random number engine, the distribution from which we wish to generate the
variate and of the variate_generator. We take a first example of generating standard
normal variates using a Fibonacci random number generator (that is, mean is 0 and standard
deviation is 1):

```
// Generating normal deviates
// RN engine
```

```
boost::lagged_fibonacci607 rng;
rng.seed(static_cast<boost::uint32_t>(std::time(0)));

// Normal distribution
boost::normal_distribution<> myDist(0,1);

// Make the 'link'
boost::variate_generator<
    boost::lagged_fibonacci607&, boost::normal_distribution<> >
    norRng(rng, myDist);

cout << "Normal variate: " << norRng() << endl;
```

We take another example. In this case we generate variates from a triangle distribution (which has applications in project planning applications). The triangle distribution needs three parameters in its constructor. Using the same random number engine rng as above we now produce the desired variate:

```
// Triangular distribution
boost::triangle_distribution<> myTriangular(0.0, 0.75, 1.0);

boost::variate_generator<boost::lagged_fibonacci607&,
    boost::triangle_distribution<> >
    triRng(rng, myTriangular);

cout << "Triangular variate: " << triRng() << endl;
```

The code for generating other distributions is similar to that just given.

15.5 Performance, Reliability, Suitability and Accuracy Requirements

We have presented a number of template classes for random number generation. The question is to decide which one is best (in some sense) in a given application. In general, the quality of a random number generator depends on the algorithm and its parameters. When creating generators we need to initialise the internal state (which may be substantial) and we also need to set the seed to a given value. Defining good seeds can be difficult and a popular tactic is to define the seed at the highest resolution possible, for example in terms of a *system clock*:

```
rng.seed(static_cast<boost::uint32_t>(std::time(0)));
```

The danger with this approach is that consecutive seeds can become close, especially on machines with a low clock resolution. In fact, the distance could be zero, thus destroying any semblance of randomness. All pseudo-random number generator instances can be copy constructed and assigned. The copied objects will generate identical random numbers as the object that they were copied from! Finally, many Random Number Generators are not thread-safe.

We determine the quality of a random number by examining the following non-exhaustive set of properties:
a) The *cycle length (period)*: number of iterations in the algorithm after which the generated numbers start repeating themselves. The larger the period the more reliable and accurate the algorithm will be.
b) Memory requirements: how many bytes does the random number generator have in its state?
c) Relative speed of execution.

We give some examples of these properties in Figure 15.1 for three generators. Further results can be found on the Boost site. The Mersenne Twister (especially `mt19937`) is a popular generator.

Generator	Cycle Length	Memory Requirements	Relative Speed
Rand 48	$2^{48} - 1$	Size of (uint64_t)	80
Mt 19937	$2^{19937} - 1$	625 * size of (uint32_t)	100
Lagged-Fibonacci607	2^{32000}	607 * size of (double)	150

Figure 15.1 Comparing random number generators

Summarising, it is advisable to test these random number generators in your applications to determine which one (or combination of generators) is most suitable.

15.6 Examples using Random Number Generators

In this section we give a number of simple examples to show how to use random number generators.

15.6.1 Calculating π: RNG 101

Consider the square and quarter-circle in Figure 15.2. We know their areas, namely r^2 and $\frac{1}{4}\pi r^2$, respectively. By dividing one area by the other, we see that we can estimate π. Now, we imagine throwing many darts at the areas in Figure 15.2. We count the number of times a dart falls in the quarter circle compared with the total number of darts thrown (we assume that all darts fall somewhere in the square). The quotient of these two numbers will be an estimate for $\frac{1}{4}\pi$. To this end, we create a loop, generate two standard uniform variates that will represent the x and y coordinates of the position when the dart has fallen. We then determine if the darts have fallen in the quarter circle or not.

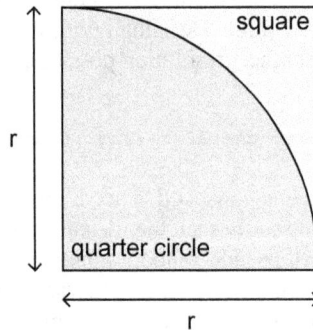

Figure 15.2 Calculating π

The code is as follows:

```
// Choose RNG and Uniform (0,1) distribution
boost::uniform_real<> uni(0.0, 1.0);
boost::hellekalek1995 rngG;
rngG.seed(static_cast<boost::uint32_t>(std::time(0)));

boost::variate_generator<boost::hellekalek1995&, boost::uniform_real<> >
    uniRngG(rngG, uni);
cout << "How many darts to throw? "; long N; cin >> N;
```

```
// Start throwing darts and count where they land
long hits = 0;
double x, y, distance;
for (long n = 1; n <= N; ++n)
{
    x = uniRngG(); y = uniRngG();
    distance = sqrt(x*x + y*y);

    if (distance <=1)
    {                       // dart has fallen within the quater circle
        hits++;
    }
}

// Produce the answer
cout << "PI is: " << hits << ", " << 4.0 * double(hits) / double (N);
```

You can use this case as the basis for testing and comparing random number generators; what is the performance and how much effort (that is, the number of draws N) is needed in order to achieve a desired accuracy?

Instead of using uniform numbers in the above code we could use the other distributions that we discussed in section 4.

15.6.2 Finding Real Roots of a Quadratic Equation

An interesting problem is to calculate the probability that the quadratic polynomial

$$ax^2 + bx + c = 0 \tag{15.1}$$

has two real roots. We know that the roots (which may be complex) are given by:

$$x_\pm = \frac{-b \pm \sqrt{b^2 - 4ac}}{2a}. \tag{15.2}$$

Much research has been done on this subject and its generalisations (see Edelman and Kostlan 1995) but our main interest in this section is to reproduce known mathematical results by using the above dart-board analogy.

The initial statement of the problem is as follows: Compute the probability that the equation (15.1) has real roots when the parameters a, b and c are standard normal variates. It has been shown that this probability value is approximately 0.6485277 and we wish to reproduce this number:

```
boost::normal_distribution<> nor(0,1);
boost::lagged_fibonacci607 rng;
rng.seed(static_cast<boost::uint32_t>(std::time(0)));

// Produce Normal (0, 1)
boost::variate_generator<boost::lagged_fibonacci607&,
                         boost::normal_distribution<> > norRng(rng, nor);

cout << "How many darts to throw? "; long N; cin >> N;

double a, b, c, factor;
long hits = 0;

// The dart board
for (long n = 1; n <= N; ++n)
{
```

```
    // Generate 3 N(0,1) variates
    a = norRng(); b = norRng(); c = norRng();
    factor = b*b - 4.0*a*c;

    if (factor >= 0.0)
    {
        hits++;
    }
}
```

We have run this code for various values of N; for N = 1 million, the probability is p = 0.648091, for N = 10 million, p = 0.648394 and for N = 100 million, p = 0.648501. We see that convergence is very slow.

15.6.3 Kernel Density Estimation

The last application is called *kernel density estimation* (also known as the *Parzen method*) and it is concerned with the computation of the probability density function of a random variable given some data about a sample of the population. A *histogram* is a collection of point samples from a kernel density estimate in which the kernel is a uniform box having the width of the histogram bin. We now introduce the Parzen method by examining the Gaussian kernel function. First, let $x_1, \ldots, x_n$ be a sequence of independent and identically distributed normal random variables. Then the *kernel density* approximation of its probability function is given by:

$$\hat{f}_h(x) = \frac{1}{nh} \sum_{i=1}^{n} K\left(\frac{x - x_i}{h}\right)$$

where h is a smoothing parameter called the *bandwidth* and K is called the *kernel* defined by:

$$K\left(\frac{x - x_i}{h}\right) = \frac{1}{\sqrt{2\pi}} e^{-\frac{(x-x_i)^2}{2h^2}}.$$

It is possible to define a variable-sized bandwidth and in this case the kernel density function becomes:

$$\hat{f}(x) = \frac{1}{n} \sum_{j=1}^{n} \frac{1}{h_j} K\left(\frac{x - x_j}{h_j}\right).$$

Instead of grouping observations in a bin – as histograms do – the kernel density estimator places small bumps at each observation. The estimator then consists of a series of bumps and the result is smoother than that produced by a histogram. The bandwidth is a free parameter and it influences the resulting estimate. It is possible to compute the optimal bandwidth but a discussion of how this is done is outside the scope of this chapter.

We now discuss the code. First, we generate a normal random variable sample:

```
// Set up normal generator
boost::normal_distribution<> nor(0.0,1.0);
boost::lagged_fibonacci607 rng;

boost::variate_generator<boost::lagged_fibonacci607&,
                 boost::normal_distribution<> > Rng(rng, nor);
// Generate n normal variates x1, x2,..., xn
```

```
const long N = 2000;
Vector<double> normalRN(N);
for (int n = normalRN.MinIndex(); n <= normalRN.MaxIndex() ; ++n)
{
   normalRN[n] =  Rng();
}
```

Next, define the kernel smoother and Gaussian kernel formulae:

```
template <typename T>
T KernelSmoother(const boost::function<T (T)>& kernel,
                 const Vector<T>& xarr, double x, double h)
{ // The sum of the terms of the kernel density function calculate
  // the value at x.

   double hinverse = 1.0/h;

   T result = kernel(hinverse * (x - xarr[xarr.MinIndex()]));

   for (long j = xarr.MinIndex() + 1; j <= xarr.MaxIndex(); ++j)
   {
       result += kernel(hinverse*(x - xarr[j]));
   }

   double factor = hinverse/xarr.MaxIndex();

   return result * factor;
}

double GaussianKernel(double x)
{ // N(0,1) variable

   const double a = 1.0 / sqrt(2.0 * 3.1415);
   return a * exp(-0.5 * x * x);
}
```

Finally, we wish plot the density function in Excel, for example:

```
long M = 60;                            // Number of mesh points in x direction
double Lower = -3.0;
double Upper = 3.0;
double h = (Upper - Lower) / M;
double increment = h;

// Now the curve/histogram/kernel density function
Vector<double, long> outputDisplay(M, 1);
Vector<double,long> xarr(outputDisplay.Size(), 1);
xarr[xarr.MinIndex()] = Lower;
xarr[xarr.MaxIndex()] = Upper;
for (long n = xarr.MinIndex()+1; n <= xarr.MaxIndex()-1; ++n)
{
   xarr[n] = xarr[n-1] + increment;
}

for (int n = outputDisplay.MinIndex(); n <= outputDisplay.MaxIndex(); ++n)
{
   outputDisplay[n] = KernelSmoother<double>
                         (GaussianKernel, normalRN, xarr[n], h);
// outputDisplay[n] = KernelSmoother<double>
//                       (QuadraticKernel, normalRN, xarr[n], h);
// outputDisplay[n] = KernelSmoother<double>
//                        (TriangularKernel, normalRN, xarr[n], h);
}
try
```

```
{
   cout << xarr.Size() << ", " << outputDisplay.Size() << endl;
   printOneExcel(xarr, outputDisplay,
                 string("Gaussian Kernel Smoother"), string(""),
                 string(""), string("Value"));

}
catch(DatasimException& e)
{
   e.print();
}
```

where the function `printOneExcel()` displays array values in the Excel spreadsheet program. The code is provided with this book. Please read the documentation on installing the software. You will need Excel running on your system.

The output from this code is shown in Figure 15.3. Other distributions that can be used are:

```
double TriangularKernel(double x)
{
   if (fabs(x) > 1.0) return 0.0;
   else return 1.0 - fabs(x);
}

double QuadraticKernel(double x)
{
   if (fabs(x) > 1.0) return 0.0;
   else return 3.0 * 0.25 * (1.0 - x*x);
}
```

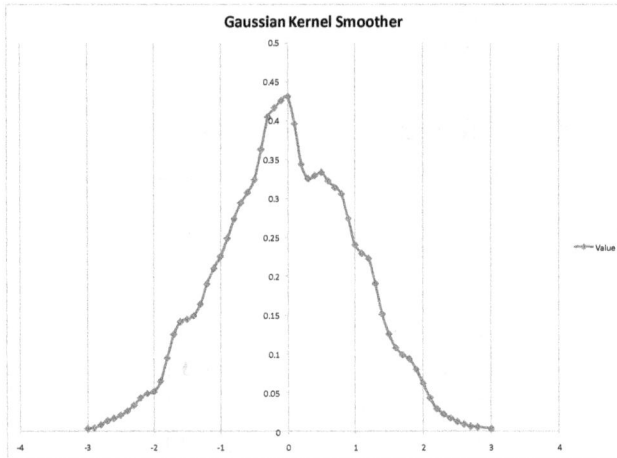

Figure 15.3 Excel output of the 'Gaussian Kernel Smoother'

15.7 Conclusions and Summary

This chapter described the Boost.Random library that provides a number of methods for calculating deterministic random numbers. Popular generators are Mersenne Twister and Lagged Fibonacci. Of particular importance is the template class `variate_generator` that joins a random number generator with a random number distribution.
We gave some simple examples on how to use the library. There are many applications for Boost.Random in finance, simulation and engineering.

16 Flyweight and Functional/Hash

16.1 Introduction and Objectives

In this chapter we introduce Boost.Flyweight that supports the efficient sharing of a large number of fine-grained objects and objects of moderate size. A *flyweight* is an object that can be simultaneously used in multiple contexts and applications. In general, a flyweight may not make assumptions concerning the context in which it operates and we then distinguish between its *intrinsic state* that is stored in the flyweight itself (and is independent of its context) and its *extrinsic state* which does depend on the flyweight's context. Extrinsic state is mutable and cannot be shared. Intrinsic state is immutable and is stored in a central repository.

The central repository that contains all shared objects is called the *flyweight factory*. Its responsibilities are:
- Locate and return a reference to an object with a given value.
- Insert a value into the repository if a copy was not previously stored.

Boost.Flyweight manages the interaction of flyweights and their factory in such a way that the programmer does not need to be aware that this relationship exists. The library uses a default factory based on a hashed container but it is also possible to employ a factory that uses a set as the internal data structure. Finally, we can to create user-defined internal data structures.

This library is close in spirit to the GOF *Flyweight* pattern (see GOF 1995) that addresses the following issues:
- Applications that use a large number of objects.
- Storage costs are high due to the large number of objects.
- We can replace groups of objects by a smaller number of shared objects when the extrinsic state has been removed.

Flyweights may incur run-time costs due to finding and computing state but these costs are offset by space savings that depend on:
- The reduction in the total number of shared instances.
- The amount of intrinsic state per object.
- Whether extrinsic state is stored or computed.

There are many applications where the *Flyweight* pattern can be used.

We use the following include file in code:

```
#include <boost/flyweight.hpp>
```

16.2 The 'Hello World' Example

In order to show how to create flyweight objects and test Boost.Flyweight functionality we design a small experiment as shown in Figure 16.1. On the right-hand side we visualise the flyweight factory that contains two immutable strings whose contents are 'Hello' and 'World'. On the left-hand side of Figure 16.1 we create strings called str1, str2, str3 and str4 whose values are shown by the arrows to the constant strings in the factory. But instead of four strings in memory we would like to have two! How do we achieve this? The answer is that we create strings `str1` to `str4` as flyweights.

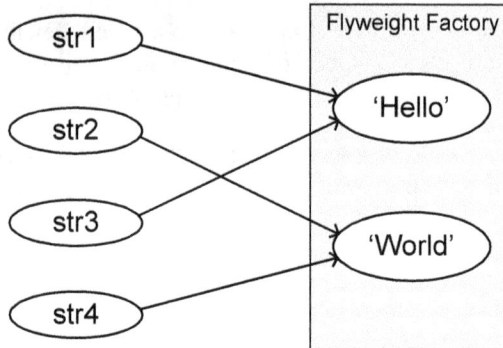

Figure 16.1 Objects and Flyweight

We define a class `MyString` that is derived from `std::string` and consequently inherits functionality that is needed in order for the flyweight to work (more on this later). We see that `MyString` has a `static` counter that is incremented each time a new instance is created:

```cpp
class MyString: public std::string
{
private:
    static int s_counter;

public:

    // Get the counter value
    static int Counter()
    {
        return s_counter;
    }

    // Default constructor
    MyString(): std::string()
    {
        s_counter++;
    }

    // Constructor with string
    MyString(const std::string& str): std::string(str)
    {
        s_counter++;
    }

    // Destructor
    ~MyString()
    {
        s_counter--;
    }

    // ...
};
```

We create the four strings that we depicted in Figure 16.1. When we run the code we shall see that only two instances of `MyString` are created because the string data is shared:

```
// Simple flyweight test with shared MyStrings. For strings created
// with 2 different strings.
cout<<"Direct boost::flyweight<MyString> test."<<endl;
boost::flyweights::flyweight<MyString> str1("Hello");
boost::flyweights::flyweight<MyString> str2("World");
boost::flyweights::flyweight<MyString> str3("Hello");
boost::flyweights::flyweight<MyString> str4("World");
cout<<"Number of strings in memory: "<<MyString::Counter()<<endl;
```

We discuss why Flyweight works the way it does. In particular, we specify the requirements on the template parameter T in order for `flyweight<T>` to be instantiable.

16.3 Flyweight Requirements

In order to interoperate with Boost.Flyweight, user-defined classes must first be *Assignable* and *Equality Comparable*. In particular, classes must implement the function `hash_value()` that computes a hash value based on their member data.

As an example, consider a class that models colours in computer graphics applications. The class models RGB (red, green, blue) colours having a transparency (alpha) value. The class interface has code for constructors, set and get functions as well as the functions that Boost.Flyweight requires. The essential interface is:

```
class Color
{
private:
    // Red, green, blue, alpha values of the color
    double m_red;
    double m_green;
    double m_blue;
    double m_alpha;

    // Static counter to see how many color objects there are
    static int s_counter;

public:

    // ...

    // Copy constructor
    Color(const Color& source)
    {
        // Copy color components
        m_red=source.m_red;
        m_green=source.m_green;
        m_blue=source.m_blue;
        m_alpha=source.m_alpha;

        // Increase counter
        s_counter++;
    }

    // Assignment operator
    Color& operator = (const Color& source)
    {
        // Copy color components
        m_red=source.m_red;
        m_green=source.m_green;
        m_blue=source.m_blue;
        m_alpha=source.m_alpha;

        return *this;
    }
```

```
    // Equal compare operator
    bool operator == (const Color& c) const
    {
        return (m_red==c.m_red && m_green==c.m_green &&
                m_blue==c.m_blue && m_alpha==c.m_alpha);
    }

    // Create a hash value for the color
    // This function is needed by the flyweight library
    friend std::size_t hash_value(const Color& color)
    {
        std::size_t seed=0;

        // Create a hash function for doubles
        boost::hash<double> hasher;

        // Hash the color components and combine them
        boost::hash_combine(seed, hasher(color.m_red));
        boost::hash_combine(seed, hasher(color.m_green));
        boost::hash_combine(seed, hasher(color.m_blue));
        boost::hash_combine(seed, hasher(color.m_alpha));

        // Return the hash value
        return seed;
    }
};
```

Regarding hash_value(), we see that it creates a hash value for a colour by combining the hash values of its parts.

Having defined the Color class we now show how it can be used in an application and how its instances can be shared. In general, we create a class hierarchy of shapes; each shape has a *fill colour* and *stroke colour* that we model as flyweights:

```
class Shape
{
private:
    // The fill and stroke colors as flyweight
    // Colors will be shared
    boost::flyweights::flyweight<Color> m_fillColor;
    boost::flyweights::flyweight<Color> m_strokeColor;

public:
    // ...

    // Set the fill color
    void FillColor(const Color& c)
    {
        m_fillColor=c;
    }

    // Set the stroke color
    void StrokeColor(const Color& c)
    {
        m_strokeColor=c;
    }
};
```

We can now create shapes, each one having its own colour. When two colours have the same value we see that they refer to the same object (colour counter has the value 1). When we set these colours to another identical colour we then see that the colour counter has the value 2:

```
// Create shapes and print the colors created. Each shape has two
// colors but they are shared. So all should print 1
cout<<endl<<"Indirect test. Shape contains flyweight<Color>."<<endl;
Shape s1;
cout<<"One shape created. Colors created: "<<Color::Counter()<<endl;
Shape s2;
cout<<"Two shapes created. Colors created: "<<Color::Counter()<<endl;

// Set two colors to another (identical) color and print the number
// of colors. Both should print 2.
s1.FillColor(Color(0.5, 1.0, 0.0));
cout<<"One color changed to "<<s1.FillColor()
    <<". Colors created: "<<Color::Counter()<<endl;
s2.StrokeColor(Color(0.5, 1.0, 0.0));
cout<<"Other color changed to "<<s2.StrokeColor()
    <<". Colors created: "<<Color::Counter()<<endl;
```

Another example is when modelling three-dimensional shapes such as cubes, spheres and cylinders. In this case we may wish to model their material properties in virtual reality applications, for example:

```
struct Material
{
    // Colors in range [0,1]
    Color diffusiveColor;
    Color emissiveColor;
    double transparency;        // [0,1]
    double ambientIntensity;    // [0,1]
    Color specularColor;        // [0,1]
    double shininess;           // [0,1]

    // Create hash value and other functions
    // that Boost.Flyweight requires
};
```

Then we could use this class in a class hierarchy similar to a two-dimensional shape hierarchy.

Summarising, what happens when a flyweight is created? The steps are:
1. The object is created using the same constructor as the flyweight constructor.
2. The hash value of the object is extracted.
3. The hash value is looked up in the flyweight's internal datastructure.
4. If the hash value has been found then the newly created object will be destroyed and the object from the internal data structure will be returned.
5. If the hash value has not been found then the newly created object will be added to the internal datastructure and returned.

One consequence is that a temporary object is created and destroyed (steps 1 and 4) and for large objects this will be a costly process. In order to avoid this possible bottleneck we need a different factory.

16.4 Key-Value Flyweights

This special factory has the form `flyweight<key_value<K,T> >` where K is the key type and T is the value type. The type K is for internal lookup of the associated values of type T. It is important to note that keys are not stored with the values and thus the key is external to the value. The consequence is that there is no need to define `hash_value()` in value

classes (the type T) whose instances are flyweights. However, we must define
hash_value() for all specialisations of the key type K.

In order to use the key-value prototype, we include the file:

```
#include <boost/flyweight/key_value.hpp>
```

The reason for using a key-value flyweight is to avoid creating a large temporary object
which we will in all probability throw away anyway. Instead, the key is used as a *gateway* to
the real object (and this object can be expensive to create). We create an object
corresponding to a key only when it does not yet exist. In this sense we see the key-value
flyweight as being similar in intent to a *Virtual Proxy* pattern (see GOF 1995).

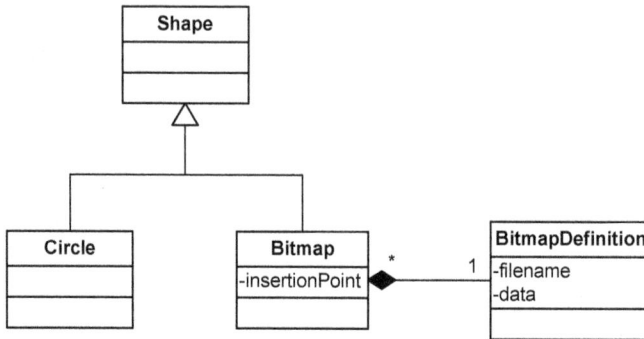

Figure 16.2 Using Key-Value Flyweight

We now give an example that simulates the creation of bitmaps in computer graphics
applications. The problem is shown in Figure 16.2 where we define a Bitmap class that
delegates to a key-value flyweight that we call BitmapDefinition. The class Bitmap
contains an insertion point and a reference to a bitmap definition. The bitmap definition is
stored as a flyweight so that multiple bitmaps referring to the same bitmap definition can
share it:

```
class Bitmap: public Shape
{
private:
    Point m_insertionPoint;     // Extrinsic state
    BitmapFlyweight m_bitmap;   // typedef: key-value flyweight, see later

public:

    // ...
};

class BitmapDefinition
{
private:
    // The filename and bitmap data (dummy at the moment)
    std::string m_filename;
    char* m_data;

    // Static counter to see how many color objects there are
    static int s_counter;

public:
```

```
   // ...
};
```

and the shorthand notation for the key-value flyweight is:

```
typedef boost::flyweights::flyweight<
   boost::flyweights::key_value<std::string, BitmapDefinition,
      BitmapDefinition::KeyExtractor> > BitmapFlyweight;
```

The class KeyExtractor is a friend of BitmapDefinition and is needed when a key-value flyweight is constructed or assigned from the value type. It is also used when a flyweight is looked up in the internal data structure. This class extracts the key value from the existing value type object:

```
class KeyExtractor
{// Key extractor class used by key-value flyweights.

public:
   const std::string& operator () (const BitmapDefinition& bd)
   {
      return bd.m_filename;
   }
};
```

An example of use is:

```
int main()
{
   cout<<"Create bitmap 1 (default constructor)"<<endl;
   Bitmap bitmap1;
   cout<<"Create bitmap 2 (default constructor)"<<endl;
   Bitmap bitmap2;
   cout<<"Create bitmap 3 (constructor with filename)"<<endl;
   Bitmap bitmap3(Point(99, 99), "c:\\test.bmp");
   cout<<"Create bitmap 4 (constructor with filename)"<<endl;
   Bitmap bitmap4(Point(10, 20), "c:\\test.bmp");
   cout<<"Create bitmap 5 (copy constructor bitmap1)"<<endl;
   Bitmap bitmap5(bitmap1);
   cout<<"Create bitmap 6 (copy constructor bitmap3)"<<endl;
   Bitmap bitmap6(bitmap3);

   cout<<"Bitmap definitions: "<<BitmapDefinition::Counter()<<endl;

   // Only possible when a key extractor is defined
   cout<<endl<<"Create flyweight from value type. ";
   cout<<"Here the bitmap definition is created and destroyed."<<endl;
   BitmapFlyweight bf(BitmapDefinition("c:\\test.bmp"));
   cout<<"Bitmap flyweight: "<<bf<<endl;
   cout<<"Bitmap definitions: "<<BitmapDefinition::Counter()<<endl;
}
```

We note that this flyweight saves memory consumption.

16.5 Flyweight Factory Specification

Boost.Flyweight supports a number of factories that implement the internal data structure to store objects:
- hashed_factory: this is the default factory based on a hashed container.
- set_factory: uses a STL set-like ordered container to implement the flyweight factory.

- `assoc_container_factory`: this can be seen as a generalisation of `hash_factory` and `set_factory` and in this case the user supplies the exact type of container on which the factory is based.

Set-based lookup and insertion of values are generally slower than those based on hashing, but hashing can be affected by pathological worst-case scenarios which can lead to poor performance.

We give some simple examples of the first two factories. First, we need to include two header files:

```
#include <boost/flyweight/hashed_factory.hpp>
#include <boost/flyweight/set_factory.hpp>
```

We now define the class for testing these factories. Please note that `hash_value` function is needed when using the `hashed_factory` and the `operator <` is needed when using the `set_factory`:

```
struct Data
{
   int i; int j;

   Data() { i = j = 0; }
   Data(int I, int J) { i = I; j = J; }

   Data& operator = (const Data& d)
   {
      // Copy Data components
      i = d.i;
      j = d.j;

      return *this;
   }

   bool operator == (const Data& d) const
   {
      return (i==d.i && j==d.j);
   }

   // Create a hash value for Data; needed by the flyweight library
   friend std::size_t hash_value(const Data& d)
   {
      std::size_t seed=0;

      // Create a hash function for doubles
      boost::hash<double> hasher;

      // Hash the components and combine them
      boost::hash_combine(seed, hasher(d.i));
      boost::hash_combine(seed, hasher(d.j));

      // Return the hash value
      return seed;
   }

   // Smaller than operator. Needed when used in flyweight that uses a
   // set as internal data structure
   bool operator < (const Data& d) const
   {
      return (i<d.i && j<d.j);
   }
};
```

We now create two flyweights:

```
// Some simple examples to show syntax
boost::flyweights::flyweight<Data, boost::flyweights::hashed_factory<> >
   myData1(Data(0,1));
boost::flyweights::flyweight<Data, boost::flyweights::set_factory<> >
   myData2(Data(1,0));
```

We continue with the classes from section 16.3 but now we use separate factories for the fill and stroke colours:

```
class Shape
{
private:
   // The fill- and stroke color as flyweight
   // Fill colors and stoke colors flyweight have different underlying
   // data structures.Thus the fill and stroke colors are separately
   // shared.
   boost::flyweights::flyweight<Color,
      boost::flyweights::hashed_factory<> > m_fillColor;
   boost::flyweights::flyweight<Color,
      boost::flyweights::set_factory<> > m_strokeColor;

   // ...
};
```

The following code creates four shapes with fill and stroke colours; the number of colours is equal to two after the four shapes have been created. This is because two different flyweight factories are used:

```
// Creating shapes
Shape s1; Shape s2; Shape s3; Shape s4;   // 2 colours in this case

cout<<"Colors created (stroke and fill): "<<Color::Counter()<<endl;

// Change stroke color of s3 & s4, number of colors now 4
// (one fill color and three stroke colors)
s3.StrokeColor(Color(0, 1, 0));
s4.StrokeColor(Color(1, 0, 0));
cout<<"Stroke colors changed: "<<Color::Counter()<<endl;
```

16.6 Tracking and Lifecycle Policies

Boost.Flyweight uses a *tracking policy* to determine when to remove objects from the internal datastructure. The options are:

- *Reference counting* (default case): this option uses a reference count mechanism; the object will be removed from memory when the flyweight does not use it anymore.
- *No tracking*: this policy performs no tracking and objects remain in memory until the program ends.

In other words, reference-counted flyweights will be removed from the internal datastructure when they go out of scope while non-tracked flyweights remain until program end, as the following code shows; (we have provided print statements to track the progress). First, we create a template function that creates a flyweight:

```
template <typename TrackingType>
void Tracking()
{
   cout<<"Start of function that creates flyweight."<<endl;
```

```
    cout<<"Create color 1"<<endl;
    boost::flyweights::flyweight<Color, TrackingType> c1;

    cout<<"Create color 2"<<endl;
    boost::flyweights::flyweight<Color, TrackingType> c2;

    cout<<"Color objects in memory: "<<Color::Counter()<<endl;

    cout<<"End of function."<<endl;
}
```

We create a test program; please note the number of instances that are created and deleted:

```
int main()
{
    cout<<"Starting scope for reference counted tracking."<<endl;
    Tracking<boost::flyweights::refcounted>();
    cout<<"Scope for ref counted ended, FW already deleted."<<endl;
    cout<<"Objects in memory: "<<Color::Counter()<<endl; // Answer: 0

    cout<<endl<<"Starting scope for no tracking."<<endl;
    Tracking<boost::flyweights::no_tracking>();
    cout<<"Scope for no tracking ended, FW not yet deleted."<<endl;
    cout<<"Objects in memory: "<<Color::Counter()<<endl; // Answer: 1

    cout<<"End of program."<<endl;
}
```

The advantage of the no-tracking option is that it is faster than reference counting and that we do not have to recreate objects. On the other hand, objects remain in memory until program end which adds to memory consumption. In other words, the choice of tracking policy is a trade-off between time and resource (memory) efficiency; references are resource-efficient and using the no-tracking option ensures that objects only need to be constructed once at the cost of having them in memory for the duration of the program.

16.7 Tagging Policies

We have already seen that if you use different flyweight factory types, each factory maintains its own flyweight objects. Thus two objects with the same state can appear in each factory. But what if you want to use only one factory type but still want to have two factories? In this case Boost.Flyweight supports the concept of *tagging* to allow the creation of different flyweight classes with each one having a separate factory. For example, consider the declarations:

```
// Case 1: A single factory for different domain concepts
boost::flyweight<string> name("localhost");
boost::flyweight<string> ipAddress("127.0.0.1");
```

It is not possible to distinguish between those strings that represent domain names and those that represent IP addresses. What we would like is to create two factories by using *tag structures*. These structs introduce an extra level of indirection and will turn a flyweight class into a completely different type. For the above example we create two structs:

```
struct NameTag
{ // Empty helper class to help create flyweight 'namespaces'
};

struct IPTag
{ // Empty helper class to help create flyweight 'namespaces'
};
```

We then use these when creating the flyweights:

```
// Case 2: A single factory for each separate domain concept
boost::flyweights::flyweight<string, boost::flyweights::tag<NameTag> >
    name2;
boost::flyweights::flyweight<string, boost::flyweights::tag<IPTag> >
    ipAddress2;

name2 = name;
ipAddress2 = ipAddress;
```

This feature promotes reliability, efficiency and maintainability of code by partitioning objects into logically distinct factories.

16.8 Holders

Each flyweight type (that is, each distinct instantiation of the template class flyweight) is associated with exactly one factory object. In most cases we are not concerned with how this factory object is created, but in some cases we do wish to control this process. In such cases we have an internal component called *holder* that is responsible for instantiating the factory; in one sense, it is a 'factory for a factory' in much the same way as the *Factory Method* pattern can be used to create *Builder* pattern objects (see GOF 1995).

There are two kinds of holder in Boost.Flyweight which are defined by a *holder specifier*:

- static_holder: this is the default holder and it produces holders in which the unique factory lives as a local static variable in the program.
- intermodule_holder: this option resolves some of the problems associated with static_holder (for example, they have problems with flyweights from different dynamic load libraries and modules (DLLs)). For example, two DLLs may contain flyweights having the same type. With a static_holder each DLL has its own flyweight factory; thus flyweight objects are not shared between DLLs. The intermodule_holder ensures that all modules of a program use the same flyweight factory instance so that flyweight objects can be shared between DLLs.

We return to the Shape class; we recall that it has two flyweight member data. We have modified the code and in this case one of the flyweights has an intermediate_holder:

```
#include <iostream>
#include <boost/flyweight.hpp>
#include <boost/flyweight/intermodule_holder.hpp>
#include "Color.hpp"

class Shape
{
private:

    // The fill- and stroke color as flyweight
    // Fill colors & stoke colors flyweight have different factory holders.
    // Therefore the fill color and stroke color will be shared separately.
    boost::flyweights::flyweight<Color,
        boost::flyweights::static_holder> m_fillColor;
    boost::flyweights::flyweight<Color,
        boost::flyweights::intermodule_holder> m_strokeColor;

public:
    // ...
};
```

A test program shows that two colour objects are created (one for each flyweight factory):

```
int main()
{
    // Creating shapes
    Shape s1; Shape s2; Shape s3; Shape s4;

    cout<<"Four shapes created with default constructor:"<<endl;
    cout<<"Shape 1: "<<s1<<endl;
    cout<<"Shape 2: "<<s2<<endl;
    cout<<"Shape 3: "<<s3<<endl;
    cout<<"Shape 4: "<<s4<<endl;

    // There are 2 flyweights here
    cout<<"Colors created: "<<Color::Counter()<<endl;

    return 0;
}
```

16.9 Locking Policies and Thread-Safe Code

The internal factory associated with each flyweight type is a shared resource and hence is potentially not thread-safe. When used in combination with a multi-threaded library (such as Boost.Thread or OpenMP) the consequences could be disastrous unless we provide a locking mechanism to protect data. The locking policies for synchronisation are:

- `simple_locking`: this is the default locking policy. It specifies native synchronisation primitives provided by the operating system.
- `no_locking`: no synchronisation is enforced and unrestricted access to the shared resource is allowed. This option leads to somewhat faster execution than in the case of the default locking policy. However, this option should be used only when you are sure that the resource is read-only when multiple threads are active. In fact, this option should only be used in single-threaded environments.

We take an example, again the `Shape` class. In this case one flyweight member data is thread-safe and the other is not:

```
class Shape
{
private:

    // The fill- and stroke color as flyweight. Fill colors
    // and stoke colors flyweight have different locking mechanisms.
    // Therefore the fill color and stroke color will be shared separately.
    boost::flyweights::flyweight<Color, boost::flyweights::simple_locking>
        m_fillColor;
    boost::flyweights::flyweight<Color, boost::flyweights::no_locking>
        m_strokeColor;

public:
    // ..
};
```

This completes our discussion of Boost.Flyweight.

16.10 Summary and Conclusions

The Boost.Flyweight library is used in applications that manage and deploy large numbers of objects of moderate size. The flyweight class is the central entity in this library and it grants access to shared data. Developers will probably only need to use the default functionality but it is possible to fine-tune and customise the library for better performance. Flyweights are common in design patterns; for example, the *State* and *Strategy* patterns can be designed as flyweights.

The Flyweight pattern has many applications that use immutable shared objects. It is a mechanism for resource handling. For example, in a document editor application we model each character as a flyweight. In this case the intrinsic state of a character corresponds to its character code and style information while its extrinsic state corresponds to its position in a document. The advantage is that we can create a large document efficiently because intrinsic data is shared rather than being copied each time a character is copied into the document. Another example of a flyweight is a layout object to produce a given look and feel in a graphics application. In many cases this object is an instance of a *Strategy* pattern (see GOF 1995 for a discussion of this pattern).

16.11 Appendix: Functional/Hash

Boost.Flyweight maintains an internal data structure to store objects and this is realised by a factory. In particular, the hashed-factory creates an internal hash table data structure. To this end, we map both built-in and user-defined types to an unsigned integer using the struct hash (which is incidentally the default hash function in the libraries Boost.Unordered, Boost.Intrusive unordered associative containers, the hash indices in Boost.MultiIndex and Boost.Bimap's unordered_set_of).

The hash function object is defined as:

```
template <typename T>
struct hash : public std::unary_function<T, std::size_t>
{
    std::size_t operator () (T const&) const;
};
```

The function call operator () calls the function hash_value() which then computes the hash value. This function is implemented for both built-in types (such as integers, floats, pointers and strings) and container types (vectors, sets, maps and so on). We now give some examples; we first define a data type and a corresponding hash function object instance and finally we compute the hash value by invoking the function call operator ():

```
Point p1;
Point p2(1.3, 3.32);
Point p3(4.4, -1.0);
Point p4 = p1;
LineSegment lineA(p1, p2);
LineSegment lineB(p3, p4);

// Hash values for built-in types
string myString("hello world etc. etc. etc.");
boost::hash<string> stringHasher;
size_t strValue = stringHasher(myString);

// Hash objects for standard container types
boost::hash<vector<double> > vectorHasher;
boost::hash<set<Point> > setHasher;    // Operator '<' must be defined
boost::hash<pair<LineSegment, LineSegment> > pairHasher;

vector<double> myVector(100, 2.0);
size_t hashValue = vectorHasher(myVector);
```

```
set<Point> mySet;
mySet.insert(p1); mySet.insert(p2);
size_t hashValue2 = setHasher(mySet);

pair<LineSegment, LineSegment> myPair(make_pair(lineA, lineB));
size_t hashValue3 = pairHasher(myPair);

// Complex numbers
complex<double> myComplex(1.0, -2.0);
boost::hash<complex<double> > complexHasher;
size_t cpxValue = complexHasher(myComplex);
```

In the case of a set hasher we must implement the operator '<' for the underlying data type.
For the above example (class Point) the code is:

```
bool Point::operator < (const Point& p2) const
{ // This inequality would be applicable in certain graphics applications

    if (x >= p2.x) return false;
    if (y >= p2.y) return false;

    return true;
}
```

We now turn our attention to creating hash values for user-defined types. This is an
incremental approach; hash values for aggregate objects are built from the hash values of
their parts; for example, a point consists of x and y coordinates and a line segment consists
of two points. To this end, we use the function hash_combine that accepts a reference
unsigned data and member data as input and that returns a hash value:

```
template <class T>
inline void hash_combine(std::size_t& seed, T const& v)
```

Each user-defined data type must support this non-member function. In the case of Point it
is:

```
friend std::size_t Point::hash_value(const Point& p);

std::size_t hash_value(const Point& p)
{
    std::size_t seed = 0;
    boost::hash_combine(seed, p.x);
    boost::hash_combine(seed, p.y);

    return seed;
}
```

while in the case of LineSegment it is:

```
friend std::size_t hash_value(const LineSegment& line);

std::size_t hash_value(const LineSegment& line)
{
    std::size_t seed = 0;
    boost::hash_combine(seed, line.startPoint);
    boost::hash_combine(seed, line.endPoint);

    return seed;
}
```

Finally, we note that it is possible to compute the hash value of an iterator range by calling
`boost::hash_range`. An example, consider the computation of a hash value of a list:

```
// Hash value for iterators
list<Point> myList(10); myList.push_back(Point(1.0, 1.0));
size_t hashValue4 = boost::hash_range(myList.begin(), myList.end());
```

We conclude this appendix with a short discussion of using a hash index with
Boost.MultiIndex. This library enables the construction of containers maintaining one or
more *indices* with different sorting and access semantics. In other words, we can create
several indices for a given data type. We take the example of class `Circle`; each circle has a
centre point and a radius. It also has member functions for the computation of radius, area
and the diameter. We now define indices based on radius, area and the reciprocal of the
diameter and in this case we use the circle member function `Radius()` and two global
functions that define these indices:

```
class Circle
{
private:
    Point centerpoint;
    double radius;

public:

    // ...

    double Radius() const
    { // Return the radius

        return radius;
    }
};
```

and

```
double AreaIndex(const Circle& c)
{ // Area

    return c.Area();
}

double InverseDiameterIndex(const Circle& c)
{
    return 1.0/c.Diameter();
}
```

We now define the multi-index collection as follows:

```
// Define a multi-index for Datasim Circle class
typedef multi_index_container
<
    Circle,
    indexed_by<
    ordered_unique
    <
        BOOST_MULTI_INDEX_CONST_MEM_FUN(Circle, double, Radius) // index 0
    >,
    ordered_non_unique
    <
        global_fun<const Circle&, double, AreaIndex>            // index 1
    >,
```

```
    ordered_non_unique
    <
        global_fun<const Circle&, double, InverseDiameterIndex> // index 2
    > >
 > CircleSet;
```

This code is not as intimidating as it looks. It describes a data structure with three indices, one of which is a member function and the other two are global functions. We describe each one by three parameters, namely the class in question, the return type of the index function and finally the name of the index function. We note that we can navigate in a circle collection CircleSet based on a given index. Thus, iterating using radius as index will give a different result to when we iterate in the collection based on the reciprocal of the diameter. To see this, let us first create an array of circles with increasing radius:

```
const int N = 5;
Circle* carr = new Circle[N];
CircleSet cSet;

for (int j = 0; j < N; ++j)
{
    carr[j] = Circle(Point(0.0, 0.0), double(j));
    cSet.insert(carr[j]);
}
```

Then the following code shows how to navigate in the collection using a given index as sorting criterium:

```
std::cout<<"\nRadius order\n"<<"---------------"<<std::endl;
for (CircleSet::iterator it = cSet.begin(); it != cSet.end(); ++it)
{
    std::cout<<it->Radius()<<std::endl;
}

std::cout<<"\nArea order\n"<<"---------------"<<std::endl;
for (nth_index<CircleSet,1>::type::iterator it1=get<1>(cSet).begin();
     it1!=get<1>(cSet).end(); ++it1)
{
    std::cout<<it1->Radius()<<std::endl;
}

std::cout<<"\nRadius order\n"<<"---------------"<<std::endl;
for (nth_index<CircleSet,0>::type::iterator it1=get<0>(cSet).begin();
     it1!=get<0>(cSet).end(); ++it1)
{
    std::cout<<it1->Radius()<<std::endl;
}

std::cout<<"\nInverse Diameter\n"<<"---------------"<<std::endl;
for (nth_index<CircleSet,2>::type::iterator it1=get<2>(cSet).begin();
     it1!=get<2>(cSet).end(); ++it1)
{
    std::cout<<it1->Radius()<<std::endl;
}
```

Further discussion of Boost.MultiIndex is outside the scope of this book. We discuss it and its applications in Volume II.

17 Integrating Legacy Applications with Boost

17.1 Introduction and Objectives

In this chapter we discuss two-dimensional geometric data structures and a corresponding C++ class library that we use in computer graphics and Computer Aided Design (CAD) applications. The authors of this book were the main designers of the library which we called CADObject. We have used it in a variety of applications ranging from mechanical and process engineering to simulation and optical technology.

The main goals of this chapter are:
- Extend and improve the functionality of CADObject by migrating existing code to Boost and by adding new functionality that CADObject did not already have.
- Show how to combine the object-oriented and generic programming models to create extendible software systems.
- Showing how applications that use design patterns can be upgraded to patterns that we implement using Boost libraries (for example, using Signals to implement the *Observer* pattern).
- Gain hands-on experience in migrating existing object-oriented code to code that uses Boost.

The process in this chapter is as follows; first, we analyse the current implementation of CADObject and we determine which parts of the code need to be modified and extended. Second, our design approach is based on understanding and reviewing UML class diagrams, in much the same way as an engineer would examine the detailed drawings of a house before renovating it. Finally, we discuss how each new feature is to be implemented using C++ and Boost.
This chapter deals with a specific application but many of the lessons learned can be applied to other object-oriented applications.

17.2 Migrating Legacy Code to Boost: The CADObject Project

This chapter is different from the previous 16 chapters − each one of which was devoted to a specific Boost library − because we now discuss the problem of designing and implementing applications that use Boost. This chapter describes our experiences when we ported a C++ application to one that uses Boost libraries.

The authors developed CADObject in the 1990's as an extendible and device-independent class library to create and manipulate two-dimensional shapes in Computer-Aided Design (CAD) and Computer Graphics (CG) applications. Some of the requirements were:
- *Suitability* and *functionality*: it shall be possible to extend and adapt the software to suit new needs and requirements. For example, we wish to create a 2d animation package on top of CADObject or we wish to create a new user-interface to a number of commercial CAD software packages.
- *Portability*: the library shall be independent of the environment in which it is used. We even consider migrating CADObject from C++ to C# (which we have done) as a project in which portability plays a major role.
- *Maintainability*: it shall be possible to extend and modify the library with a minimum of effort. In particular, the software changes must not lead to instability. In order to realise these goals we used the object-oriented features in C++ at the time (in particular its support for dynamic polymorphism and data encapsulation) in combination with a

number of design patterns. We have found the following patterns to be of particular value.

- *Composite*: the ability to create complex (nested, recursive) objects and whole-part hierarchies.
- *Adapter*: this pattern promotes reusability and extendibility by allowing us to convert the interface of a class into the interface of another class that clients expect.
- *Bridge*: decoupling of classes in CADObject from their 'implementations'. For example, we create graphical objects using a variety of user interface devices such as the console, pointing devices (mouse, joystick) and data files.
- *Visitor*: this important pattern allows us to extend the functionality of the class hierarchy in a non-intrusive way. Different users will have different requirements and each new requirement is coded as a dedicated *Visitor* class; for example, all I/O drivers are visitors and this implies that application objects and their interaction with the environment are separated.
- *Strategy*: defining families of algorithms and making them interchangeable. An example is a mesh generator in two dimensions. We would like to choose an algorithm at run-time based on time and resource efficiency considerations. Encapsulating algorithms in semi-independent strategy classes also promotes their reusability.

We started on this project at a time when templates were not supported. The Standard Template Library (STL) was in its infancy and we created many of the containers and algorithms that were later to be supported in STL. In this sense CADObject contains (internal) legacy code that should be ported to STL and Boost.

In the next sections we discuss the steps we took to migrate the legacy code in CADObject to a version that uses modern generic programming techniques in combination with Boost. The format is similar in all three cases; first, we present the current design using a combination of UML class diagrams and C++ code, second we show how to use the library and finally we analyse the design with a view to improving it in the following version of the software. From a project management point of view we use the *Risk-driven Spiral Model* (see Boehm 1986) because it allows us to combine the strengths of top-down analysis and bottom-up design.

In order to scope the following sections, we discuss the essential design, classes and code in the library.

17.3 CADObject Architecture: Version One

There are a number of class hierarchies in CADObject, two of which we discuss in this section. First, the data hierarchy is shown in Figure 17.1. We make a distinction between *basic classes* (such as `Line` and `Circle`) and *composite classes*. The latter classes allow us to create tree-structures and whole-part hierarchies. The classes in Figure 17.1 have essential functionality in the form of constructors, set/get operations and some geometrical operations that are needed by most applications. Furthermore, we avoid placing member data in `Shape` because this would be inherited by derived classes and can lead to unwanted behaviour:

```
class Shape
{
   public:
      // Constructors & destructor.
      Shape();                              // Default constructor
      Shape(const Shape& source);           // Copy constructor
      virtual ~Shape();                     // Destructor

      // Functions
```

```
        virtual Shape* Clone() const=0;               // Prototype pattern
        virtual void Accept(ShapeVisitor& visitor)=0;  // Visitor Pattern
        virtual string ToString() const;

        // Operators
        Shape& operator = (const Shape& source);
        friend ostream& operator << (ostream& os, const Shape& s);
    };
```

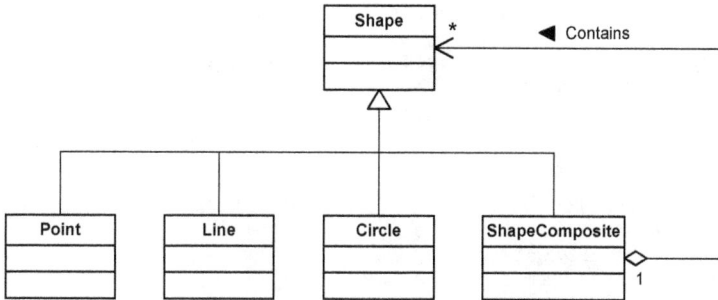

Figure 17.1 Shape class hierarchy

We take one basic class to show what its interface is:

```
class Circle: public Shape
{
    private:
        Point m_centrePoint;      // The centre point of the circle
        double m_radius;          // The radius of the circle

    public:
        // Constructors & destructor
        Circle();                                      // Default constructor
        Circle(const Point& centre, double radius);   // Centre/radius
        Circle(const Circle& source);                 // Copy constructor
        virtual ~Circle();                             // Destructor

        // Selectors
        const Point& CentrePoint() const;             // Get the centre point
        double Radius() const;                        // Get the radius

        // Modifiers
        void CentrePoint(const Point& centrePoint);   // Set centre point
        void Radius(double radius);                   // Set the radius

        // Functions
        double Area() const;           // Calculate the area of the circle
        double Circumference() const;  // Calculate the circumference
        virtual Shape* Clone() const;                 // Clone the circle
        virtual void Accept(ShapeVisitor& visitor);   // Visitor
        virtual string ToString() const;              // Return a description

        // Operators
        Circle& operator = (const Circle& source);   // Assignment
    };
```

We now discuss the implementation of the composite class in Figure 17.1. In this version we implement it using an STL `list` and it has the following STL-compatible interface:

```
class ShapeComposite: public Shape
{
```

```
    private:
        list<Shape*> m_shapes;                          // Storage of Shape*
        void Copy(const ShapeComposite& source);

    public:
        // User can use the STL iterator
        typedef list<Shape*>::iterator iterator;
        typedef list<Shape*>::const_iterator const_iterator;

        // Constructors & destructor
        ShapeComposite();
        ShapeComposite(const ShapeComposite& source);
        virtual ~ShapeComposite();

        // Selectors
        int Count() const;

        // Add functions
        void Insert(const Shape& shape);
        void Insert(Shape* shape);
        void Append(const Shape& shape);
        void Append(Shape* shape);

        // Remove functions.
        void RemoveFirst();
        void RemoveLast();
        void RemoveAll();

        // Iterator functions
        iterator begin();
        const_iterator begin() const;
        iterator end();
        const_iterator end() const;

        // Abstract functions.
        virtual Shape* Clone() const;
        virtual void Accept(ShapeVisitor& visitor);
        virtual string ToString() const;

        // Operators
        ShapeComposite& operator = (const ShapeComposite& source);
};
```

Some of the improvements that we now wish to implement are:

- R1: The member data is a list which may not always be the most suitable data structure in all cases; we would like to use vectors and graphs, for example.
- R2: The class supports Shape pointers; we would like to create composites containing other polymorphic objects such as GUI widgets and algorithms, for example.
- R3: Standard pointers: the composite class is responsible for its children; in this case when the composite goes out of scope it removes its children from memory:

```
void ShapeComposite::RemoveAll()
{
    // Create iterator for the source list
    list<Shape*>::const_iterator it;
    list<Shape*>::const_iterator end=m_shapes.end();

    // Delete all shapes in the list
    for (it=m_shapes.begin(); it!=end; it++) delete (*it);

    // Remove the shape* from the list
    m_shapes.clear();
}
```

```
ShapeComposite::~ShapeComposite()
{
    RemoveAll();
}
```

This situation is far from ideal; one major problem will occur when composites have shared objects. The question is: who is responsible for these shared objects? It is clear that we can make the code more reliable, reusable and generic if we can find ways to resolve requirements R1, R2 and R3.

Continuing, we now examine how we have extended the functionality of the classes in Figure 17.1 using the *Visitor* pattern. We discovered this pattern independently of GOF 1995 and at the time we called it a *Driver*; in fact, a driver or a visitor is an action on an object. We show the *Visitor* class hierarchy in Figure 17.2 and we can see that we have visitors for geometric transformations, serialisation and for searching. We also have a special class for Boost serialisation that is not a visitor and we will discuss this issue later in this chapter.

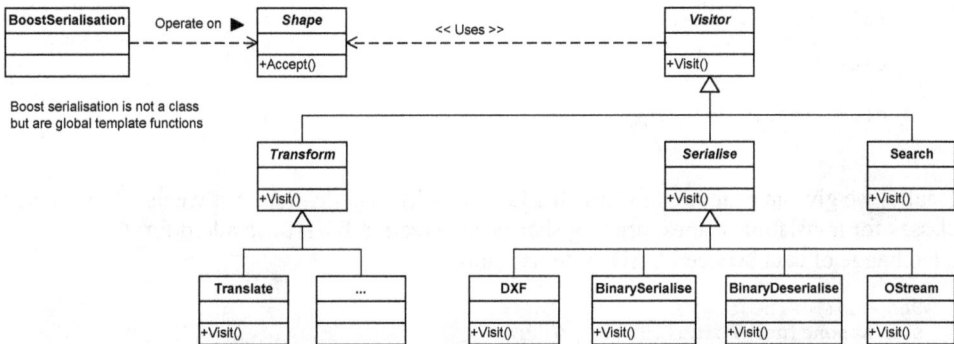

Figure 17.2 Extending shape functionality

The base class ShapeVisitor in Figure 17.2 has the interface:

```
class ShapeVisitor
{
public:
    // Constructors and destructor
    ShapeVisitor();
    ShapeVisitor(const ShapeVisitor& source);
    virtual ~ShapeVisitor();

    // The pure virtual visit functions
    virtual void Visit(Point& p)=0;            // Visit a point
    virtual void Visit(Line& l)=0;             // Visit a line
    virtual void Visit(Circle& c)=0;           // Visit a circle
    virtual void Visit(ShapeComposite& sc);    // Visit a composite

    // Operators.
    ShapeVisitor& operator = (const ShapeVisitor& source);
};
```

Derived classes must implement the above pure virtual member functions; for example, here is the body of the functions for translating points, lines and circles:

```
// Visit a point
void TranslateVisitor::Visit(Point& p)
```

```
{
    p.X(p.X()+m_xOffset);
    p.Y(p.Y()+m_yOffset);
}

// Visit a line
void TranslateVisitor::Visit(Line& l)
{
    Point p1(l.P1());
    Point p2(l.P2());

    Visit(p1);
    Visit(p2);

    l.P1(p1);
    l.P2(p2);
}


// Visit a circle
void TranslateVisitor::Visit(Circle& c)
{
    Point pc(c.CentrePoint());

    Visit(pc);

    c.CentrePoint(pc);
}
```

Finally, we give an example of using this functionality in code; note that we use three visitor classes for translating shapes, printing shapes and creating DXF (a standard for the interchange of data between CAD systems) output:

```
ShapeComposite sc1;
sc1.Append(new Point(10.33, 20));
sc1.Append(new Line(Point(0, 0), Point(10.33, 20)));
sc1.Append(new Circle(Point(10.22, 20), 10));

ShapeComposite sc2;
sc2.Append(new Circle(Point(25, 25), 5.5));
sc2.Append(sc1.Clone());
sc2.Append(new Line(Point(20, 25), Point(30, 25)));
TranslateVisitor(10, 20).Visit(sc2);
OStreamVisitor(cout).Visit(sc2);
cout<<endl;

// Print to DXF.
cout<<"DXF:"<<endl;
DxfVisitor dxf(cout, "My comment");
dxf.Visit(sc2);
dxf.Close();
```

This completes the description of the classical object-oriented design of CADObject. We continue with an analysis of the requirements R1, R2 and R3 above.

17.4 CADObject Architecture: Version Two

The next phase involves improving the robustness, reliability and reusability of the code by using shared pointers (as discussed in chapter 5) and creating a template composite class which can then be specialised to a ShapeComposite class. To this end, we first create a *smart generic composite* whose member data is (still) implemented by an STL list:

```
template <typename T>
class SmartComposite: public T
{
private:
    // The storage of the data in smart pointers. No deep copies
    // Data is shared.
    list<boost::shared_ptr<T> > m_data;

public:
    // User can use the STL iterator
    typedef typename list<boost::shared_ptr<T> >::iterator iterator;
    typedef typename list<boost::shared_ptr<T> >::const_iterator
        const_iterator;

    // Constructors & destructor
    SmartComposite();
    SmartComposite(const SmartComposite<T>& source);   // Not deep
    virtual ~SmartComposite();

    // Selectors
    int Count() const;        // Return the number of elements

    // Add functions
    // 1. Add an element at the beginning of the composite
    // 2. Add an element at the beginning of the composite
    //    Ownership will be transfered to smart pointer
    // 3. Add an element at the end of the composite
    // 4. Add an element at the end of the composite
    //    Ownership will be transfered to smart pointer

    // Add functions
    void Insert(boost::shared_ptr<T> data);     // 1
    void Insert(T* data);                       // 2
    void Append(boost::shared_ptr<T> data);     // 3
    void Append(T* data);                       // 4

    // Remove functions
    void RemoveFirst();          // Remove the first element
    void RemoveLast();           // Remove the last element
    void RemoveAll();            // Remove all elements

    // Iterator functions
    iterator begin();                    // Iterator at begin of composite
    const_iterator begin() const;  // Const iterator at begin of composite
    iterator end();                      // Iterator after end of composite
    const_iterator end() const;    // Const iterator after end of composite

    // Operators
    SmartComposite<T>& operator = (const SmartComposite<T>& source);
};
```

In this case the composite is a template class. Note that it derives from its template parameter T. We also see that shared pointers are used instead of raw pointers. The amount of coding is reduced because memory management is taken care of by Boost.SmartPtr. For example, removing elements when the composite goes out of scope has the particularly simple form:

```
template <typename T> void SmartComposite<T>::RemoveAll()
{
    // No need to delete the pointers first.

    // Clear the list.
    m_data.clear();
}
```

This class can now be used in many applications by use of template specialisation. In the current case we have:

```
class ShapeComposite: public SmartComposite<Shape>
{
private:

public:
    // Constructors & destructor
    ShapeComposite();
    ShapeComposite(const ShapeComposite& source);
    virtual ~ShapeComposite();

    // Functions
    virtual Shape* Clone() const;
    virtual void Accept(ShapeVisitor& visitor);
    virtual string ToString() const;

    // Operators
    ShapeComposite& operator = (const ShapeComposite& source);
};
```

An example of using the new composite is (memory deallocation is now automatic):

```
ShapeComposite sc1;
sc1.Append(p2.Clone());
sc1.Append(l2.Clone());
sc1.Append(c2.Clone());
```

The requirements R2 and R3 have now been resolved; all memory is reference-counted and we have a generic solution. However, the container type of m_data is still hard-coded and we shall now resolve requirement R1 using template-template parameters.

17.5 CADObject Architecture: Version Three

We resolve requirement R1 by employing *template-template parameters*. The new smart generic composite has the same member functions as the Composite class in section 4 but now we have a new level of indirection because the member data type is a generic parameter. We implement the smart composite in the header file. You need to specify the TAlloc parameter even when there is a default allocator in the corresponding STL container. The new interface is now:

```
template <typename T,
          template <typename T, typename TAlloc> class TContainer=list,
          typename TAlloc=std::allocator<T> >
class SmartComposite: public T
{
private:
    TContainer<boost::shared_ptr<T>, TAlloc> m_data;

public:
    // User can use the STL iterator
    typedef typename TContainer<boost::shared_ptr<T>, TAlloc>::iterator
        iterator;
    typedef typename TContainer<boost::shared_ptr<T>,
                    TAlloc>::const_iterator const_iterator;
    // interface as before
};
```

We see that the default implementation is an STL `list`. Of course, we can use another implementation provided it implements the member functions:

```
push_back()
pop_back()
size()
clear()
default constructor.
```

We now create some shapes, each one having its own data member:

```
// Use smart composite directly (needed to make shape not abstract)
Datasim::Utilities::SmartComposite<Shape> sc_1;        // Default
Datasim::Utilities::SmartComposite<Shape, list> sc_2;   // List
Datasim::Utilities::SmartComposite<Shape, vector> sc_3; // Vector

sc_1.Append(p2.Clone()); sc_1.Append(l2.Clone()); sc_1.Append(c2.Clone());
sc_2.Append(p2.Clone()); sc_2.Append(l2.Clone()); sc_2.Append(c2.Clone());
sc_3.Append(p2.Clone()); sc_3.Append(l2.Clone()); sc_3.Append(c2.Clone());
```

We are finished; we have a defined smart template composite class whose implementation (member data) is also a customisable template parameter. Please see the full source code accompanying the book.

17.6 Using Boost.Serialization

We have introduced Boost.Serialization in chapter 5. In this section we serialise shapes to disk. We use non-intrusive serialisation and this entails creating free functions for each class in the `Shape` hierarchy. In fact, we define two functions for each class, one for serialisation and the other for deserialisation. We now describe the steps to produce this serialisation and deserialisation code.

First, we include the header files:

```
#include <boost/serialization/serialization.hpp>  // Most of serialization
#include <boost/serialization/split_free.hpp>      // Split free macro
#include <boost/serialization/export.hpp>          // Export guid macro
#include <boost/serialization/shared_ptr.hpp>      // Serialise shared_ptr
```

Next, we need to distinguish between load and save operations:

```
BOOST_SERIALIZATION_SPLIT_FREE(Datasim::CADObject::Point);
BOOST_SERIALIZATION_SPLIT_FREE(Datasim::CADObject::Line);
BOOST_SERIALIZATION_SPLIT_FREE(Datasim::CADObject::Circle);
BOOST_SERIALIZATION_SPLIT_FREE(
    Datasim::Utilities::SmartComposite<Datasim::CADObject::Shape>);
```

Then we pre-register the classes to be serialised and this is needed when we serialise base class pointers that are assigned to addresses of derived class instances:

```
BOOST_CLASS_EXPORT_GUID(Datasim::CADObject::Shape, "Shape");
BOOST_CLASS_EXPORT_GUID(Datasim::CADObject::Point, "Point");
BOOST_CLASS_EXPORT_GUID(Datasim::CADObject::Line, "Line");
BOOST_CLASS_EXPORT_GUID(Datasim::CADObject::Circle, "Circle");
BOOST_CLASS_EXPORT_GUID(
    Datasim::CADObject::ShapeComposite, "ShapeComposite");
    BOOST_CLASS_EXPORT_GUID(Datasim::Utilities::SmartComposite<
    Datasim::CADObject::Shape>, "SmartComposite");
```

Finally, we give the serialisation/deserialisation code for each class:

```
namespace boost
{
    namespace serialization
    {
        // Serialise a shape (both load and save)
        template <typename Archive> inline void serialize(Archive& ar,
            Datasim::CADObject::Shape& shape,const unsigned int file_version)
        {
            // No data to serialise
        }

        // Serialise a point (save)
        template <typename Archive> inline void save(Archive& ar,
            const Datasim::CADObject::Point& point,
            const unsigned int file_version)
        {
            double tmp;

            // Serialise base object
            ar<<base_object<Datasim::CADObject::Shape>(point);

            // So we use a temporally variable.
            tmp=point.X(); ar<<tmp;
            tmp=point.Y(); ar<<tmp;
        }

        // Deserialise a point (load)
        template <typename Archive> inline void load(Archive& ar,
            Datasim::CADObject::Point& point,
            const unsigned int file_version)
        {
            // Deserialise base object
            ar>>base_object<Datasim::CADObject::Shape>(point);

            double tmp;
            ar>>tmp; point.X(tmp);
            ar>>tmp; point.Y(tmp);
        }

        // Serialise a line (save)
        template <typename Archive> inline void save(Archive& ar,
            const Datasim::CADObject::Line& line,
            const unsigned int file_version)
        {

            // Serialise base object.
            ar<<base_object<Datasim::CADObject::Shape>(line);

            ar<<line.P1();
            ar<<line.P2();
        }

        // Deserialise a line (load)
        template <typename Archive> inline void load(Archive& ar,
                Datasim::CADObject::Line& line,
            const unsigned int file_version)
        {

            // Deserialise base object
            ar>>base_object<Datasim::CADObject::Shape>(line);

            Point tmp;
            ar>>tmp; line.P1(tmp);
```

```cpp
      ar>>tmp; line.P2(tmp);
   }

   // Serialise a circle (save)
   template <typename Archive> inline void save(Archive& ar,
      const Datasim::CADObject::Circle& circle,
      const unsigned int file_version)
   {
      double tmp;

      // Serialise base object
      ar<<base_object<Datasim::CADObject::Shape>(circle);

      // So we use a temporally variable.
      ar<<circle.CentrePoint();
      tmp=circle.Radius(); ar<<tmp;
   }

   // Deserialise a circle (load)
   template <typename Archive> inline void load(Archive& ar,
      Datasim::CADObject::Circle& circle,
      const unsigned int file_version)
   {
      // Deserialise base object
      ar>>base_object<Datasim::CADObject::Shape>(circle);

      Point tmpPoint;
      double tmpDouble;
      ar>>tmpPoint; circle.CentrePoint(tmpPoint);
      ar>>tmpDouble; circle.Radius(tmpDouble);
   }

   // Serialise a smart composite of shapes (save)
   template <typename Archive> inline void save (Archive& ar,
      const Datasim::Utilities::SmartComposite<
         Datasim::CADObject::Shape>& sc,
      const unsigned int file_version)
   {
      int tmpInt;

      // Serialise base object
      ar<<base_object<Datasim::CADObject::Shape>(sc);

      // Write the number of elements.
      tmpInt=sc.Count(); ar<<tmpInt;

      // Serialise all elements
      // Get composite iterators
      Datasim::Utilities::SmartComposite<
         Datasim::CADObject::Shape>::const_iterator it;
      Datasim::Utilities::SmartComposite<
         Datasim::CADObject::Shape>::const_iterator end=sc.end();

      // Serialise all shapes in the composite
      boost::shared_ptr<Datasim::CADObject::Shape> data;
      for (it=sc.begin(); it!=end; it++)
      {
         data=*it;
         ar<<data;
      }
   }

   // Deserialise a smart composite of shapes (load)
   template <typename Archive> inline void load(Archive& ar,
      Datasim::Utilities::SmartComposite<
```

```
              Datasim::CADObject::Shape>& sc,
          const unsigned int file_version)
      {
          // Deserialise base object
          ar>>base_object<Datasim::CADObject::Shape>(sc);

          // Deserialise the number of elements
          int count; ar>>count;

          // Deserialise all elements
          boost::shared_ptr<Datasim::CADObject::Shape> data;
          for (int i=0; i<count; i++)
          {
              ar>>data;
              sc.Append(data);
          }
      }

      // Serialise a shape composite (both load and save)
      template <typename Archive> inline void serialize(Archive& ar,
          Datasim::CADObject::ShapeComposite& sc,
          const unsigned int file_version)
      {
          // Serialise/deserialise base object
          ar&base_object<Datasim::Utilities::SmartComposite<
              Datasim::CADObject::Shape> >(sc);
      }
  }
}
```

17.7 Factories and Deserialisation

The *Visitor* pattern can be used instead of a *Factory Method pattern* to create objects. In this case we note that we first have to create shapes (using a default constructor, for example) and then pass them to Visitor::visit().

To take an example, the interface and code body for a binary serialiser is:

```
class BinaryDeserialiseVisitor: public SerialiseVisitor
{
private:
    istream& m_is;                 // The stream to read from

    BinaryDeserialiseVisitor();
    BinaryDeserialiseVisitor(const BinaryDeserialiseVisitor& source);

    void ReadHeader();             // Read header
public:
    // Constructors and destructor
    BinaryDeserialiseVisitor(istream& is);
    virtual ~BinaryDeserialiseVisitor();

    // The visit functions
    virtual void Visit(Point& p);            // Visit a point
    virtual void Visit(Line& l);             // Visit a line
    virtual void Visit(Circle& c);           // Visit a circle
    virtual void Visit(ShapeComposite& sc);  // Visit composite

private:
    // Operators
    BinaryDeserialiseVisitor& operator = (
        const BinaryDeserialiseVisitor& source);
};
```

We give two examples of how to code `Visit()`:

```
// Visit a circle
void BinaryDeserialiseVisitor::Visit(Circle& c)
{
   // Visit the centre point of the circle
// Point tmpPoint;
// Visit(tmpPoint); c.CentrePoint(tmpPoint);    // One possibility
   Visit(const_cast<Point&>(c.CentrePoint())); // Also possible

   // Read the radius
   double tmpDouble;
   m_is.read((char*)&tmpDouble, sizeof(tmpDouble));
   c.Radius(tmpDouble);
}

// Visit a Shape composite
void BinaryDeserialiseVisitor::Visit(ShapeComposite& sc)
{
   // Read the number of shapes
   int count;
   m_is.read((char*)&count, sizeof(count));

   // Read all the shapes
   for (int i=0; i<count; i++)
   {
      // First read the shape type
      int type;
      m_is.read((char*)&type, sizeof(type));

      // Create the shape depending on the type
      Shape* shape;
      switch (type)
      {
         case otPoint:          shape=new Point();           break;
         case otLine:           shape=new Line();            break;
         case otCircle:         shape=new Circle();          break;
         case otShapeComposite: shape=new ShapeComposite();  break;
         default: throw "Unknown shape type.";
      }

      // Load the shape by sending the visitor to it
      shape->Accept(*this);

      // Add the loaded shape to composite who takes ownership
      sc.Append(shape);
   }
}
```

We give an example of how to use the `BinarySerialiseVisitor` and `BinaryDeserialiseVisitor`:

```
// Serialise visitor
{
   cout<<"\n\nSerialising point, line, circle & shape composite"<<endl;

   ofstream ofs("Output.bin", ios_base::out | ios_base::binary);

   // Create visitor and send shapes to it.
   BinarySerialiseVisitor v(ofs);
   v.Visit(p2);   // Serialise a point
   v.Visit(l2);   // Serialise a line
   v.Visit(c2);   // Serialise a circle
   v.Visit(sc2);  // Serialise a shape composite
}
```

```
// Deserialise visitor
{
   cout<<"\n\nDeserialising point, line, circle & shape composite"<<endl;

   ifstream ifs("Output.bin", ios_base::in | ios_base::binary);

   Point p; Line l; Circle c; ShapeComposite sc;

   // Create visitor and send shapes to it.
   BinaryDeserialiseVisitor v(ifs);

   v.Visit(p);
   v.Visit(l);
   v.Visit(c);
   v.Visit(sc);

   cout<<"Deserialised point: "<<p<<endl;
   cout<<"Deserialised line: "<<l<<endl;
   cout<<"Deserialised circle: "<<c<<endl;
   cout<<"Deserialised shape composite: "<<endl;
   OStreamVisitor(cout).Visit(sc);
   cout<<endl;
}
```

17.8 Conclusions and Summary

In this chapter we examined a number of topics related to porting C++ legacy code to code that makes use of the libraries in Boost. It was meant to give some guidelines and pointers for more extended applications. In our experience, up-front design is essential because well-designed code is easier to manage than code that is not well-designed.

We have presented two class hierarchies in Figures 17.1 and 17.2 that describe the data classes and the functionality that operate on these classes, respectively. This combination is a pattern that we can apply to any problem that models product hierarchies. In particular, we can apply design patterns to extend the functionality of these hierarchies and improve the reliability and efficiency of the resulting code. We have already seen how to do this using smart pointers and Boost.Serialization. It is possible to use other Boost libraries, for example:

- Thread: improve the performance of algorithms in CADObject using parallel design patterns such as *Master/Worker, Geometric Decomposition and Loop Parallelism* (see Mattson 2005 for an introduction to parallel design patterns.)
- Function: we use this library to create flexible and device-independent algorithms and drivers. In particular, the *Strategy* and *Bridge* pattern are suitable candidates. We need to determine what the performance requirements are.
- Signals: dependencies between objects and event-notification patterns such as *Observer* and *Mediator*.
- Flyweight: shared objects are needed in CAD applications and the Flyweight library can be used.
- Xpressive: creating scripts to create and access shapes.

A discussion of using Boost and design patterns is given in Appendix B.

18 An Introduction to Thread

18.1 Introduction and Objectives

In this chapter we discuss how to create C++ code that make use of multi-core processors. In particular, we introduce the *thread* concept. A thread is a software entity and it represents an independent unit of execution in a program. We design an application by creating threads and letting them execute separate parts of the program code with the objective of improving the speedup of an application. We define the *speedup* as a number that indicates how many times faster a parallel program is than its serial equivalent. The formula for the speedup $S(p)$ on a CPU with p processors is:

$$S(p) = T(1)/T(p)$$

where the factor $T(p)$ is the total execution time on a CPU with p processors. When the speedup equals the number of processors we then say that the speedup is *perfectly linear*. The improved performance of parallel programs comes at a price and in this case we must ensure that the threads are synchronised so that they do not destroy the integrity of the shared data. To this end, Boost.Thread has a number of synchronisation mechanisms to protect the program from *data races,* and ensuring that the code is *thread-safe*. We also show how to define locks on objects and data so that only one thread can update the data at any given time.

When working with Boost.Thread you should use the following header file:

```
#include <boost/thread.hpp>
```

and the following namespaces:

```
using namespace boost;
using namespace boost::this_thread;
```

This chapter is a gentle introduction to multi-threading. We recommend that you also run the source code that accompanies the book to see how multi-threaded code differs from sequential code. In Volume II we use Thread as the basis for the implementation of parallel design patterns (Mattson 2005).

18.2 An Introduction to Threads

A *process* has a collection of resources to enable the execution of program instructions. Examples of resources are (virtual) memory, I/O descriptors, run-time stack and signal handlers. It is possible to create a program that consists of a collection of cooperating processes. What is the structure of a process?
- A read-only area for program instructions.
- A read-write area for global data.
- A heap area for memory that we allocate dynamically using the `new` operator or the `malloc` system call.
- A stack where we store the automatic variables of the current procedure.

Processes have control over their resources. Processes can communicate with each other using IPC (*Inter Process Communication)* mechanisms and they can be seen as *heavyweight* units of execution. Context-switching between processes is expensive.

A *thread* is a *lightweight unit of execution* that shares an address space with other threads. A process has one or more threads. Threads share the resources of the process. The execution context for a thread is the data address space that contains all variables in a program. This includes both global variables and automatic variables in routines as well as dynamically allocated variables. Furthermore, each thread has its own stack within the execution context. Multiple threads invoke their own routines without interfering with the stack frames of other threads.

18.3 The Life of a Thread

Each process starts with one thread, the *master* or main thread. Before a new thread can be used, it must be created. The main thread can have one or more *child threads*. Each thread executes independently of the other threads.

What is happening in a thread after it has been created and before it no longer exists? A general answer is that it is either executing or not executing. The latter state may have several causes:

- It is sleeping.
- It is waiting on some other thread.
- It is blocked, that is it is waiting on system resources to perform an input or output operation.

An application should make the best use of its threads because each thread may run on its own processor and the presence of idle threads is synonymous with resource waste.

18.3.1 How Threads Communicate

A multi-threaded application consists of a collection of threads. Each thread is responsible for some particular task in the application. In order to avoid anarchy we need to address a number of important issues:

- *Synchronisation*: ensuring that an event in one thread notifies another thread. This is called *event synchronisation*. This signals the occurrence of an event among multiple threads. Another type of synchronisation is *mutual exclusion* that gives a thread exclusive access to a shared variable or to some other resource for a certain amount of time. This ensures the integrity of the shared variable when multiple threads attempt to access and modify it. We place a lock on the resource and failure to do this may result in a *race condition*. This occurs when multiple threads share data and at least one of the threads accesses this data without using a defined synchronisation mechanism.
- *Scheduling*: we order the events in a program by imposing some kind of *scheduling policy* on them. In general, there are more concurrent tasks to be executed than there are processors to run them. The scheduler synchronises access to the different processors on a CPU. Thus the scheduler determines which threads are currently executing on the available processors.

18.4 What Kinds of Applications are suitable for Multi-Threading?

The main reason for creating a multi-threaded application is performance and responsiveness. As such, threaded code does not add new functionality to a serial application. There should be compelling reasons for using parallel programming techniques. In this section we give an overview of a number of issues to address when developing parallel applications (see Mattson 2005 and Nichols 1996). First, we give a list of criteria that help us determine the categories of applications that could benefit from parallel processing. Second, having determined that a given application should be parallelised we discuss how to analyse and design the application with *'parallelism in mind'*.

18.4.1 Suitable Tasks for Multi-threading

The ideal situation is when we can design an application that consists of a number of independent tasks in which each task is responsible for its own input, processing and output. In practice, however tasks are inter-dependent and we must take this into account.

Concurrency is a property of software systems in which several computations are executing simultaneously and potentially interacting with each other. We maximise concurrency while we minimise the need for synchronisation. We identify a task that will be a candidate for threading based on the following criteria (Nichols 1996):

- Its degree of independence from other tasks. Does the task need results or data from other tasks and do other tasks depend on its results? These questions determine the *provide/require* constraints between tasks. An analysis of these questions will lead us to questions concerning task dependencies and resource sharing.
- Does a task spend a long time in a suspended state and is it blocked in potentially long waits? Tasks that consume resources are candidates for threads. For example, if we dedicate a thread for I/O operations then our program will run faster instead of having to wait for slow I/O operations to complete.
- Compute-intensive routines. In many applications we may be able to dedicate threads to tasks with time-consuming calculations. Examples of such calculations are array processing, matrix manipulation and random number generation.

18.5 **The Boost** `thread` **class**

This class represents a thread. It has member functions for creating threads, firing up threads, thread synchronisation and notification, and finally changing thread state. We discuss the functionality of the thread class in this chapter.

There are three constructors in `thread`:
- Default constructor.
- Create a thread with an instance of a *callable type* (which can be a function object, a global function or static function) as argument. This function is run when the thread fires up that is, after thread creation.
- Create a thread with a callable type and its bound arguments to the thread constructor.

We discuss the second option. The callable type – which plays the role of the thread function – can be a free function, a static member function or a function callable object. The thread function has a `void` return type and when it has finished the thread that called it will stop executing.
We give some code to show how to create a simple '101' multi-threaded program. There are two threads, namely the main thread (in the `main()` function) and a thread that we explicitly create in `main()`. The program is simple – each thread prints some text on the console.

The first case is when we create a thread whose thread function is a free (global) function:

```
// Global function called by thread
void GlobalFunction()
{
    for (int i=0; i<10; ++i)
```

```
    {
        cout<< i << "Do something in parallel with main method." << endl;
        boost::this_thread::yield(); // 'yield' discussed in section 18.6
    }
}
```

We now create a thread with `GlobalFuntion()` as thread function and we fire the thread up:

```
int main()
{
    boost::thread t(&GlobalFunction);

    for (int i=0; i<10; i++)
    {
        cout << i <<"Do something in main method."<<endl;
    }

    return 0;
}
```

Each thread prints information on the console. There is no coordination between the threads and you will get different output each time you run the program. The output depends on the thread scheduler. You can run the program and view the output.

We now discuss how to create a thread whose thread function is a static member function of a class and that is a functor at the same time.

```
class CallableClass
{
private:
    // Number of iterations
    int m_iterations;

public:

    // Default constructor
    CallableClass()
    {
        m_iterations=10;
    }

    // Constructor with number of iterations
    CallableClass(int iterations)
    {
        m_iterations=iterations;
    }

    // Copy constructor
    CallableClass(const CallableClass& source)
    {
        m_iterations=source.m_iterations;
    }

    // Destructor
    ~CallableClass()
    {
    }

    // Assignment operator
    CallableClass& operator = (const CallableClass& source)
    {
        m_iterations=source.m_iterations;
```

```
         return *this;
      }

      // Static function called by thread
      static void StaticFunction()
      {
         for (int i=0; i < 10; i++)   // Hard-coded upper limit
         {
            cout<<i<<"Do something in parallel (Static function)."<<endl;
            boost::this_thread::yield(); // 'yield' discussed in section 18.6
         }
      }

      // Operator() called by the thread
      void operator () ()
      {
         for (int i=0; i<m_iterations; i++)
         {
            cout<<i<<" - Do something in parallel (operator() )."<<endl;
            boost::this_thread::yield();  // 'yield' discussed in section 18.6
         }
      }

};
```

We can now create threads based on the static member function `StaticFunction()` and on the fact that `CallableClass` is a function object:

```
int main()
{
    boost::thread t(&CallableClass::StaticFunction);

    for (int i=0; i<10; i++)
    {
       cout<<i<<" - Do something in main method."<<endl;
    }

    return 0;
}
```

and

```
int main()
{
    // Using a callable object as thread function
    int numberIterations = 20;
    CallableClass c(numberIterations);
    boost::thread t(c);

    for (int i=0; i<10; i++)
    {
       cout<< i <<" - Do something in main method." << endl;
    }

    return 0;
}
```

Finally, when a thread's destructor is called then the thread of execution becomes detached and it no longer has an associated `boost::thread` object. In other words, the member function `Thread::detach()` is called while the thread function continues running.

18.6 The Life of a Thread

In general, a thread is either doing something (running its thread function) or is doing nothing (wait or sleep mode). The state transition diagram is shown in Figure 18.1. The scheduler is responsible for some of the transitions between states:

- *Running*: the thread has been created and is already started or is ready to start (this is a *runnable state*). The scheduler has allocated processor time for the thread.
- *WaitSleepJoin*: the thread is waiting for an event to trigger. The thread will be placed in the *Running* state when this event triggers.
- *Stopped*: the thread function has run its course (has completed).

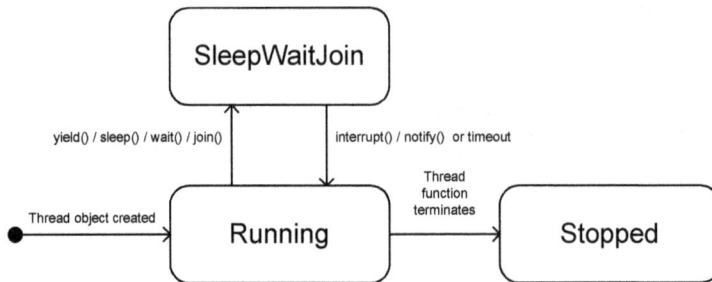

Figure 18.1 Thread Lifecycle

We now discuss some of the member functions that appear in Figure 18.1. First, we note that multi-tasking is not guaranteed to be *preemptive* and this can result in possible performance degradation because a thread can be involved in a computationally intensive algorithm. *Preemption* relates to the ability of the operating system to stop a running thread in favour of another thread. In order to give other threads a chance to run, a running thread may voluntarily give up or *yield control*. Control is returned as soon as possible. For example, we use the global function `yield()` in the `boost::this_thread` namespace. As an example, consider a callable object that computes the powers of numbers (this class could be adapted to compute powers of very large matrices which would constitute a computationally intensive algorithm):

```
class PowerClass
{
private:

    // Version II: m will be a large matrix
    int m, n;        // Variables for m^n

public:
    double result;   // Public data member for the result

    // Constructor with arguments
    PowerClass(int m, int n)
    {
        this->m=m; this->n=n;
        this->result=0.0;
    }

    // Calculate m^n. Supposes n>=0
    void operator () ()
    {
        result=m;                              // Start with m^1
        for (int i=1; i<n; ++i)
```

```
      {
         result*=m;                           // result=result*m
         boost::this_thread::yield();
      }
      if (n==0) result=1;                     // m^0 is always 1
   }
};
```

A thread can put itself to sleep for a certain duration (the units can be a POSIX time duration, hours, minutes, seconds, milliseconds or nanoseconds). We use the *sleep* option when we wish to give other threads a chance to run and for tasks that fire at regular intervals. The main difference is that with yield the thread will continue executing as soon as possible while with sleep the thread will continue executing after the specified amount of time.

We give an example to show how to put a thread to sleep. We simulate an animation application by creating a thread whose thread function displays some information, then sleeps only to be awoken again by the scheduler at a later stage. The thread function is modelled as AnimationClass:

```
class AnimationClass
{
private:
   boost::thread* m_thread;       // The thread runs this object
   int m_frame;                   // The current frame number

   // Variable that indicates to stop and the mutex to
   // synchronise "must stop" on (mutex explained later)
   bool m_mustStop;
   boost::mutex m_mustStopMutex;

public:
   // Default constructor
   AnimationClass()
   {
      m_thread=NULL;
      m_mustStop=false;
      m_frame=0;
   }

   // Destructor
   ~AnimationClass()
   {
      if (m_thread!=NULL) delete m_thread;
   }

   // Start the thread
   void Start()
   {
      // Create thread and start it with myself as argument.
      // Pass myself as reference since I don't want a copy
      m_thread=new boost::thread(boost::ref(*this));
   }

   // Stop the thread
   void Stop()
   {
      // Signal the thread to stop (thread-safe)
      m_mustStopMutex.lock();
      m_mustStop=true;
      m_mustStopMutex.unlock();
```

```
        // Wait for the thread to finish.
        if (m_thread!=NULL) m_thread->join();
    }

    // Display next frame of the animation
    void DisplayNextFrame()
    {
        // Simulate next frame
        cout<<"Press <RETURN> to stop. Frame: "<<m_frame++<<endl;
    }

    // Thread function
    void operator () ()
    {
        bool mustStop;

        do
        {
            // Display the next animation frame
            DisplayNextFrame();

            // Sleep for 40ms (25 frames/second).
            boost::this_thread::sleep(boost::posix_time::millisec(40));

            // Get the "must stop" state (thread-safe)
            m_mustStopMutex.lock();
            mustStop=m_mustStop;
            m_mustStopMutex.unlock();
        }
        while (mustStop==false);
    }
};
```

Note that the boost thread is created in the `Start()` function passing itself as thread function. This function object will loop until we call `Stop()`. In the current case the `main()` function will call this member function. The code corresponding to the second thread is:

```
int main()
{
    // Create and start the animation class
    AnimationClass ac;
    ac.Start();

    // Wait for the user to press return
    getchar();

    // Stop the animation class
    cout << "Animation stopping..." << endl;
    ac.Stop();
    cout << "Animation stopped." << endl;

    return 0;
}
```

We note the presence of the variable `boost::mutex m_mustStopMutex` and the call `lock()` and `unlock()` on that variable in the `Stop()` and `operator ()` functions. We discuss mutexes in section 18.7.

The next question is: how does a thread 'wait' for another thread to finish before proceeding? The answer is to use `join()` (wait for a thread to finish) or `timed_join` (wait for a thread to finish for a maximum amount of time). The effect in both cases is to put the calling thread into *WaitSleepJoin* state. It is used when we need to wait on the result of a lengthy calculation. To give an example, we revisit the class `PowerClass` and we use it in `main()` as follows:

```
int main()
{
    int m=2;
    int n=200;

    // Create a m^n calculation object
    PowerClass pc(m, n);

    // Create thread and start m^n calculation in parallel
    // Since we read the result from pc, we must pass it as reference,
    // else the result will be placed in a copy of pc
    boost::thread t(boost::ref(pc));

    // Do calculation while the PowerClass is calculating m^n
    double result=m*n;

    // Wait till the PowerClass is finished
    // Leave this out and the result will be bogus
    t.join();

    // Display result.
    cout << "(" << m << "^" << n << ") / (" << m << "*" << n
        << ") = "<<pc.result/result<<endl;
}
```

Here we see that the main thread does some calculations and it waits until the computationally intensive thread function in `PowerClass` has completed.

18.7 Basic Thread Synchronisation

One of the attention points when writing multi-threaded code is to determine how to organise threads in such a way that access to shared data is done in a controlled manner. This is because the order in which threads access data is non-deterministic and this can lead to inconsistent results; called *race conditions*. A classic example is when two threads attempt to withdraw funds from an account at the same time. The steps in a sequential program to perform this transaction are:
1. Check the balance (are there enough funds in the account?).
2. Give the amount money to be withdrawn.
3. Commit the transaction and update the account.

When there are two threads involved then steps 1, 2 and 3 may be interleaved which means the threads can update data in a non-deterministic way. For example, the scenario in Figure 18.2 shows that after withdrawing 70 and 90 money units the balance is -60 money units which destroys the *invariant condition*. This states in this case that the balance may never become negative. Why did this transaction go wrong?

Thread 1	Thread 2	balance
if (70>balance)		100
	if (90>balance)	100
balance-=70		30
	balance-=90	-60

Figure 18.2 Thread Synchronisation

The solution is to ensure that steps 1, 2 and 3 constitute an atomic transaction by which we mean that they are locked by a single thread at any one moment in time. Boost.Thread has a number of classes for thread synchronisation. The first class is called mutex (*mutual exclusion*) and it allows us to define a lock on a code block and release the lock when the thread has finished executing the code block. To do this, we create an Account class containing an embedded mutex:

```
class Account
{
private:

    // The mutex to synchronise on
    boost::mutex m_mutex;

    // more...
};
```

We now give the code for withdrawing funds from an account. Notice the *thread-unsafe version* (which can lead to race conditions) and the *thread-safe version* using mutex:

```
// Withdraw an amount (not synchronized). Scary!
void Withdraw(int amount)
{
    if (m_balance-amount>=0)
    {
        // For testing we now give other threads a chance to run
        boost::this_thread::sleep(boost::posix_time::seconds(1));

        m_balance-=amount;
    }
    else throw NoFundsException();
}

// Withdraw an amount (locking using mutex object)
void WithdrawSynchronized(int amount)
{
    // Acquire lock on mutex.
    // If lock already locked, it waits till unlocked
    m_mutex.lock();

    if (m_balance-amount>=0)
    {
        // For testing we now give other threads a chance to run
        boost::this_thread::sleep(boost::posix_time::seconds(1));

        m_balance-=amount;
    }
    else
    {
        // Release lock on mutex. Forget this and it will hang
        m_mutex.unlock();
        throw NoFundsException();
    }

    // Release lock on mutex. Forget this and it will hang
    m_mutex.unlock();
}
```

Only one thread has the lock at any time. If another thread tries to lock a mutex that is already locked it will enter the *SleepWaitJoin* state until the lock is released by the other thread. Summarising, only one thread can hold a lock on a mutex and the code following the call to mutex.lock() can only be executed by one thread at a given time.

A major disadvantage of using mutex is that the system will *deadlock* ('hang') if you forget to call `mutex.unlock()`. For this reason we use the `unique_lock<Lockable>` adapter class that locks a mutex in its constructor and that unlocks a `mutex` in its destructor. The new version of the withdraw member function will be:

```
// Withdraw an amount (locking using unique_lock)
void WithdrawSynchronized2(int amount)
{
    // Acquire lock on mutex. Will be automatically unlocked
    // when lock is destroyed at the end of the function
    boost::unique_lock<boost::mutex> lock(m_mutex);
    if (m_balance-amount>=0)
    {
        // For testing we now give other threads a change to run
        boost::this_thread::sleep(boost::posix_time::seconds(1));
        m_balance-=amount;
    }
    else throw NoFundsException();
}  // Mutex automatically unlocked here
```

Note that it is not necessary to explicitly unlock the mutex in this case.

18.8 Thread Interruption

A thread that is in the *WaitSleepJoin* state can be interrupted by another thread which results in the former thread transitioning into the *Running* state. To interrupt a thread we call the thread member function `interrupt()` and then an exception of type `thread_interrupted` is thrown inside the thread function. We note that `interrupt()` only works when the thread is in the *WaitSleepJoin* state. If the thread never enters this state, you should call `boost::this_thread::interruption_point()` to specify a point where the thread can be interrupted.

The following function contains a *defined interruption point*:

```
// The function that will be run by the thread
void ThreadFunction()
{
    // Never ending loop. Normally the thread will never finish
    while(true)
    {
        try
        {
            // Interrupt can only occur in wait/sleep or join operation.
            // If you don't do that, call interuption_point().
            // Remove this line, and the thread will never be interrupted.
            boost::this_thread::interruption_point();
        }
        catch(const boost::thread_interrupted&)
        {
            // Thread interruption request received, break the loop
            cout<<"- Thread interrupted. Exiting thread."<<endl;
            break;
        }
    }
}
```

We now use this function in a test program; in this case we start a thread with `ThreadFunction()` as thread function. We let it run and then we interrupt it.

```
int main()
{
```

```
    // Create and start the thread
    boost::thread t(&ThreadFunction);

    // Wait 2 seconds for the thread to finish
    cout<<"Wait for 2 seconds for the thread to stop."<<endl;
    while (t.timed_join(boost::posix_time::seconds(2))==false)
    {
        // Interupt the thread
        cout<<"Thread not stopped, interrupt it now."<<endl;
        t.interrupt();
        cout<<"Thread interrupt request sent. "'
        cout<<"Wait to finish for 2 seconds again."<<endl;
    }

    // The thread has been stopped
    cout<<"Thread stopped"<<endl;
}
```

18.9 Thread Notification

In some cases a thread *A* needs to wait for another thread *B* to perform some activity. Boost.Thread provides an efficient way for thread notification using the condition_variable class and its member functions:

- wait(): thread *A* releases the lock when wait() is called; *A* then sleeps until another thread *B* calls notify().
- notify(): signals a change in an object related to thread *B*. Then one waiting thread (in this case *A*) wakes up after the lock has been released.
- notify_all(): this has the same intent as notify() except that all waiting threads wake up.

We shall see examples of this mechanism when we discuss synchronising queues and the Producer-Consumer pattern in section 18.11 and 18.12.

18.10 Thread Groups

Boost.Thread contains the class thread_group that supports the creation and management of a group of threads as one entity. The threads in the group are related in some way. The functionality is:

- Create a new thread group with no threads.
- Delete all threads in the group.
- Create a new thread and add it to the group.
- Remove a thread from the group without deleting the thread.
- join_all(): call join() on each thread in the group.
- interrupt_all(): call interrupt() on each thread object in the group.
- size(): give the number of threads in the group.

We shall give an example of how to use this class when we discuss the *Producer-Consumer* pattern in which a producer group writes data (*enqueue*) to a *synchronised queue* while threads in a consumer group extract (*dequeue*) the data from this queue.

18.11 Shared Queue Pattern

This pattern is a specialisation of the *Shared Data Pattern* (Mattson 2005). It is a thread-safe wrapper for the STL queue<T> container. It is a *blocking queue* because a thread wishing to dequeue the data will go into sleep mode if the queue is empty and it will wake up when it receives a notify() from another thread. This notification implies that new data is in the queue. Waiting threads are notified using a *condition variable*. A condition variable provides a way of naming an event in which threads have a general interest.

The interface is:

```
// Queue class that has thread synchronisation
template <typename T>
class SynchronisedQueue
{
private:
    std::queue<T> m_queue;              // Use STL queue to store data
    boost::mutex m_mutex;              // The mutex to synchronise on
    boost::condition_variable m_cond;  // The condition to wait for

public:

    // Add data to the queue and notify others
    void Enqueue(const T& data)
    {
        // Acquire lock on the queue
        boost::unique_lock<boost::mutex> lock(m_mutex);

        // Add the data to the queue
        m_queue.push(data);

        // Notify others that data is ready
        m_cond.notify_one();

    } // Lock is automatically released here

    // Get data from the queue. Wait for data if not available
    T Dequeue()
    {

        // Acquire lock on the queue
        boost::unique_lock<boost::mutex> lock(m_mutex);

        // When there is no data, wait till someone fills it.
        // Lock is automatically released in the wait and obtained
        // again after the wait
        while (m_queue.size()==0) m_cond.wait(lock);

        // Retrieve the data from the queue
        T result=m_queue.front(); m_queue.pop();
        return result;

    } // Lock is automatically released here
};
```

We now use this class as a data container in the *Producer-Consumer* pattern.

18.12 The Producer-Consumer Pattern

This pattern is useful in a variety of situations. There are many applications of this pattern (POSA 1996, Mattson 2005, GOF 1995). In general, one or more *producer agents* write information to a synchronised queue while one or more *consumer agents* extract information from the queue. It is possible to extend the pattern to support multiple queues. The Producer-Consumer Pattern is depicted in Figure 18.3.

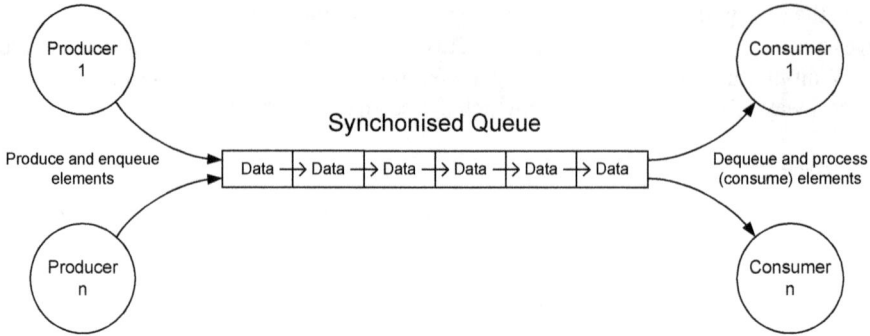

Figure 18.3 Producer-Consumer Pattern

We create a producer class as follows:

```
// Class that produces objects and puts them in a queue
class Producer
{
private:
    int m_id;                          // The id of the producer
    SynchronisedQueue<string>* m_queue;   // The queue to use

public:

    // Constructor with id and the queue to use
    Producer(int id, SynchronisedQueue<string>* queue)
    {
        m_id=id;
        m_queue=queue;
    }

    // The thread function fills the queue with data
    void operator () ()
    {
        int data=0;
        while (true)
        {
            // Produce a string and store in the queue
            string str = "Producer: " + IntToString(m_id) +
                         " data: " + IntToString(data++);
            m_queue->Enqueue(str);
            cout<<str<<endl;

            // Sleep one second
            boost::this_thread::sleep(boost::posix_time::seconds(1));
        }
    }
};
```

Similarly, the interface for the consumer class is given by:

```
// Class that consumes objects from a queue
class Consumer
{
private:
    int m_id;                          // The id of the consumer
    SynchronisedQueue<string>* m_queue;   // The queue to use

public:
    // Constructor with id and the queue to use.
```

```
    Consumer(int id, SynchronisedQueue<string>* queue)
    {
       m_id=id;
       m_queue=queue;
    }

    // The thread function reads data from the queue
    void operator () ()
    {
       while (true)
       {
          // Get the data from the queue and print it
          cout<<"Consumer "<<IntToString(m_id).c_str()
             <<" consumed: ("<<m_queue->Dequeue().c_str();

          // Make sure we can be interrupted
          boost::this_thread::interruption_point();
       }
    }
};
```

Finally, the following code creates thread groups for producers and consumers using the `thread-group` class:

```
#include "Producer.hpp"
#include "Consumer.hpp"

using namespace std;

int main()
{
   // Display the number of processors/cores
   cout<<boost::thread::hardware_concurrency()
      <<" processors/cores detected."<<endl<<endl;
   cout<<"When threads are running, press enter to stop"<<endl;

   // The number of producers/consumers
   int nrProducers, nrConsumers;

   // The shared queue
   SynchronisedQueue<string> queue;

   // Ask the number of producers
   cout<<"How many producers do you want? : ";
   cin>>nrProducers;

   // Ask the number of consumers
   cout<<"How many consumers do you want? : ";
   cin>>nrConsumers;

   // Create producers
   boost::thread_group producers;
   for (int i=0; i<nrProducers; i++)
   {
      Producer p(i, &queue);
      producers.create_thread(p);
   }

   // Create consumers
   boost::thread_group consumers;
   for (int i=0; i<nrConsumers; i++)
   {
      Consumer c(i, &queue);
      consumers.create_thread(c);
   }
```

```
    // Wait for enter (two times because the return from the
    // previous cin is still in the buffer)
    getchar(); getchar();

    // Interrupt the threads and stop them
    producers.interrupt_all(); producers.join_all();
    consumers.interrupt_all(); consumers.join_all();
}
```

18.13 Thread Local Storage

We know that global data is shared between threads. In some cases we may wish to give each thread its own copy of global data. To this end, we use `thread_specific_ptr<T>` that is a pointer to the data (it is initially set to NULL). Each thread must initialise this pointer by calling `reset()` and subsequentially the data can be accessed by dereferencing the pointer. The data is automatically deleted when the thread exits.

Here is an example of a thread function that defines it own copy of global data:

```
    // Global data. Each thread has its own value
    boost::thread_specific_ptr<int> threadLocalData;

    // Callable function
    void CallableFunction(int id)
    {
        // Initialise thread local data (for the current thread)
        threadLocalData.reset(new int);
        *threadLocalData=0;

        // Do this a number of times
        for (int i=0; i<5; i++)
        {
            // Print value of global data and increase value
            cout<<"Thread: "<<id<<" - Value: "<<(*threadLocalData)++<<endl;

            // Wait one second
            boost::this_thread::sleep(boost::posix_time::seconds(1));
        }
    }
```

We now initialise the copy of the global data, we also create a thread group and we add a number of threads to it, each one having its own copy of the global data:

```
    int main()
    {
        // Initialise thread local data (for the main thread)
        threadLocalData.reset(new int);
        *threadLocalData=0;

        // Create threads and add them to the thread group
        boost::thread_group threads;
        for (int i=0; i<3; i++)
        {
            boost::thread* t=new boost::thread(&CallableFunction, i);
            threads.add_thread(t);
        }

        // Wait till they are finished
        threads.join_all();

        // Display thread local storage value, should still be zero
        cout<<"Main - Value: "<<(*threadLocalData)<<endl;
```

```
    return 0;
}
```

18.14 Summary and Conclusions

We have included a chapter on multi-threading using Boost.Thread. It is now possible to create parallel applications in C++. We see a future for multi-threaded applications and for this reason we decided to give an introduction to the most important functionality in this library.

Boost.Thread contains low-level operations or mechanisms that we use to design and implement multi-threaded applications. It contains the building blocks that can be used with parallel design patterns (see Mattson 2005). We summarise the main steps in the process of creating a multi-threaded application:
1. *Finding Concurrency*: we decide if a problem is a suitable candidate for a parallel solution. System decomposition based on tasks or data allows us to find potentially concurrent tasks and their dependencies. In particular, we need a way of grouping tasks and ordering the groups to satisfy temporal constraints. An initial design is produced.
2. *Algorithm Structure Design*: we elaborate the initial model to move it closer to a program. We pay attention to forces such as efficiency, simplicity, portability and scalability. The algorithm structure will be determined by tasks on the one hand or by data on the other hand. Examples of high-level algorithms are *Divide and Conquer*, *Geometric Decomposition* and *Pipeline*.
3. *Supporting Structures Design*: in this phase we decide how to model program structure and shared data. For example, the program could be designed as a *SPMD (Single Program Multiple Data)*, *Master Worker* or *Loop Parallelism* pattern. Possible data structures are *Shared Data* and *Shared Queue* whose implementation we discussed in section 18.11.
4. *Implementation Mechanisms*: in this phase we deploy the functionality of Boost.Thread to implement the design.

We discuss this process and its applications in Volume II.

Appendix A: Generic Programming

Introduction and Objectives

In this appendix we discuss a number of generic C++ design techniques that are used in Boost. We feel that it is important to know what these are and how to use them. For more detailed discussions, see Alexandrescu 2001 and Abrahams 2005.

Some Useful Techniques

When creating template classes with several template parameters it is possible to define default policy. In other words, template parameters are used to express *policies* and *traits*. The default argument provides the most common or *default policy*. To give an example, we examine a class for one-dimensional vectors:

```
template <typename Value = double, int N = 10>
class SimpleVector
{ // Simple vector class

private:
    Value arr[N];

public:
    // member functions
};
```

In this case there are two default parameters. Thus, it is possible to create vectors with two, one or zero parameters, for example:

```
SimpleVector<double, 20> vec1;
SimpleVector<string> vec2;
SimpleVector<> vec3;
```

In this case the first vector contains 20 doubles; the second vector contains 10 strings while the third vector contains 10 doubles. We note that default template arguments can be user-defined types.

The main advantage of using default template parameters is that it reduces cognitive overload by allowing the developer to use the most common policy in a transparent way.

An effective way to create new generic data structures is to use template classes as parameters for other template classes. We say that one class is *nested* in another class. We also speak of an *inner class* and an *outer class*, respectively.

We take an example to show nesting. We consider creating a square sparse matrix class. To this end, we implement a dynamic sparse matrix as a map of maps. We specialise the underlying parameter types for convenience and we define a synonym for readability purposes:

```
// Specific data types, can be generalised
typedef map<int, double> SparseRow;
```

Now we define a sparse matrix structure as follows:

```
template <int N> struct SparseMatrix
{ // Compile-time matrix (stack-based)

    map<int, SparseRow> data;
};
```

We take an example of using this class. In this case we create a sparse matrix by populating its rows. We also print the sparse matrix using the following function:

```cpp
template <int N> void print(SparseMatrix<N>& sm)
{
    SparseRow sr;
    SparseRow::const_iterator it;
    for (int row = 0; row < N; ++row)
    {
        SparseRow sr = sm.data[row];
        // Now iterate over row
        for (it=sm.data[row].begin();it!=sm.data[row].end(); ++it)
        {
            cout << (*it).second << ", ";
        }
        cout << endl;
    }
}
```

The code for initialisation is:

```cpp
int main()
{
    const N = 500000;

    // Create some rows
    SparseRow current;
    current.insert(pair<int, double>(0, -2.0));
    current.insert(pair<int, double>(1, 1.0));

    // Create a sparse matrix and populate its first row
    SparseMatrix<N> sparseMat;
    sparseMat.data[0] = current;

    int currentIndex = 0;

    // Populate the matrix with multiple rows
    for (int row = 1; row < N-1; row++)
    {
        current.clear();
        current.insert(pair<int, double>(currentIndex, 1.0));
        current.insert(pair<int, double>(currentIndex+1, -2.0));
        current.insert(pair<int, double>(currentIndex+2, 1.0));
        sparseMat.data[row] = current;
        currentIndex++;
    }

    print(sparseMat);

    return 0;
}
```

This sample shows how it is possible to write code using C++ templates.

A *template member function* is a member function that uses one or more additional template parameters in addition to those defined in the class containing it. Let us suppose that we wish to multiply the elements of a vector by a scalar; this scalar belongs to a *field type* and the corresponding template class and template member function are defined as follows:

```cpp
template <typename Value, int N>
class SimpleVector
{
    … // Other members
```

```
    // Member function version of the scaling function
    template <typename F> void scale(const F& scalar)
    {
        for (int i=0; i < N; ++i)
        {
            arr[i]  = scalar * arr[i];
        }
    }
};
```

An example of use is:

```
// Create vector
double value = 10.0;
SimpleVector<double, 6> vec(value);

// Now scale using a member function
// Notice the use of template argument
double factor = 2.0;
vec.scale<double>(factor);
vec.print();
```

Please note that we have inserted the type of the scaling factor in the call to the scaling function. This makes calls unambiguous and ensures we do not get cryptic compiler error messages. Finally, another example is to define a scaling function (non-member) using operator overloading:

```
template <typename Value, int N>
class SimpleVector
{
    ... // Other members

    // Premultiplication by a field value
    template <typename F> SimpleVector<Value, N>
    friend operator * (const F& scalar,
                       const SimpleVector<Value, N>& myArray)
    {
        SimpleVector<Value, N> result;
        for (int i= 0; i < N; ++i)
        {
            result.arr[i] = scalar * myArray.arr[i];
        }
        return result;
    }
};
```

An example of use is:

```
// Scale using a templated friend function
double factor = 0.5;
SimpleVector<double, 6> scaledVector = factor * vec;
scaledVector.print();
```

Traits Classes

A *trait* is a small object whose main purpose is to carry information that is needed by another object or algorithm, thus allowing us to determine *policy*. The main reason for using a trait is to provide a consistent interface to clients and to avoid embedding *magic numbers* in code.

The STL and Boost libraries contain built-in traits classes. An important trait is
`numeric_limits<T>` and it contains a wealth of information on numeric data types, for
example:

- Minimum and maximum values.
- Binary and decimal accuracy estimates.
- Whether a numeric type is signed.
- Whether a numeric type is integer.
- Machine precision information.
- Details about rounding.

This class can be used when creating scientific and numeric applications that use numeric
data types such as `float` and `double`, for example. By instantiating the traits class you will
be given the appropriate set of parameters and values. A template function to print some of
these numerical properties is:

```cpp
template <typename Numeric> void print(string& s)
{ // Numeric properties

    Numeric largest = numeric_limits<Numeric>::max();
    Numeric smallest = numeric_limits<Numeric>::min();

    // calculations done on a type are free of rounding errors.
    bool exactYN = numeric_limits<Numeric>::is_exact;

    // has integer representation
    bool integerRepYN = numeric_limits<Numeric>::is_integer;

    // etc. for the interested developer, see online documentation

    cout << endl << "Numeric type is: " << s << endl;
    cout << "Max, min: " << largest << ", " << smallest << endl;

    // This function ensures values are printed as text, not 0 or 1
    boolalpha(cout);
    cout << "Free of rounding errors: " << exactYN << endl;
    cout << "Integer representation: " << integerRepYN << endl;
}
```

We can then instantiate this template function by replacing the generic data type by built-in
types:

```cpp
print<double>(string("double"));
print<int>(string("int"));
print<long>(string("long"));
print<unsigned int>(string("unsigned int"));
print<unsigned long>(string("unsigned long"));
```

The output from this program is:

```
Numeric type is: double
Max, min: 1.79769e+308, 2.22507e-308
Free of rounding errors: false
Integer representation: false

Numeric type is: int
Max, min: 2147483647, -2147483648
Free of rounding errors: true
Integer representation: true

Numeric type is: long
```

```
Max, min: 2147483647, -2147483648
Free of rounding errors: true
Integer representation: true

Numeric type is: unsigned int
Max, min: 4294967295, 0
Free of rounding errors: true
Integer representation: true
```

Numeric type is: unsigned long
Max, min: 4294967295, 0
Free of rounding errors: true
Integer representation: true

Concluding, the use of traits in this case promotes portability and reusability of code.

An Introduction to Policy-based Design (PBD)

The authors saw this term in Alexandrescu 2001 where it is used in the context of C++ template programming. We generalise it here to make it applicable to a wider range of software techniques including *component-based design*, UML modelling and template programming. See Leavens 2000 for an introduction of software component design.
The need for, and power of the PBD approach is that we can think about the design of a system by decomposing it into loosely coupled components. A component is a piece of software that offers services in the form of functions (called *interfaces*) to other potential client components. In order to design a component we need to address the following issues:
- The products, services and data that the component provides.
- The input data that the component requires from other components.
- The steps that map the input data to output data.

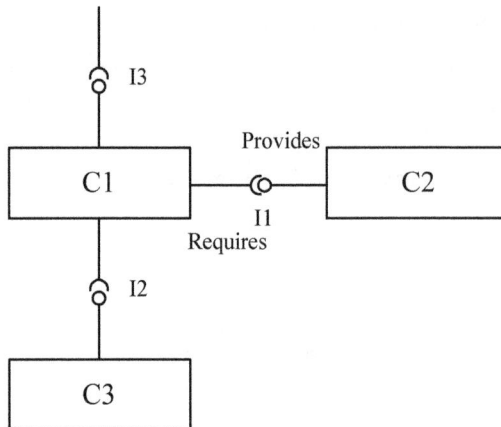

Figure 1 UML Component Diagram

Executing these activities is part of the software design process and the end result is a network of components, each one having well-defined responsibilities. We model these responsibilities by interfaces. The resulting UML *component diagram* is shown in Figure 1 for the case of a component called C1 that *provides* an interface I3 to potential clients and that *requires* interfaces I1 and I2 from server/components C2 and C3. In other words, C1 offers services but it also requires services from other server components. These components C2 and C3 typically have responsibilities for services such as:

- S1: Object creation and initialisation of simple and complex objects.
- S2: Authentication and authorisation (allowing access to C1).
- S3: Execution of commands on behalf of component C1.
- S4: Execution of algorithms and extended functions of C1 (for example, *Strategy* and *Visitor* patterns).

We strive to create the components in Figure 1 so that they have little orthogonal functionality and each one should have one major responsibility. Let us take an example in which we model scenario S1. In this case we model components that create objects (this example is based on Alexandrescu 2001, page 8). Clients delegate to these factory components when they need an object to be created. We depict the situation in Figure 2. A client object delegates to factory objects. The base factory describes an interface:

```
template <typename T> class Factory
{ // Base class for all factories

public:
    virtual T* Create() = 0;
};
```

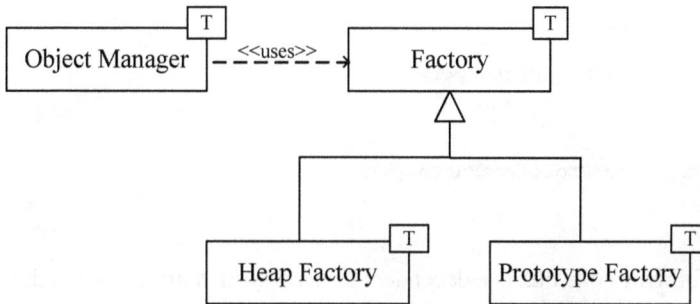

Figure 2 Creational Policies

Derived classes are:

```
template <typename T> class HeapFactory: public Factory<T>
{
public:
    virtual T* Create()
    {
        cout << "Creating heap object\n";
        return new T();
    }
};

template <typename T> class PrototypeFactory: public Factory<T>
{
private:
    T* proto;

public:
    PrototypeFactory () { proto = new T; }
    PrototypeFactory (T* prototype) { proto = prototype; }
    ~PrototypeFactory() { delete proto; }

    virtual T* Create()
```

```
    {
        cout << "Creating prototype object\n";
        return new T(*proto);
    }
};
```

We now define the client classes that use these generic factory classes:

```
template <typename CreationPolicy>
class ObjectManager: public CreationPolicy
{
public:
    ObjectManager() {}
};
```

Now we can use these classes in applications; in this case we manage two-dimensional points. First, we create a template function that prompts the user to choose which specific factory to use in subsequent code. This function can be described as a '*factory for a factory*':

```
template <typename T> Factory<T>* GetFactory()
{
    int choice = 1;
    cout << "Factories: 1) Heap 2) Prototype ";
    cin >> choice;

    if (choice == 1)
    {
        return new HeapFactory<T>();
    }
    else
    {
        return new PrototypeFactory<T>();
    }
}
```

Finally, we can write code that is independent of the way memory is allocated; we call a factory to create memory. We then create some numbers and points:

```
typedef ObjectManager<HeapFactory<Point> > MyHeapPointMgr;

int main()
{
    // Create a double
    Factory<double>* fac = GetFactory<double>();

    double* myval = fac->Create();
    *myval = 0.001;
    cout << "double is: " << *myval << endl;

    // Create a point by choosing a factory
    Factory<Point>* fac2 = GetFactory<Point>();
    Point* pt2 = fac2->Create();
    (*pt2).print();

    // Create a point using heap allocation
    MyHeapPointMgr myPoint;
    Point* pt = myPoint.Create();
    pt->x = 1.0;
    pt->y = 2.0;
    (*pt).print();

    delete pt; delete pt2;
    delete myval;
```

```
      delete fac; delete fac2;

      return 0;
}
```

Curiously Recurring Template Pattern (CRTP)

This pattern dates from the 1990's (developed by Jim Coplien) and it is a technique to
simulate *dynamic polymorphism*. It is used to achieve the same effect as virtual functions
without experiencing the possible performance costs associated with vtable structures,
method lookup and multiple inheritance. In general, CRTP is applicable in situations where
we have a class hierarchy in which the base class has a combination of one or more default
virtual and pure virtual member functions and where these member functions may/must be
overridden in derived classes, for example:

- Algorithms (*Strategy* and *Template Method Patterns*).
- Polymorphic copy construction (*Prototype* pattern).
- UML Statecharts in Boost.Statechart.
- Windows Active Template Library (ATL).
- Simulating multiple inheritance.
- Metaprogramming techniques (Alexandrescu 2001).
- Simulating interfaces.

We give examples of this pattern. The first example is the case of a base class and a derived
class that together implement *static polymorphism* We give this example to show how the
principle works:

```cpp
template <typename Derived> struct Base_A
{
   void interface()
   {
      // ...
      static_cast<Derived*>(this)->implementation();
      // ...
   }

   static void static_func()
   {
      // ...
      Derived::static_sub_func();
      // ...
   }
};
```

We see the absence of the keyword 'virtual' and the presence of 'policy' functions
implementation() and static_sub_func(). We take examples of classes that
implement these functions:

```cpp
struct Derived_A: Base_A<Derived_A>
{
   void implementation() { cout << "Derived A" << endl; }
   static void static_sub_func() { cout << "Static derived A" << endl; }
};

struct Derived_B: Base_A<Derived_B>
{
   void implementation() { cout << "Derived B" << endl; }
   static void static_sub_func() { cout << "Static derived B" << endl; }
};
```

An example is:

```
Derived_A d1;
d1.interface(); d1.static_func();

Derived_B d2;
d2.interface(); d2.static_func();
```

The appropriate functions in the derived classes will be called, as expected.

The second example is based on the *Template Method pattern* (see GOF 1995). This pattern defines the skeleton of an algorithm in an operation, deferring some steps to derived classes. It lets subclasses redefine certain steps of an algorithm without changing the algorithm's structure. The example we take concerns an algorithm that consists of three parts, namely *preprocessing, computation* and *postprocessing*. The first and third parts must be implemented by derived classes. The base class has the interface:

```
// CRTP pattern
template <typename D>
struct Base_B
{
    double algorithm(double x)
    { // Template method pattern

        // Variant part I
        double y = Preprocess(x);

        // Invariant part
        y += 2.0;
        if ( y <= 21.0) y = 3.3;
        else y = 3.4;

        // Variant part II
        double z = Postprocess(x);

        // Postcondition
        return y * z;
    }

    inline double Preprocess(double x)
    {
        return static_cast<D*>(this) -> Preprocess(x);
    }

    inline double Postprocess(double x)
    {
        return static_cast<D*>(this) -> Postprocess(x);
    }

    virtual ~Base_B() {}
};
```

An example of a class that conforms to the interface is:

```
struct DerivedCRTP: Base_B<DerivedCRTP>
{
    inline double Preprocess(double x) { return exp(-x*x); }
    inline double Postprocess(double x) { return tanh(x); }
};
```

In some cases, CRTP improves performance when compared to the use of virtual functions. The third example implements multiple inheritance. To this end, we create a class that inherits from both `Base_A` (as defined at the beginning of the CRTP section) and `Base_B`:

```
template <typename Derived> struct Base_B
{
    void calculate()
    {
        // ...
        static_cast<Derived*>(this)->calculate();
        // ...
    }
};

// Multiple inheritance
struct Derived_AB : Base_A<Derived_AB>, Base_B<Derived_AB>
{
    void calculate() { cout << "Derived AB from Base_B" << endl; }
    void implementation() {cout<< "Derived AB from Base_A" << endl; }

    static void static_sub_func()
    {
        cout << "Static derived AB from Base_A" << endl;
    }
};
```

Creating instances of `Derived_AB` proceeds as follows:

```
cout << "Multiple inheritance\n";
Derived_AB d12;
d12.calculate(); d12.interface(); d12.static_func();
```

An understanding of CRTP is useful in a number of application areas.
The last example concerns polymorphic copy construction (also known as the *Prototype* design pattern). In the object-oriented approach we define a *polymorphic copy* member function in a base class:

```
class Shape
{
public:
    virtual Shape* Clone() const = 0;
    virtual ~Shape() {}
};
```

We apply CRTP to create a derived class of `Shape` that has a copy function:

```
template <typename Derived>
class Shape_CRTP: public Shape
{
public:
    Shape* Clone() const
    {
        return new Derived(dynamic_cast<Derived const&>(*this));
    }
};
```

For example, we can create specific classes as follows:

```
class Circle: public Shape_CRTP<Circle> {};
```

In this case we applied the CRTP pattern to avoid implementing the same code for each derived class and not necessarily to improve performance.
An example of using the code is:

```
int main()
{
    Shape* s = new Circle;
    Shape* sClone = s -> Clone();

    delete s; delete sClone;
    return 0;
}
```

Some of the advantages of CRTP are that it is more efficient than using dynamic polymorphism, both in terms of run-time behaviour and human effort. The resulting code is also easier to maintain in many cases.

The Boost Categories

Looking at the site **www.boost.org** we note that each library is classified into one or more categories. The relationship between libraries and categories is many-to-many. Knowing what these categories are and what they offer will help you to determine if a Boost library can be used in your applications. We include those libraries that we have discussed in this book. Please consult the Boost site for a complete list.

1. *String and Text Processing*
   - Conversion: polymorphic and lexical casts.
   - Lexical Cast: general literal text conversions (for example, between `int` and `string`).
   - Regex: regular expression library.
   - String Algo: string algorithm library.
   - Tokenizer: break a string or other character sequence into a series of tokens.
   - Xpressive: regular expressions that can be written as strings and expression templates.

2. *Containers*
   - Array: STL-compliant container wrapper for constant-size arrays.
   - Multi-Array: a generic n-dimensional array concept definition and common implementations of that interface.
   - Variant: safe, generic, stack-based discriminated union container.

3. *Iterators*
   - Tokenizer.

4. *Algorithms*
   - String Algo.
   - Range: infrastructure for generic algorithms based on iterator concepts.

5. *Function Objects and Higher-Order Programming*
   - Bind: generalisation of `std::bind1st` and `std::bind2nd` and more.
   - Function: function object wrappers for deferred calls and callbacks.
   - Functional/Hash: hash function object that can be extended to hash user-defined types.
   - Signals: managed signals and slots callback implementation.
   - Signals2: thread-safe managed signals and slots callback implementation.

6. *Generic Programming*
    - Concept Check: Tools for generic programming.

7. *Template Metaprogramming*
    - None discussed in this book.

8. *Preprocessor Metaprogramming*
    - None discussed in this book.

9. *Concurrent Programming*
    - Thread: portable C++ multi-threading.

10. *Maths and Numerics*
    - Math Octonian: Octonians.
    - Math Quaternion: Quaternions.
    - Multi-Array.
    - Random: random number generation.
    - Rational: a rational number class.
    - Math Common Factor: greatest common divisor and least common multiple.

11. *Correctness and Testing*
    - Concept Check: Tools for generic programming.

12. *Data Structures*
    - Any: safe, generic container for single values of different value types.
    - Tuple: class for n-tuples.
    - Multi-Index: Containers with one or more indices.

13. *Image Processing*
    - None discussed in this book.

14. *Input/Output*
    - Serialization: serialisation for persistence and marshalling.
    - Assign: filling containers with constant or generated data.

15. *Inter-Language Support*
    - None discussed in this book.

16. *Memory*
    - SmartPtr: smart pointer class templates.

17. *Parsing*
    - None discussed in this book.

18. *Programming Interfaces*
    - Function.

19. *Miscellaneous*
    - Conversion.
    - Lexical Cast.
    - Numeric Conversion: optimised policy-based numeric conversions.
    - Flyweight: design pattern to manage large quantities of highly redundant objects.

Concepts

Introduction

One of the important and practical issues when using the Boost libraries is to know what these libaries expect of classes that developers use as instantiated template parameters. In other words, these classes should implement certain member functions such as default constructor and an equality operator ==, for example. Failure to implement these functions will result in a compiler error and a resulting, cryptic error message.

There are many reasons why C++ template code does not compile, some of which are:
a)   Syntax error: the code is not well-formed.
b)   The instantiated template parameter does not provide the interface that the client class requires.

A discussion of problem a) is outside the scope of this book. We focus on problem b) and in particular we discuss which interface implementations Boost requires. This issue is a special case of policy-based design that we have already discussed in this appendix. In this section we give an overview of the required interfaces that Boost libraries expect. These are called concepts in C++. A *concept* is a set of requirements that a type must fulfill in order to be correctly used as an argument to a generic algorithm. In C++ concepts are represented by formal template parameters to function templates and there is no explicit mechanism for representing concepts. In fact they are just placeholders and their names are chosen to reflect the interfaces they represent.

The Boost libraries are based on template programming techniques. In many cases assumptions are made about the functionality provided by the type that is passed as template argument. In other words, for some Boost templates the type you pass as template argument must implement certain functionality. An example from Boost is the array class. If you create a `boost::array` specifying the size, it uses the default constructor of the type to be stored in the array. Thus the underlying type must provide a default constructor.

There are a number of predefined concepts that are used in the Boost libraries. Each concept describes a piece of functionality. It may be required that a class implements more than one concept. Frequently used concepts are:
• DefaultConstructible.
• CopyConstructible.
• Assignable.
• EqualityComparable.
• LessThanComparable.

• InputIterator.
• OutputIterator.
• ForwardIterator.
• BidirectionalIterator.
• RandomAccessIterator.

• SinglePassRange, ForwardRange, BidirectionalRange and RandomAccessRange.

These concepts and the generalisation/specialisation relationship between them are depicted in Figure 3. Note that it is not a class diagram in the usual sense. Concepts are not classes.

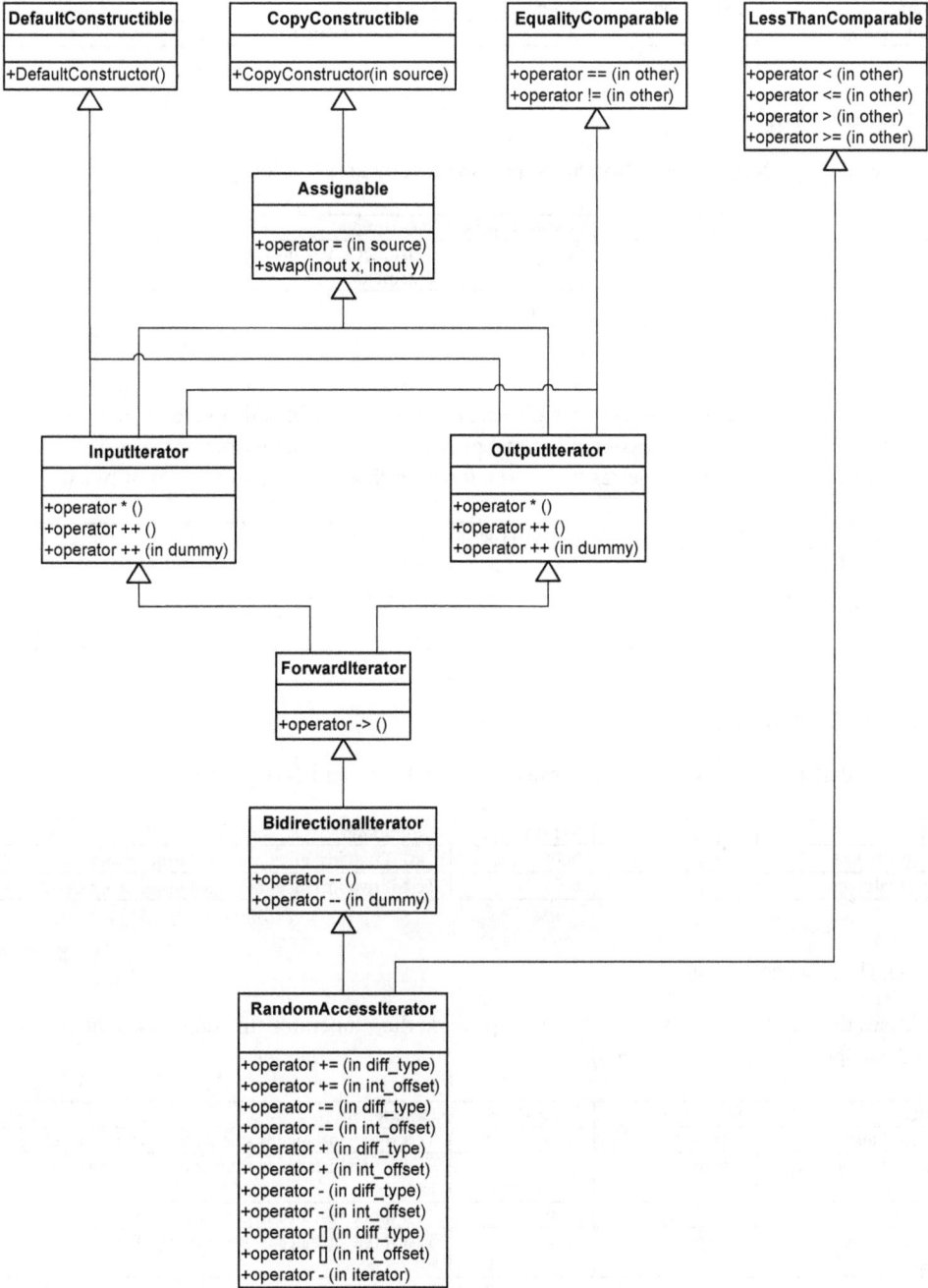

Figure 3 Concept 'conceptual' hierarchy

We now discuss each concept in Figure 3.

DefaultConstructible

Classes that are default constructible must provide a default constructor.

Name	Expression	Return Type	Description
Construction	X()	X	Construct a default instance of type X

CopyConstructible

Classes that are copy constructible must provide a copy constructor.

Name	Expression	Return Type	Description
Copy Construction	X(x)	X	Construct a new instance of type X using the copy constructor

Assignable

Assignable is an extension to the *CopyConstructible* concept. In addition to a copy constructor, classes that are assignable must provide an assignment operator (operator =). In some cases *Assignable* requires a swap() function that swaps the contents of two objects.

Name	Expression	Return Type	Description
Assignment	x=y	X&	Copy values from one instance to another using operator =
Swap (optional)	swap(x, y)	void	Exchange values of two instances using swap() function

EqualityComparable

Classes that are equality comparable must provide the == and != operators.

Name	Expression	Return Type	Description
Equality test	x==y	bool	Test if two instances are equal using operator ==
Inequality test	x!=y	bool	Test if two instances are equal using operator !=

LessThanComparable

Classes that are less than comparable must provide the < operator. In some cases the >, <= and >= operators are also required.

Name	Expression	Return Type	Description
Less than	x<y	bool	Test if one instance is smaller than another instance
Less than or equal	x<=y	bool	Test if one instance is smaller or equal to another instance
Greater than	x>y	bool	Test if one instance is greater than another instance
Greater than or equal	x>=y	bool	Test if one instance is grater or equal to another instance

InputIterator

Classes that are an input iterator provides functionality to read a sequence of values. An input iterator represents a position in a sequence and can move through a sequence in the forward direction and can read the values of the sequence (read-only). Only sequential navigation is possible. Additionally, an input iterator is *single pass* meaning that you can read the value at the current position only once. An input iterator must implement the

Assignable, *DefaultConstructible* and *EqualityComparable* concepts. Additionally it must implement the *dereference* (`operator *`), *pre-increment* and *post-increment* operators (`operator ++`).

Name	Expression	Return Type	Description
Dereference	`*i`	const T&	Read access to the current element
Pre-increment	`++i`	Iter&	Set iterator to next element and return the iterator
Post-increment	`i++`	Iter	Return iterator to current element and set iterator to the next element

OutputIterator

An output iterator is similar to an input iterator but can only write the values of a sequence (write-only). It can move in the forward direction and it is *single pass*.

Name	Expression	Return Type	Description
Dereference	`*i`	T&	Write access to the current element
Pre-increment	`++i`	Iter&	Set iterator to next element and return the iterator
Post-increment	`i++`	Iter	Return iterator to current element and set iterator to the next element

ForwardIterator

A forward iterator is a combination of the *InputIterator* and *OutputIterator* concepts. It can read and write a value at the current position and it can iterate in the forward direction only. Additionally, it is *multi-pass* which means that the value at the current position can be read/written more than once. In addition to the *dereference* operator (`operator *`), it must also provide the *member access* operator (`operator ->`).

Name	Expression	Return Type	Description
Dereference	`*i`	T&	Read/Write access to the current element
Member access	`i->`	T*	Access to member

BidirectionalIterator

A bidirectional iterator is an extension of the *ForwardIterator* concept and it can move in both directions. It thus provides the *pre-* and *post-decrement* operators (`operator --`).

Name	Expression	Return Type	Description
Pre-decrement	`--i`	Iter&	Set iterator to previous element and return the iterator
Post-decrement	`i--`	Iter	Return iterator to current element and set iterator to the previous element

RandomAccessIterator

A random access iterator is an extension of the *BidirectionalIterator* concept and the *LessThanComparable* concept. In addition to the bidirectional iterator, it can jump through the sequence by more than one step. It provides the +, -, +=, -= and `[]` operators for both *integer offsets* and an *iterator difference type* (difference between two iterators (i1-i2)). The + operator must be defined for both 'iterator+offset' and 'offset+iterator' forms.

Finally, an `operator` – must be defined that subtracts two iterators resulting in an *iterator difference type*.

Name	Expression	Return Type	Description
Motion (diff type)	`i+=n`	Iter&	Move to element using difference type
Motion (int offset)	`i+=offset`	Iter&	Move to element using integer offset
Motion (diff type)	`i-=n`	Iter&	Move to element using difference type
Motion (int offset)	`i-=offset`	Iter&	Move to element using integer offset
Addition (diff type)	`i+n`	Iter	New iterator at a difference from current
Addition (int offset)	`i+offset`	Iter	New iterator at an offset from current
Addition (diff type)	`n+i`	Iter	New iterator at a difference from current
Addition (int offset)	`offset+i`	Iter	New iterator at an offset from current
Subtraction (diff type)	`i-n`	Iter	New iterator at a negative difference from current
Subtraction (int offset)	`i-offset`	Iter	New iterator at a negative offset from current
Distance	`i1-i2`	diff_type	Difference between two iterators
Element access (diff type)	`i[n]`	T&	Read/write access to element at a difference from current
Element access (int offset)	`i[offset]`	T&	Read/write access to element at an offset from current

Range Concepts

The range concept contains a start- and end-iterator as one object. Functions can accept a single range instead of a separate start- and end-iterator. Functions can also return a single range which is easier than returning two iterators.

All range concepts must provide `begin()` and `end()` functions that return an iterator. The type of iterator returned depends on the range type. These iterator types are not the same as the iterator concepts described above but they are similar in the sense that they are refinements of the above concepts.

- *SinglePassRange* concept returns *SinglePassIterator* which is similar to the *InputIterator* concept.
- *ForwardRange* concept returns *ForwardTraversalIterator* which is similar to the *ForwardIterator* concept.
- *BidirectionalRange* concept returns *BidirectionalTraversalIterator* which is similar to the *BidirectionalIterator* concept.
- *RandomAccessRange* concept returns *RandomAccessTraversalIterator* which is similar to the *RandomAccessIterator* concept.

Name	Expression	Return Type	Description
Begin position	`boost::begin(r)`	Iter	Get the iterator at the begin position
End position	`boost::end(r)`	Iter	Get the iterator at the end position
Is empty	`boost::empty(r)`	bool	Is the begin position the same as the end position?

Boost Concept Check Library (BCCL)

We now introduce the Boost Concept Check Library (BCCL). This library has functions to check if a class implements a given concept. It also has mechanisms for inserting compile-time checks on template parameters at the point of instantiation. We examine each of these topics.

The first example concerns a C++ class that implements some (but not all) of the concepts in Figure 3:

```cpp
class Point
{
private:
    double x;                       // X coordinate
    double y;                       // Y coordinate

public:
    // Constructors
    Point();                              // Default constructor
    Point(const Point& pt);               // Copy constructor
    Point(double xval, double yval);      // Initialize with x and y value

    ~Point();

    // Accessing functions
    double X() const ;                    // The x-coordinate
    double Y() const;                     // The y-coordinate

    Point operator + (const Point& p2) const;
    double distance(const Point& p2) const;   // Distance between 2 points

    Point& operator = (const Point& pt);

    // Comparing points
    bool operator == (const Point& pt) const; // EqualityComparable
    bool operator != (const Point& pt) const; // EqualityComparable
    bool operator < (const Point& pt) const;  // LessThanComparable

    // Modifiers
    void X(double newX);
    void Y(double newY);
};
```

We now create a program to test if the class implements certain concepts:

```cpp
#include <boost/concept_check.hpp>
#include "Point.hpp"

int main()
{
    // All these concepts are supported by Point; code compiles
    boost::function_requires< boost::DefaultConstructible<Point> >();
    boost::function_requires< boost::CopyConstructible<Point> >();
    boost::function_requires< boost::Assignable<Point> >();
    boost::function_requires< boost::EqualityComparable<Point> >();
    boost::function_requires< boost::LessThanComparable<Point> >();

    // Concepts not supported by Point; code does NOT compile and an error
    // message will be given
// boost::function_requires< boost::InputIterator<Point> >();

    return 0;
}
```

The program compiles and is runnable. However, it does not support input iterators and when we ran the program (with the comments in the last line removed) we got the following error messages (many!):

```
Error 1  error C2039: 'iterator_category' : is not a member of 'Point'
c:\program files\microsoft visual studio 9.0\vc\include\xutility 764
ConceptCheck
```

```
Error 2  error C2146: syntax error : missing ';' before identifier
'iterator_category'
c:\program files\microsoft visual studio 9.0\vc\include\xutility 764
ConceptCheck
Error 3  error C4430: missing type specifier - int assumed.
Note: C++ does not support default-int
c:\program files\microsoft visual studio 9.0\vc\include\xutility 764
ConceptCheck
Error 4  error C2602: 'std::iterator_traits<_Iter>::iterator_category'
is not a member of a base class of 'std::iterator_traits<_Iter>'
c:\program files\microsoft visual studio 9.0\vc\include\xutility 764
ConceptCheck
Error 5  error C2868: 'std::iterator_traits<_Iter>::iterator_category' :
illegal syntax for using-declaration; expected qualified-name
c:\program files\microsoft visual studio 9.0\vc\include\xutility 764
ConceptCheck
Error 6  error C2039: 'value_type' : is not a member of 'Point'
c:\program files\microsoft visual studio 9.0\vc\include\xutility 765
ConceptCheck
Error 21 error C2039: 'reference' : is not a member of 'Point'
c:\program files\microsoft visual studio 9.0\vc\include\xutility 769
ConceptCheck
Error 22 error C2146: syntax error : missing ';' before identifier
'reference' c:\program files\microsoft visual studio 9.0
\vc\include\xutility 769   ConceptCheck
Error 23 error C4430: missing type specifier - int assumed.
Note: C++ does not support default-int
c:\program files\microsoft visual studio 9.0\vc\include\xutility 769
ConceptCheck
Error 24 error C2602: 'std::iterator_traits<_Iter>::reference'
is not a member of a base class of 'std::iterator_traits<_Iter>'
c:\program files\microsoft visual studio 9.0\vc\include\xutility 769
ConceptCheck
Error 25 error C2868: 'std::iterator_traits<_Iter>::reference' :
illegal syntax for using-declaration; expected qualified-name
c:\program files\microsoft visual studio 9.0\vc\include\xutility 769
ConceptCheck

And more...
```

If you look hard at the output you will see that the compiler is complaining about iterators. This might give some hints on where to start debugging. In this particular case the class Point does not support the concept InputIterator.

We now turn our attention to defining *constraints* in template classes. The following example is a class that requires its underlying template parameter to implement default and copy constructors. The interface is given by:

```
template <typename T>
class MyClass
{
    BOOST_CONCEPT_ASSERT((boost::DefaultConstructible<T>));
    BOOST_CONCEPT_ASSERT((boost::CopyConstructible<T>));

private:
    T data;

public:
    MyClass() : data(T()) {}
    MyClass(const T& t) : data(t) {}
};
```

When we instantiate this class the compiler checks that the underlying type T will support the concept. For example, the following code will compile:

```
MyClass<Point> myClass;
```

while the following code will not compile:

```
MyClass<Nope> myNope;
```

where we have defined the class:

```
class Nope
{
private:
   Nope() {}
   Nope(const Nope& n2) {}
};
```

We also can check if STL containers support concepts, for example:

```
typedef std::map<int, double> Map;
boost::function_requires<boost::SortedAssociativeContainer<Map> >();
boost::function_requires<boost::UniqueAssociativeContainer<Map> >();
boost::function_requires<boost::PairAssociativeContainer<Map> >();
```

For more information, please consult the Boost online documentation.

Finally, we remark that it does no harm to document classes by the component diagram as the example in Figure 4 shows; here we see that a class C requires its templates arguments to implement the CopyConstructible and EqualityComparable concepts.

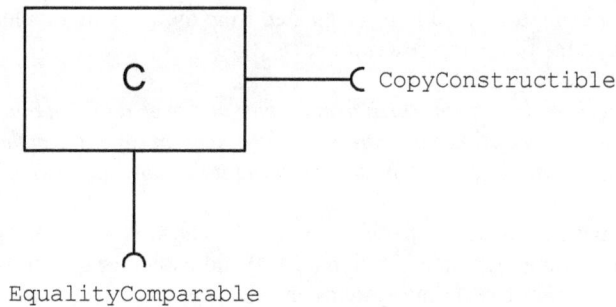

Figure 4 UML component diagram for Concepts

Appendix B: Boost, Design Patterns and Applications

Introduction and Objectives

In this appendix we discuss the use of Boost libraries as building blocks in software development projects. There will be reasons for using the libraries and developers may wish to employ them in different ways. It is impossible to discuss (or even know!) how a given group of developers will use the libraries. It is advisable to design problems before implementing them and we had decided to use Design Patterns (GOF 1995, POSA 1996) and the Unified Modeling Language (UML) as important modelling constructs in the software process.

In order to show how to apply Boost in a design-oriented approach to software projects, we discuss the following topics:
- A short overview of Design Patterns.
- Which Boost libraries directly implement design patterns?
- Which Boost libraries can I use to implement a given design pattern?
- How can I write applications using Boost and Design Patterns?

An Overview of Design Patterns

The origins of design patterns for software systems date back to the 1980's. They were published by Eric Gamma and co-authors (GOF 1995). This influential book spurred interest in the application of design patterns to software development projects in C++.

The motivation for using design patterns originated from the work of architect Christopher Alexander who used the following description:

'Each pattern describes a problem which occurs over and over again in our environment, and then describes the core of the solution to that problem, in such a way that you can use this solution a millions times over, without ever doing it the same way twice'

The authors have been using design patterns since 1993 and we have applied them in applications such as Computer Aided Design (CAD) and computer graphics, optical technology, process control, real time systems and finance. Once you learn how a pattern works in a certain context, you will find that it is easy to apply in new situations. The GOF patterns model *object lifecycle*, namely object creation, the structuring of objects into larger configurations and modelling how objects communicate using *message passing*. The main categories are:
- *Creational*: these patterns abstract the instantiation (*object creation*) process. The added-value of these patterns is that they ensure that an application can use objects without having to be concerned with how these objects are created, composed or internally represented. This is called *information hiding*. To this end, we create dedicated classes whose instances (objects) have the responsibility for creating other objects. In other words, instead of creating all our objects in `main()` we can delegate the object creation process to dedicated *factory objects*. The creational patterns are:
  - *Builder* (for complex objects).
  - *Factory Method* (define an interface for creating an instance of a class).

- *Abstract Factory* (defines an interface for creating hierarchies of objects or families of related objects).
- *Prototype* (create an object as a copy of some other object).
- *Singleton* (create a class that has only one instance).
- *Structural*: these patterns compose classes and objects to form larger structures. We realise these new relationships by the application of modelling techniques such as *inheritance, association, aggregation* and *composition*. The structural patterns are:
- *Composite* (recursive aggregates and tree structures).
- *Adapter* (convert the interface of a class into another interface that clients expect).
- *Façade* (define a unified interface to a system instead of having to access the objects in the system directly).
- *Bridge* (a class that has multiple implementations).
- *Decorator* (add additional responsibilities to an object at run-time).
- *Flyweight* (an object that is shared among other objects).
- *Proxy* (an object that is a surrogate/placeholder for another object to control access to it).
- *Behavioural*: these are patterns for inter-object communication, in particular the implementation of algorithms. These patterns describe run-time control and data flow in an application. We can further partition these patterns as follows:
- *Variations*: patterns that customise the member functions of a class in some way. In general, these patterns externalise the code that implements member functions. The main patterns are:
  - *Strategy* (families of interchangeable algorithms).
  - *Template Method* (define the skeleton of an algorithm in a base class; some variant steps are delegated to derived classes; common functionality is defined in the base class).
  - *Command* (encapsulate a request as an object; execute the command).
  - *State* (allows an object to change behaviour when its internal state changes).
  - *Iterator* (provide a means to access the elements of an aggregate object in a sequential way, without exposing its internal representation).
- *Notifications*: these patterns define and maintain dependencies between objects.
  - *Observer* (define one-to-many dependency between a *publisher* object and its dependent *subscribers*).
  - *Mediator* (define an object that allows objects to communicate without being aware of each other; this pattern promotes *loose coupling*) between objects.
  - *Chain of Responsibility* (avoid coupling between *sender* and *receiver* objects when sending requests; give more than one object a chance to handle the request).
- *Extensions*: patterns that allow us to add new functionality (in the form of member functions) to classes and to classes in a class hierarchy. There is one pattern in this category:
  - *Visitor* (define a new operation on the classes in a class hierarchy in a non-intrusive way).

Boost and Design Patterns

Having understood what a design pattern is and how it can be deployed we will need to implement it in C++. The emergence and the growing popularity of Boost presents developers with a number of opportunities:

- S1: Use Boost libraries to implement the GOF and POSA patterns.
- S2: Replacing legacy code by Boost code.

Scenario S1 is similar to the implementation guidelines in GOF 1995 but with a number of differences; first, we can implement the patterns using a combination of object-oriented and generic (template) programming models whereas the GOF patterns are primarily based on the object-oriented paradigm. Second, we can use many of the Boost libraries to speed up development time because we can apply them without any modification. Finally, there are a number of Boost libraries that are direct implementations of design patterns; a typical example is *Flyweight*.

Scenario S2 entails creating new classes and code using Boost libraries or modifying existing code with the objective of replacing our own data structures and functionality by new code from Boost. Some examples are:

- Using `boost::any` instead of `void*` to model variant data.
- Using `boost::function` instead of C function pointers.
- Replacing proprietary matrix structures by those in uBLAS and MultiArray.
- Using Boost.Random in simulation applications.
- See also chapter 17.

This is a short list of the possibilities and you will be able to find many more examples of use when you work with Boost. The first question we should ask before we reinvent the wheel is: does Boost already have the functionality that we need? It is advisable to search in the Boost documentation (ideally by category as discussed in Appendix A) to determine if the required functionality already exists?

Which Boost Libraries 'Bootstrap' the GOF Design Patterns?

The design patterns in GOF 1995 use a combination of dynamic polymorphism and composition to achieve flexibility.

The two main questions that we ask are:

- Given a design pattern, which Boost libraries can I use to implement it?
- Given a Boost library, which design pattern is it 'good' for?

We give a partial answer to these questions, first in pictorial form in Figure 1. The open circle signifies a 'medium' link, a filled circle signifies a 'strong' link while a triangle signifies a 'weak' link. Unfilled cells mean that there is no relationship or that we have not yet discovered a relationship.

	Function	Signals	Regex Xpressive	Statechart	Flyweight	Phoenix Bind
Chain	△	⊘				△
Command	⊘		△	△		
Interpreter			⊘			
Observer		⊘				
Strategy	⊘			△	○	○
State			⊘			
Proxy	○				⊘	○
Prototype					⊘	

Figure 1 Relationship between some Design Patterns and Boost libraries

We now describe why we have filled in the cells in Figure 1 the way we did:

- *Chain of Responsibility*: involves sending messages between sender and receiver. The data in the chain might be bound which implies that Boost.Bind or the Bind component in Boost.Phoenix can be used.
- *Command*: this is where `boost::function` is useful, as we saw in Chapter 1. Some text and string processing may be needed in the user interface to create command objects and regular expressions. Commands may also have state, in which case Boost.Statechart can be used.
- *Interpreter*: Boost.Xpressive.
- *Observer*: Boost.Signals and Boost.Signals2 implement the Observer pattern. We can also use Signals to implement the *Mediator* pattern.
- *Strategy* (and *Template Method Pattern*): these are algorithms. Then the ability to define functions will be important. Algorithms may have embedded states.
- *State*: Boost.Statechart is a complete implementation of UML Statechart and hence implements the *State* pattern.
- *Proxy*: this pattern has to do with access to objects via published functions, hence `boost::function` is useful. In some cases it may be useful to consider using this pattern in combination with Boost.Flyweight.
- *Prototype*: this pattern creates an object as a copy of another object. In this case we could possibly think of using Boost.Flyweight as a repository for (shared) objects.

Creating Layered Software Systems

There are many ways to design and implement software systems. One particular approach is to create software modules in layers (see the discussion of the *Layers* pattern in POSA 1996). In the current situation we are interested in combining design patterns and the Boost libraries to promote reliability of code. We have five conceptual layers, each one containing software modules:

- Layer 1: STL and Boost libraries that provide foundation classes, algorithms and data structures.
- Layer 2: The GOF patterns adapted to use Boost as 'engine' or a direct implementation of a design pattern by a Boost library.
- Layer 3: System patterns such as *Command Processor*, *Layers*, *Presentation-Abstraction-Control* (PAC) and *Blackboard*. These patterns use the modules in layer 3 as well as the Boost libraries.
- Layer 4: Multi-threaded and parallel patterns and modules (see Mattson 2005). The modules we can use here are Boost.Thread, Boost.Asio and the OpenMP library, for example.
- Layer 5: The application layer, including user-interface modules and modules for object configuration and management.

In general, we build modules in a given layer by combining the modules from lower layers. For example, we can use inheritance, composition, traits and policies.

Finally, we note that multi-threaded technology puts a new complexion on the problem; in this case, ad hoc bottom-up software development techniques will probably be sub-optimal and other top-down decomposition methods are needed before we start writing multi-threaded code (see Mattson 2005, Quinn 2004).

Appendix C: Exercises and Projects

Introduction and Objectives

In this appendix we assemble a number of exercises, self-test questions and projects that apply the techniques in this book. Just reading the chapters without attempting to write, compile and debug code that uses the Boost libraries is not optimal in our experience and in this sense we feel that it is necessary to gain hands-on skills with these libraries. And this means programming. Investing some time to solve these problems is recommended.

1. (Creating Tuples)

We take an example of a 3-tuple that models geographic data relating to cities in a country.

The components of the 3-tuple are:
- The x,y coordinates of the city relative to some fixed origin.
- The number of metres above (or below) sea-level of the city.
- The name of the city.

The 3-tuple is then defined as:

```
typedef boost::tuple<Point, double, std::string> City;
```

where `Point` is the C++ class that models points in two-dimensional geometry.

Answer the following questions:
a) Create instances of `City` using a combination of tuple constructor and the free function `boost::make_tuple()`.
b) Create a function to print instances of `City` (use the `get<int>()` member function or free function `get<int>()`, whichever one is more suitable for your purposes).
c) Create a `std::set<City>` and insert some instances into it.
d) Write a function to determine if a given `City` instance is in a `set<City>` (use the comparison operators in section 6.5 of the book).
e) Given a `Point` instance pt and a `set<City>` instance find the name of the city whose coordinates are closest to pt (you will need to use `Point::distance()` and *tieing* as explained in section 6.7).
f) Given a `Point` instance pt and a `set<City>` instance find the names of the cities whose coordinates are closest to pt and farthest away from pt. The return type of this function is `tuple<string, string>` (again, section 6.7 will guide you).
g) Use a manipulator (see section 6.6) to create instances of City from the console.

2. (Migrating Legacy Code to Any)

This exercise determines how to port C++ code to code that uses the Boost.Any library. In this case we have defined classes whose member data can be initialised using maps; the keys of these maps are strings and the corresponding values will be member data. We need some way of associating each key value with the appropriate member data. Another problem is that the data types corresponding to the keys can be of any type . In the pre-Boost days developers used `void*` but in our case we created a class called `AnyType` and a corresponding template class called `Wrapper<T>` that help us treat types uniformly. The class interfaces are:

```
class AnyType
{ // Base class for all wrapped types
```

```
public:
   AnyType() {}
   virtual ~AnyType(){}
};

template <typename T>
class Wrapper: public AnyType
{ // Generic wrapper for any data type

public:
   T obj;

   Wrapper() { obj = T(); }
   virtual ~Wrapper(){}

   T GetObj()
   {
      return T(obj);
   };

   Wrapper(T wrappedObject) { obj = wrappedObject; }

   // Need to know if current type is same as another type
   // This is a template member function
   template <typename T2> bool sameType(const T2& t2)
   {
      if (typeid(Wrapper<T>) == typeid(t2))
      {
         return true;
      }
      return false;
   }
};
```

These classes are somewhat 'rough and ready' but they satisfied our needs. We show how they are used by taking an example of a class that models a person entity having names and age attributes:

```
class Person
{
private:

   // Member data
   string fName;      // first name
   string lName;      // last name
   int age;           // how old?

public:
   Person();

   // Initialise the member data with a map
   Person(map<string, AnyType*>& pset);

   void print() const;
};
```

Here we see that we can initialise the member data through a map of defining properties:

```
Person::Person(map<string, AnyType*>& pset)
{
   // Get all the values from property set; no exception handling yet
   Wrapper<std::string>* type_string =
      dynamic_cast<Wrapper<std::string>*>(pset["FirstName"]);
   fName = type_string->GetObj();
```

```
    type_string = dynamic_cast<Wrapper<std::string>*>(pset["SecondName"]);
    lName = type_string->GetObj();

    Wrapper<int>* type_int = dynamic_cast<Wrapper<int>*>(pset["Age"]);
    age = type_int->GetObj();
}
```

A typical example of use is:

```
map<string, AnyType*> personTable;
personTable["FirstName"] = new Wrapper<string>("John");
personTable["SecondName"] = new Wrapper<string>("Smith");
personTable["Age"] = new Wrapper<int>(42);

Person myPerson(personTable);
myPerson.print();
map<string, AnyType*>::iterator it;
for (it = personTable.begin(); it != personTable.end(); ++it)
{
    delete it->second;
}
personTable.clear();
```

We now reengineer this code, in particular we execute the following action points:
- Using Boost.Any instead of `AnyType` and `Wrapper<T>`.
- More robust code, for example exception handling and ensuring that the key-value pair is 'compatible' with the names, types and values of the member data in the class.

We recommend taking an incremental approach by first inspecting and running the original code and then introducing new code in a step-by-step manner.

Answer the following questions:
a) Replace the functionality provided by `AnyType` and `Wrapper<T>` by equivalent code that *any* provides. Test the program.
b) Make the code more robust; there are a number of things that can go wrong when initialising the member data:
   - The size of the map is not the same as the number of member data in this class.
   - The map contains an unknown property name.
   - The value in the map cannot be converted to the type of the corresponding member data.
   - Some keys in the map have not been initialised.

Determine how to modify the code in order to accommodate these situations. Consider the applicability of `any_cast` (section 7.2) and `polymorphic_cast` and the other cast functions from section 9.7.

3. (Variant)
In some applications we wish to write code that works with a range of data types. For example, in numerical analysis applications we write code that uses fixed-sized Boost arrays and dynamic STL vectors. To this end, we use `boost::variant` to encapsulate these data structures:

```
const int M = 20;
typedef boost::variant<double, boost::array<double, M>,
                       std::vector<double> > NumericDataType;
```

Since this is a variant structure it can hold a `double`, Boost `array` or STL `vector` at any one time.

As a test case, suppose that we write code to negate a `double`, `array` or `vector` and then print it. For both negation and printing functionality we use derived classes of `static_visitor` (as discussed in section 8.5 of the book):

```
void doSomething(NumericDataType& myType)
{
    // Visitor class derived from boost::static_visitor<NumericDataType>
    Negate_Visitor nvis;
    myType = boost::apply_visitor(nvis, myType);

    // Visitor class derived from boost::static_visitor<void>
    Print_Visitor pvis;
    boost::apply_visitor(pvis, myType);
}
```

The interfaces for the visitors `Negate_Visitor` and `Print_Visitor` are:

```
class Variant_Visitor: public boost::static_visitor<NumericDataType>
{
public:
};

class Negate_Visitor: public Variant_Visitor
{ // A visitor with function object 'look-alike'

public:
    NumericDataType operator () (double d)
    {
        // todo
    }

    NumericDataType operator () (const boost::array<double, M>& arr)
    {
        // todo
    }

    NumericDataType operator () (const std::vector<double>& vec)
    {
        // todo
    }
};

class Print_Visitor: public boost::static_visitor<void>
{ // A visitor with function object 'look-alike'

public:
    void operator () (double d)
    {
        // todo;
    }

    void operator () (const boost::array<double, M>& arr)
    {
        // todo
    }

    void operator () (const std::vector<double>& vec)
    {
        // todo
    }
};
```

Answer the following questions:

a) Implement the bodies of the functions in the *Visitor* classes `Negate_Visitor` and `Print_Visitor`.

b) Create a test program:

```
int main()
{
    // Using declaration, for readability purposes
    using boost::variant;

    // Populate elements of variant
    double d = 1.234;

    using namespace boost::assign;
    vector<double> myVec;

    // Using Boost.Assign (section 7.6 of book)
    myVec += 10.34,11.87,45.0,80.1,23.23,-99.99;

    boost::array<double, M> myArr;
    for (int j = 0; j < M; j++)
    {
        myArr[j] = j;
    }

    NumericDataType myType;
    myType = d;
    myType = myVec;
    myType = myArr;

    Negate_Visitor vis;
    myType = boost::apply_visitor(vis, myType);

    Print_Visitor pvis;
    boost::apply_visitor(pvis, myType);

    myType = myVec;
    doSomething(myType);

    return 0;
}
```

Experiment with the code and convince yourself that it works no matter what the current value of `myType` is.

Using `boost::variant` in this way (that is, using `Visitor` to define type-safe methods on variants) has many applications.

4. (Review Questions on Data Types)

This exercise tests your knowledge of the data types that we discuss in chapters 6 (Tuple), 7 (Any) and 8 (Variant). A common question is when to use a particular library rather than another one in a particular context. In all cases we are modelling data and operations on that data. To summarise, we wish to examine:

```
Tuple, Any, Variant, C struct, C union
```

Answer the following questions:

a) When would you use tuples instead of structs? How do they differ in their treatment of data and functions?

b) Discuss how you can define polymorphic functions and how to promote type-safeness using Boost variants.

c) When would you use structs and unions?

d) Compare `any` and `variant`

5. (Greatest Common Divisor and Least Common Multiple)

The greatest common divisor (gcd) of two or more non-zero integers is the largest positive integer that divides these numbers without producing a remainder. The least common multiple (lcm) of two integers a and b (denoted lcm(a,b)) is the smallest positive number that is an integer multiple of both a and b. See section 9.5.

Answer the following questions:

a) For a range of values of integers a and b, verify that:

$$gcd(a, b) = a.b/lcm(a, b)$$

$$gcd\left(2^a - 1, 2^b - 1\right) = 2^{gcd(a,b)} - 1$$

$$gcd(a, lcm(b, c)) = lcm(gcd(a, b), gcd(a, c)).$$

b) Modify the code in section 9.5.1 that computes the gcd of a collection of n integers so that it can be used to compute the lcm of a collection of n integers.

6. (Tokenizer)

The objective of this exercise is to use the Tokenizer library to extract comma-separated data (CSV) from a text-file (record-by-record) and store the information in an STL container. In order to scope the problem, we assume that each record contains integer data separated by commas, for example 1, 22, -879, 77. The output is the STL nested data structure `map<int, vector<int> >` where the key corresponds to the line number in the file and the vector contains the data. We write this information to a second file.

Answer the follow questions:

a) Use file streams for I/O processing.

b) The record data in the input file needs to be screened for leading and trailing tabs, blanks and double commas. Use String Algorithm library to preprocess and 'clean' record data before creating map data (see section 10.2).

c) Use the functionality to create a `vector<int>` corresponding to each record.

d) Introduce exception handling by demanding that only integer values are allowed. For example, the record "1, 2., hello, *" is not allowed.

e) Each record is written to a second file; each record's line number and vector data from the input file is stored in the output file.

7. (Boost Array)

The objective of this exercise is to implement a class representing points in N-dimensional space. We provide the specification of the interface by:

```
template <typename Type, int n> class NPoint
{
private:

    // Originally: Type arr[n]
    boost::array<Type, n> arr;

public:
```

```
// Constructors & destructor
NPoint();
NPoint(const Type& value); // All elements get this value
NPoint(const NPoint<Type, n>& source);
virtual ~NPoint();

// Selectors
int Size() const;
int MinIndex() const;
int MaxIndex() const;

// Some properties
Type distance(const NPoint<Type, n>& p2) const;    // Euclidean distance
Type innerProduct(const NPoint<Type, n>& p2) const; // Dot product
friend NPoint<Type, n> operator * (const NPoint<Type, n>& pt,
                                    const Type& scalar);
friend NPoint<Type, n> operator * (const Type& scalar,
                                    const NPoint<Type, n>& pt);

// Operators
const Type& operator [] (int index) const;       // Index operator const
Type& operator [] (int index);                   // non const

    NPoint<Type, n>& operator = (const NPoint<Type, n>& source);
};
```

Answer the following question:

a) Implement this class and create a program to test its member functions (we discuss Boost
   arrays in sections 14.8 and 14.9)

   An important application is when we calculate the distance between two points.

$$L_m = \left(\sum_{j=1}^{n} |x_j - y_j|^m \right)^{1/m}$$

where $x = (x_1, \ldots, x_n)$ and $y = (y_1, \ldots, y_n)$ are n-dimensional points. Special cases
are when m = 1 (the so-called *city block* or *Manhattan distance*) and when m = 2 (the
Euclidean distance), the latter being defined by:

$$L_2 = \sqrt{ \sum_{j=1}^{n} \Delta x_j^2 }, \quad \Delta x_j = |x_j - y_j|.$$

The objective now is to implement the above metrics. Implement them as template
member functions (see Appendix A) and as free functions. The focus is to produce the
correct results.

8. (MultiArray)

In chapter 14 we gave a detailed introduction to the functionality of Boost multi-arrays. The
emphasis was on the creation of multi-arrays and accessing their elements.

When developing applications we may need to define new functionality relating to multi-
arrays, for example:

- Serialisation and deserialisation of multi-arrays.
- Mathematical properties of multi-arrays (maximum/minimum elements, averages).
- Interfacing multi-arrays with other libraries.

In this exercise we compute the maximum 'distance' between two multi-arrays. In order to give a hint, we first provide the code that finds and computes the maximum value in a multi-array:

```cpp
int const Dim = 3;
typedef boost::multi_array<double, Dim> BoostTensor;

double MaxNorm(const BoostTensor& tensor)
{ // Compute the largest element of a 3d numeric matrix

    // For readability, define start and end indices for each dimension
    // We need to get the start and end bounds to use indices in for loops
    BoostTensor::size_type size0 = tensor.shape()[0];
    BoostTensor::index start0 = tensor.index_bases()[0];
    BoostTensor::index end0 = start0 + size0;

    BoostTensor::size_type size1 = tensor.shape()[1];
    BoostTensor::index start1 = tensor.index_bases()[1];
    BoostTensor::index end1 = start1 + size1;

    BoostTensor::size_type size2 = tensor.shape()[2];
    BoostTensor::index start2 = tensor.index_bases()[2];
    BoostTensor::index end2 = start2 + size2;

    double result = tensor[start0][start1][start2];
    double tmp;

    for (BoostTensor::index row=start0; row<end0; row++)
    {
        for (BoostTensor::index column=start1; column<end1; column++)
        {
            for (BoostTensor::index layer=start2; layer<end2; layer++)
            {
                if (tensor[row][column][layer] > result)
                {
                    tmp = tensor[row][column][layer];
                    if (tmp > result)
                    {
                        result = tmp;
                    }
                }
            }
        }
    }

    return result;
}
```

Please note that the return type is a `double`. Answer the following questions:

a) Modify the above code so that both the maximum value and its position in the multi-array are returned. In this case we define the tuple structure:

```cpp
typedef tuple<double, BoostTensor::index, BoostTensor::index,
    BoostTensor::index> HotSpot;
```

b) Create a function to compute the maximum distance between two multi-arrays: the function prototype is given by:

```cpp
HotSpot MaxNorm(const BoostTensor& m1, const BoostTensor& m2)
{ // Compute the largest element of the m1 - m2 and where it occurs

    // todo
}
```

9. (Combining MultiArray and Boost Function)

In some applications we compute the values of scalar-valued functions with one or more arguments. This feature is useful when approximating the coefficients of differential equations in numerical schemes. For example, we can define a scalar-valued function having four input arguments representing three-dimensional space and one-dimensional time. In many cases we discretise the space dimension first and we keep the time variable t continuous.

The function we wish to discretise has the following form:

```
typedef boost::function<double (double x, double y, double z ,double t)>
    FourdFunction;
```

We now create a three-dimensional multi-array that contains the discrete values of instances of the above function at given *discrete* x, y and z mesh points and a given continuous time t. We provide the function prototype:

```
BoostTensor CreateDiscreteFunction
(
    // The function to be discretised
    const FourdFunction& function,

    // Meshes using the Datasim Vector class
    const Vector<double, long>& xmesh,
    const Vector<double, long>& ymesh,
    const Vector<double, long>& zmesh,

    // The t value where we create the tensor
    double t
)
{
    // todo
}
```

Answer the following questions:
a) Implement the function `CreateDiscreteFunction()`.
b) Create a program to test this function.

10. (Boost Flyweight)

We introduced flyweights in chapter 16.

In section 16.3 we created a `Shape` class that used flyweights to store associated colours. Extend this example with a `LineType` class. The line type will be a flyweight data member of the `Shape` class. Since a complex line type definition uses memory, using a flyweight can save memory.

a) Start by creating the class `LineType`. The line type has a *name* (`std::string`) and a pattern. Define the pattern as a `std::vector<char>`. Each value in the vector defines the length of the pattern segment. The *even indices* specify the line and the *odd indices* define the spacing. For example, the pattern [10, 5] defines a line type with 10 pixels on and 5 pixels off (spacing).
b) In order to use the line type as a flyweight, the line type class should implement a copy constructor, assignment operator (=), equal (==) and not equal (!=) operators. It should also implement a `hash_value()` function.
c) Add a `LineType` data member as flyweight to the `Shape` class. Make sure you use the colon syntax to initialise the members. Include the `<boost/flyweight.hpp>` header file to the `Shape` class if it is not already there. Test how the flyweight works by

counting the number of line type objects in memory (static counter variable that is increased/decreased in the constructors/destructor, respectively).

When flyweight objects are constructed, the system first creates the object for the flyweight, then checks if the object is already in the flyweight's internal data structure. If the object is already available, it is destroyed. With key-value flyweights (see section 16.4) we can avoid constructing unnecessary objects.

Answer the following questions:
a) Make the `LineType` class suitable as a key-value flyweight. The name of the line type is used as the key so that the constructor with the name can be used for key-value flyweights. Give the `LineType` class a nested `KeyExtractor` class that implements the function call operator that accepts a `LineType` object. The functor returns the key's value for the line type which in this case is the name. Furthermore, print a message so that you can see when this function is called.

The key extractor is used when we create a flyweight directly from a line type object. With the key extractor it gets the key of the input object so that we can determine if that key is already in the flyweight's internal data structure. When it is already there the object is not copied to the flyweight again.
Note that the `hash_value()` function of the line type is not used anymore but it will use the `hash_value()` function of the key type (in this case `std::string`).
b) In the `Shape` class, change the flyweight definition to a key-value flyweight:

```
typedef boost::flyweights::flyweight<
    boost::flyweights::key_value<std::string, LineType,
        LineType::KeyExtractor>
> LineTypeFlyweight;
```

Include the `<boost/flyweight/key_value.hpp>` header file.
c) In the `Shape` class create a constructor with the line type name. Make sure that you use the colon syntax to initialise the line type data member. Can you create a constructor with a line type name and a line type definition?
Also create a constructor that accepts a `LineType` object.
d) Check that no temporary line type objects are created when using the `Shape` default constructor, the constructor with line type name, the copy constructor and the constructor with the `LineType` object.
Comment out the line type's `hash_value()` function to see if it still works with the key-value flyweight.

You can specify the factory for the internal data structure to be used by the flyweight (see section 16.5). By default this is the `boost::flyweights::hashed_factory<>` factory.

a) Change the factory type to `boost::flyweights::set_factory<>`. Do not forget to include the `<boost/flyweight/set_factory.hpp>` header file. Note that the key value should support the less than (<) operator. Since you use the key-value flyweight, the key type is `std::string` that already supports the < operator. If you do not use the key-value flyweight, then the `LineType` class should support the < operator.

11. (Multi-threading)
We introduced the boost multi-threading library in chapter 18.

In this exercise we create a program that calculates the dot product of two vectors:

$$ab = \sum_{i=1}^{n} a_i b_i = a_1 b_1 + a_2 b_2 + \ldots + a_n b_n.$$

To speed up calculation we start multiple threads that execute each part of the data structure. The workload can be equally distributed. For example, when the data structure has ten elements and there are two threads, the first thread can process the first five elements of the data structure and the second thread can process the last five elements of the data structure. The result from each thread is combined when the threads have finished.

To make it easier to divide the work we use `std::vector` to store the data since it can be indexed by the [] operator.

a) Create a `DotProduct` class. It will receive references to the two input vectors. Make sure that it does not create a copy of the vectors. It will also receive the start- and end-index of the part it should process [start, end) (closed-open interval).

b) Add a function call operator `()` in the class that will be run by a thread. The operator `()` should multiply the elements of the range it processes and add them to the *current sum*. At each iteration of the loop you should *yield* the thread. This ensures that other threads get a chance to run.

c) The main program creates two vectors with values and you need to determine how many threads to use. Then it instantiates the correct number of `DotProduct` instances with the range it should process. For each instance of the `DotProduct` class, create a thread. (You can use thread groups as explained in section 18.10).

Make sure you pass the `DotProduct` class as a `boost::ref` to the thread. Otherwise, a copy of the `DotProduct` class will be run and the result will disappear when the thread has finished.

d) You have to wait for the threads to finish. Use a `join` to wait. After joining the threads, add the result of each `DotProduct` object and print the total result.

e) Test the application. If you have a multi-core/multi-processor machine, is it faster if you start two threads instead of one? You can use the `boost::timer` to measure time. Note that the number of elements in the vector must not be too small; typically, you should create large vectors (for example at least 10,000 elements) to notice any effect. Also comment out the call to `join`. Does it still print the correct result?

When multiple threads share the same data, then access to that data must be synchronised. Instead of allowing the main thread to sum the results of each thread, we can also allow the thread to add its result to a static variable in the class. Make sure that data does not become corrupted and to this end we need to synchronise access to the static variable (See section 18.7).

a) Add a static variable to the `DotProduct` class that holds the total dot product result and create a corresponding static function to read the value of that static variable. Add a static `boost::mutex` member.

b) When you have finished with your calculation, update the static variable. Before you update the static variable from the thread, obtain a lock on the mutex. When you have finished the update, release the lock on the mutex.

Note: you can also update the static variable at each iteration of the loop instead of using a local total for each `DotProduct` instance. However, with locking, you increase the risk that other threads have to wait so you should try to limit the number of times you obtain a lock.

c) In the main function, remove the code that computes the addition of the results (this is now done in the `DotProduct` instance) and read the static total result variable from the `DotProduct` class. It should still give the same result as before.

d) To automatically unlock the mutex, use the `boost::unique_lock<boost::mutex>` wrapper class.

The second exercise is an application of the Producer-Consumer pattern.

We synchronise the flow of data when multiple threads run that are dependent on each other. A simple way to do this is to use a *synchronised queue*. Instead of polling to check if a thread has produced data, the queue uses a *condition variable* that will wake the thread up when data is available.

Use the synchronised queue in combination with the Producer-Consumer pattern (see sections 18.11 and 18.12) to create a queue of dot product operations.

a) Add the `SynchronisedQueue` to your project.

b) Create a *producer functor class* that has a pointer to a `SynchronisedQueue<boost::shared_ptr<std::vector<double> > >`. We use smart pointers in the queue.

c) In the body of the function call operator `()` create a loop that instantiates vectors with random numbers. You can use the *Boost Random library*. The number of elements per vector should be the same for each vector. Add the created vector to the queue. At each iteration we sleep for one second in order to ensure that not too many vectors are created.

d) In the `DotProduct` instance remove the static total variable previously added.

e) Create a *consumer functor class* that has a pointer to a `SynchronisedQueue<boost::shared_ptr<std::vector<double> > >`.

f) In the body of the function call operator `()` create a loop that retrieves two vectors from the queue. Create a `DotProduct` instance with those vectors and call the functor. You thus use the `DotProduct` instance in the current thread instead of starting separate threads. Then retrieve and print the result. Furthermore, use an *interruption point* (see section 18.8) so that the thread can be interrupted.

g) Create a main program that creates the queue as well as multiple producers, consumers and their threads. Use a thread group.
Add code to wait for a key after which you interrupt the producers and wait until they have completed (using `join`). Then interrupt the consumers and wait until they have completed.

h) Test the program.
You can adapt the consumer so that it processes a vector pair in parallel by starting extra threads for each `DotProduct` object.

Epilogue and Volume II Contents

The second volume introduces some other libraries in Boost.
In particular, we discuss advanced data structures, container, networking and interprocess communication libraries as well as mathematical libraries for special functions and statistical distributions. Our plan is to discuss the following libraries (for more details, please see www.boost.org), in arbitrary order:

- Date and Time (date-time libraries).
- Dynamic Bitset (data structure that implements a set of bits).
- Intrusive (advanced containers that store objects directly rather than creating copies).
- Bimap (bidirectional maps in which both parameters can be used as keys).
- Fusion (library for working with tuples, containers and algorithms).
- MultiIndex (containers having multiple search and sort indices).
- Graph (BGL) (Boost's implementation of graphs and their algorithms).
- Property Map (interfaces that map keys to values).
- Property Tree (tree data that is used for storing configuration data).

- uBLAS (matrix and vector classes; basic linear algebra routines).
- Math Special Functions (special functions for use in mathematical physics and applications).
- Math Statistical Distributions (univariate statistical distributions and related operations).
- Accumulators (calculation and collection of statistical data).
- Units (library for Dimensional Analysis and unit quantity manipulation/conversion).
- Interval (the Boost library for interval arithmetic).

- Asio (portable networking software).
- Interprocess (share memory and related functionality).
- Pool (memory pool management).
- Statechart and Meta State Machine (implementations of UML Statechart).

- Spirit (LL parser framework).
- Filesystem (query and manipulate paths, files and directories).

In Volume II we design and implement a number of applications in domains such as computational finance, engineering, optimisation and real-time as well as more generic applications.

Bibliography

Abrahams, D. 2005 *C++ Template MetaProgramming* Addison Wesley.

Aho, A. and Ullman, J. D. 1977 *Principles of Compiler Design* Addison Wesley.

Alexandrescu, A. 2001 *Modern C++ Design* Addison Wesley.

Andrews, G.E. 1971 *Number Theory* Dover.

Ayers, F. 1965 *Modern Algebra* Schaum's Outlines McGraw-Hill.

Baez, J. 2001 *The Octonions* University of California Press.

Boehm, B. 1986 *Software Engineering Economics* Prentice-Hall.

Coplien, J. 1992 *Advanced C++ Programming Styles and Idioms* Addison Wesley.

Date, C. 1981 *An Introduction to Data-base Systems* Addison Wesley.

Duffy, D. J. 2004 *Financial instrument pricing using C++* John Wiley & Sons.

Duffy, D.J. 2006 *Finite difference methods in financial engineering* John Wiley & Sons.

Duffy, D.J. and Kienitz, J. 2009 *Monte Carlo frameworks Building Customisable High Performance C++ Applications* John Wiley & Sons.

Edelman, A. and Kostlan, E. 1995 *How many zeros of a random polynomial are real?* Bull. Amer. Math. Soc. 32 (1).

GOF 1995 Gamma, E., Helm, R., Johnson, R. and Vlissides, J. *Design Patterns: Abstraction and Reuse of Object-Oriented Design* Addison Wesley.

Golub, G. and Van Loan, C. F. 1996 *Matrix Computations* Johns Hopkins University Press.

Hsu, H. P. 1995 *Signals and Systems* Schaum's Outlines McGraw-Hill.

Hunter, J. 1964 *Number Theory* Oliver and Boyd.

Jagannathan, V., Dodhiawada, R. and Baum, L.S. (eds.) 1989 *Blackboard Architectures and Applications*.

Josuttis, N. M. 1999 *The C++ Sandard Library* Addison Wesley Boston.

Josuttis, N. M. and Vandervoorde, D. 2003 *C++ Templates* Addison Wesley Boston.

Karlsson, B. 2006 *Beyond the C++ Standard Library An Introduction to Boost* Addison Wesley.

Kernighan, B. and Ritchie, D.M. 1988 *The C Programming Language* Prentice-Hall.

Leavens, G. T. and Sitaraman, M. 2000 *Foundations of Component-Based Systems* Cambridge University Press.

Lipschutz, S. and Lipson, M. 1997 *Discrete Mathematics* Schaum's Outlines McGraw-Hill.

Mattson, T.G., Sanders, B. A., Massingill, B. L. 2005 *Patterns for Parallel Programming* Addison Wesley.

Mitchell, A. R. and Griffiths, D. F. 1980 *The Finite Difference Method in Partial Differential Equations* John Wiley & Sons.

Nichols, B., Buttlar, D. and Farrell, J. P. 1996 *Pthreads Programming* O'Reilly.

OMG 2000 *Object Lifecycle Services* Object Management Group www.omg.org.

POSA 1996 Buschmann, F., Meunier, R., Rohnert, H., Sommerlad, P. and Stal, M. *Pattern-Oriented Software Architecture* John Wiley & Sons.

Press, W. H., Teukolsky, S. A., Vetterling, W. T. and Flannery, B. P. 2002 *Numerical Recipes in C++* Cambridge University Press.

Quinn, P. 2004 *Parallel Programming in C with MPI and OpenMP* Addison Wesley.

Spiegel, M. 1999 *Complex Variables* Schaum's Outlines McGraw-Hill.

Stroustrup, B. 2000 *The C++ Programming Language* Addison Wesley.

Index

Book Registration Form

In order to receive the source code for this book please fill in the original (**not a copy**) registration form and send it to:

Datasim Education BV
't Veer 1
1832 AK Koedijk
The Netherlands

Do not lose this form as we cannot accept copies.

Name: ....

Title: ....

Company: ....

Address: ....

City: ....

Postal Code: ....

Country: ....

Email-address*: ....

Terms:
I agree that this code is for my own personal use and ownership cannot be transferred. I also accept the user terms of the User Agreement.

☐ Keep me informed on new developments

* We need your e-mail address in order to send you the source code.

User Agreement

The following terms govern use of the book 'An Introduction to the Boost C++ Libraries –
Volume I – Foundations', by Robert Demming and Daniel J. Duffy, ISBN 978-94-91028-
01-4 and its accompanied software and code examples (the *product*).

a) The entire contents of the *product* are protected by copyright.

b) You may not copy, distribute, transmit or otherwise reproduce material from the *product*
in any form or media other than for your own personal use.
This is not meant to prohibit quotations for purposes of comment, criticism or similar
scholarly purposes.

c) The *product* may provide links to third party websites. Where such links exist, Datasim
Education BV disclaims all responsibility and liability for the content of such third party
websites. Users assume the sole responsibility for the accessing of third party websites
and the use of any content appearing on such websites.

d) You may compile, test and run the provided code examples and they may serve as
inspiration for software you create. But code examples are provided for educational
reasons only. They come without any warranty and usage is at your own risk.

e) The *product* is provided on an 'as is' basis, without warranties of any kind. The use of
the material in the *product* is at your own risk. Neither Datasim Education BV nor
anyone else involved in creating the *product* shall be liable for any direct or indirect
damages arising from using the *product* or the inability to use the *product*.

www.ingramcontent.com/pod-product-compliance
Lightning Source LLC
Chambersburg PA
CBHW082003190326

41458CB00010B/3059